# MINISTRY AFTER FREUD

# MINISTRY AFTER FREUD

## FREUD

|||||||||||||||||||||||||||||||||||||||||||||||||||||||||||||||||||||||||||||||||||||||||||||||||||||||

## ALLISON STOKES

THE PILGRIM PRESS
*New York*

Copyright © 1985 The Pilgrim Press
All rights reserved

The scripture quotations in this book are from the *Revised Standard Version of the Bible,* copyright 1946, 1952 and © 1971, 1973 by the Division of Christian Education, National Council of Churches, and are used by permission.

**Library of Congress Cataloging-in-Publication Data**

Stokes, Allison, 1942–
Ministry after Freud.

Bibliography: p. 219.
Includes index.
1. Pastoral psychology—United States—History—
20th century.  I. Title.
BV4012.S64     1985     261.5'15'0973     85-12356
ISBN 0-8298-0563-X
ISBN 0-8298-0569-9 (pbk.)

The Pilgrim Press, 132 West 31 Street, New York, NY 10001

# Contents

# Preface

> *You can tell a liberal by his attitude, an ex-liberal by his disillusionment, and one who never dared to be liberal by his clinging-vine tactics of assuming that everything important is at hand. The true liberal does not attack people, but evils and deficiencies. His vision is always greater than his indignation. By these fruits is he to be known.*
>
> —SEWARD HILTNER[1]

WHAT WAS THE impact of Freud's comprehensive, psychological theory of human motivation and behavior on the practice of American Protestant ministry? Surprisingly, there has been no systematic study of the question. Historians have long been fascinated by Darwin's enormous impact on the churches and have written at length about Protestant liberalism's accommodation of scientific, evolutionary concepts. But they have ignored the influence of Freud and have failed to identify and describe a significant movement in American religious history that is a product of Protestant liberalism's accommodation of scientific, dynamic psychological concepts.

As a result of this scholarly vacuum, numerous misconceptions have arisen. It is assumed, for example, that the churches initially reacted to Freudian psychoanalysis with hostility and only later were receptive. Although there were strenuous objections—particularly among fundamentalists, who thought (incorrectly) that Freud was an advocate of sexual libertinism and who took offense at his atheism—what is remarkable is the readiness with which many Protestant leaders accepted Freud's teaching.

At the turn of the century, pastoral care in the United States had reached a nadir, and an alarmed clergy was searching for effective ways to meet the increasingly apparent need of Americans for healing and wholeness. Many intelligent and highly educated pastors turned to the newly emerging scientific psychology for assistance. In Boston in 1906 the launching of the Emmanuel Movement marked the first effort of Protestant liberals to bring together religion and science in healing ministry. Ironically, in the history books this movement is mistakenly lumped with the religious phenomena its leaders sought to combat—Christian Science, New Thought, and Mind Cure. By grossly misunderstanding the enterprise of the Rev. Dr. Elwood Worcester, historians have generally failed to perceive the intellectual antecedent of the efforts to reconcile religion and depth psychology.

One scholar, in particular, who has contributed to the confusion by lumping together "pop psychology" and religion and health is Prof. Donald Meyer. His updated study, *The Positive Thinkers, Religion as Pop Psychology from Mary Baker Eddy to Oral Roberts* (1980), blends astute observations, a refreshing style, rash judgments, and personal bias against "religion-as-therapy" in an exasperating way.

In the past decades there have been various criticisms of the secular direction taken by clinical pastoral education, pastoral counseling, pastoral psychology, and pastoral theology. Because many of these criticisms are either ahistorical or historically confused, they are misguided. Two examples will illustrate the point. Psychologist Hobart Mowrer has bewailed the widespread influence of Freud in American Protestantism[2] and has suggested, as a corrective measure, a return to the thinking of the Rev. Anton Boisen, founder of clinical pastoral education. What Mowrer fails to appreciate—and he is not alone—is the deep affinity of Boisen's thought with Freud's. As we will see in chapter 3, from his experience of psychotic illness, Boisen drew conclusions that were confirmed for him by reading Freud.

Another critic, theologian Thomas Oden, charges that today Christian pastoral care is captive to accommodationist thinking, to a series of successive psychologies:

The average pastor has come to a saturation point with fads. He or she has likely done the TA trip, the T Group trip, microlabs, and perhaps some Gestalt training, probably dabbled with psychoanalysis and/or any number of other available therapeutic strategies: client-centered, bioenergetics, Jungian, Adlerian, rational-emotive therapy, parent effectiveness training, E.S.T., and the list goes on.[3]

In calling for a return to classic (i.e., pre-Freudian) models of pastoral care, Oden evidences little appreciation for the *distinctive* achievement of Freud and of historical efforts of theological liberals to grapple with and use his theories of human behavior in the service of ministry. It is not uncommon for scholars who might be expected to know better to equate Freud's achievement with that of lesser men or to base comments about Freud's clinical theories on popular, distorted conceptions of them. That pioneers of clinical pastoral education and pastoral psychology recognized in Freud one of the most outstanding thinkers of the twentieth century, a brilliant mind with which it was necessary to come to terms, is too little understood.

How we interpret the past will determine the meaning we find in the present and the action we take in the future. Ideas, as John Dewey once remarked, are the most practical things in the world.[4] The time has come for an accurate assessment of Freud's influence on American Protestant ministry so that pastors, seminary students, theologians, counselors, historians, and interested laypeople may appreciate the heritage of the past and knowledgeably evaluate directions for the future. *Are* we "children of the progressives"?[5] *Do* we want to—indeed can we—return to pre-Freudian models of pastoral care for our bearings?

As soul guides, pastors for centuries necessarily relied on their intuitive gifts and life experience to understand human beings in their conflict and self-alienation. (The apostle Paul's lament, "For the good that I would I do not: but the evil which I would not, that I do [Rom. 7:19]," expresses a universal human dilemma.[6]) With the Freudian revolution, however, ministers are now drawing on dynamic psychology—concepts of the unconscious, repression, transference, aggression, projection, and so on—for insight into the human psyche. Effective pastoral care and counseling are considered teachable, for they are based on an understanding of the scientifically demonstrable laws of health.

There have been histories of the cure of souls and of the church and healing.[7] These deal tangentially, if at all, with the impact of dynamic psychology on ministry. In a recent study E. Brooks Holifield describes Freud's influence in pastoral care as primarily limited to the New York-based wing of the clinical training movement. This seems to reflect Holifield's narrow understanding of Freud's achievement and the significance of his contribution.[8]

A survey of the literature shows that observations about ministry after Freud are unfocused, scattered like pieces of an unworked jigsaw puzzle. This book is an effort to synthesize available materials in a radically new way. It is an effort to put the puzzle together, to see the whole elephant.

What has generally not been understood is that a number of apparently discrete developments—Emmanuel, clinical pastoral education, pastoral counseling, pastoral psychology—are actually part of a larger, more comprehensive movement. Sociologist Samuel Klausner describes this as the "Religio-Psychiatric" Movement. I have avoided his term (its awkwardness probably accounts for the fact that it has not gained acceptance) and instead have settled on a phrase often used by the movement's leaders: Religion and Health. Reference will be made in the following chapters, for example, to the Religion and Health Commission of the Federal Council of Churches; to Seward Hiltner's first book, *Religion and Health;* to the Columbia University seminar on Religion and Health; to Granger Westberg's appointment to the University of Chicago as Associate Professor of Religion and Health; and to the *Journal of Religion and Health,* published for many years by the Institutes of Religion and Health in New York City.

I am indebted to Professor Klausner for identifying and clarifying the nature of this movement. As he points out, there are two senses in which the word movement is used. Sociologists restrict the term to social movements in which groups are organized in pursuit of a common goal, but in regular usage:

> "Movement" signifies a convergence in the work of a number of individuals. . . . They need never meet in a face-to-face group, identify with each other, or espouse a common objective. Some-

times their designation as "members" of the same movement awaits their historian.[9]

It is in this second sense that, as its historian, I write of the Religion and Health Movement.

Although I have chosen to use the term Religion and Health to designate the movement, it should be clear that I am *not* writing about the relationship between religion, or ministry, and health in general (which might bring to mind the hospital chaplaincy movement, for example), or about persons or sects that have spiritual healing as their religious focus (which might bring to mind Mary Baker Eddy, or Christian Science, for example).

Chapter 1 argues that the impetus for the development of the Religion and Health Movement was that tradition or impulse in American Protestantism which perennially attempts to make the ancient Christian message both credible and relevant to the modern age—the liberal tradition. Histories of religious liberalism in the United States, in the past, focused either on Unitarianism and Transcendentalism or on "classic" liberalism, that is, the response during the Gilded Age to scientific biblical criticism and Darwin's biological discoveries. Until now, efforts to mediate the gospel in light of Freud's psychological discoveries have not been studied as a more recent expression of the liberal, or modernist, impulse.

Chapter 2 focuses on the Emmanuel Movement, in which the Rev. Dr. Elwood Worcester pioneered in the use of psychotherapeutics as a scientific tool for healing ministry. This experiment in religion and medicine, begun in the Emmanuel Episcopal Church in Boston in 1906, was a pre-Freudian antecedent to the Religion and Health Movement.

Chapter 3 examines the role of the Rev. Anton T. Boisen in promoting Religion and Health. In the 1920s and 1930s Boisen founded and developed the Council for the Clinical Training of Theological Students (now the Association for Clinical Pastoral Education). His insistence, stemming from his own experience of mental breakdown, on the study of "living human documents," not books and traditions, as the proper approach to theological problems is a familiar story to many, especially those who have taken a quarter of clinical pastoral education.

Chapter 4 relates the story of the one woman who made an

outstanding contribution to the early Religion and Health venture: Helen Flanders Dunbar. A brilliant student and colleague of Boisen's and a pioneer in psychosomatic medicine, Dunbar held Ph.D., B.D., and M.D. degrees from Columbia, Union, and Yale, respectively. Dunbar broke new ground as she headed the Joint Committee on Religion and Medicine of the New York Academy of Medicine and the Federal Council of Churches.

Chapter 5 tells of the seemingly unlikely alliance between an advocate of positive thinking, the Rev. Norman Vincent Peale, and an analysand of Freud's, Dr. Smiley Blanton. Together this minister-psychiatrist team established in 1937 a Religio-Psychiatric Clinic at the Marble Collegiate Church on Fifth Avenue in New York City. This venture expanded phenomenally to become a significant factor in the growth of the Religion and Health Movement.

Chapter 6 reveals the existence of an exclusive gathering that has heretofore been generally unknown to the scholarly community: the New York Psychology Group.[10] Between 1941 and 1945 private monthly seminars of specially invited theologians, psychiatrists, psychotherapists, and social scientists—including Ruth Benedict, Erich Fromm, Seward Hiltner, Rollo May, David Roberts, Carl Rogers, and Paul Tillich—were held in the home of Union Theological Seminary professor Harrison Elliott. The extraordinary story of this wartime group is told in this chapter.

Chapter 7 draws conclusions about the working assumptions of Religion and Health founders, including their beliefs that the laws of mental health are progressively discoverable and that psychoanalysis is scientifically valid. Chapter 8 focuses on the debate about whether or not Freud's theories were scientific and the bearing of that debate on the Religion and Health Movement.

In a fascinating interview the Rev. Dr. Wayne Oates, prominent Religion and Health leader and evangelical liberal from the Southern Baptist tradition, told me the story of his unpublished Th.D. thesis, "The Significance of the Work of Sigmund Freud for the Christian Faith." This is found in Appendix A. Appendix B is a chronology that locates particular Religion and Health developments in historical context.

Protestantism is the exclusive focus of this study because Freudian ideas have impinged on Protestant consciousness for more than three-quarters of a century with demonstrable effect. The more recent Jewish and Roman Catholic responses to Freud, fascinating in their own right, deserve separate studies. Rabbi Joshua Liebman's brilliant effort to integrate theology and psychoanalysis in *Peace of Mind* (1946) and Bishop Fulton Sheen's polemic against psychoanalysis in *Peace of Soul* (1949) would highlight stories that, unfortunately, cannot be taken up here.

About terminology: In the Religion and Health literature, authors write variously about religion *and* . . . psychiatry, psychology, psychoanalysis, psychotherapy, and depth psychology. The subject has no single accepted term. *Psychoanalysis* describes Freud's own system and can be used to designate Freudian theory or Freudian therapy, a specific form of *psychotherapy*. *Depth psychology* usually refers to the psychology of the unconscious, which, in the historical evolution of psychoanalysis, yielded to *ego psychology*. *Dynamic psychiatry* derives from the late nineteenth century, when theories of mental energy were modeled on the physical theory of energy: it views mental life as the interplay of reciprocally urging and checking forces.[11] *Psychiatry* is the discipline that encompasses all of these. Because my subject is Freudian psychology—which includes the discoveries not only of Freud, but also of those who modified and carried on his work—I use the terms psychoanalysis and, more generally, dynamic psychology.

Some readers may object that my reference to Freudian psychology and my description of Freud's influence are too broad, too inclusive. I am reminded of a statement that Albert Outler made in 1953: "The nuclear motifs of modern psychotherapy are still those supplied by Freud; they have influenced subsequent developments more than they have been altered by it."[12] This was certainly so in 1945, the year that marked the take-off of the Religion and Health Movement. I believe that it is so today.

Both Reichian psychology and Jungian psychology have their own descriptive terms. I do not discuss the disruptive influence of Wilhelm Reich's orgonomy theory, an elusive chapter of the past that calls for an in-depth study of its own. (Edward Thornton briefly alluded to Reich's role in his *Professional Education for Ministry, A History of Clinical Pastoral Education.*[13]) Nor do I discuss Carl Jung's distinctive impact, which has been deeply felt in recent years, especially within the Episcopal and Roman Catholic churches, and which bears close observation by historians of American religion.

To be more explicit about the content of Freudian theory, I quote the psychological model formulated by Peter Berger in his attempt to isolate key propositions in a configuration derived from the psychoanalytic movement that is now operative in everyday life. My analysis of Freud's influence basically follows this psychological model:

> Only a relatively small segment of the total self is present to consciousness. The unconscious is the matrix of decisive mental processes. The conscious self is moved out of these unknown depths into actions the true meaning of which it does not understand. Men are typically ignorant of their own motives and incapable of interpreting their own symbolizations. Specific and scientifically verifiable hermeneutic procedures have to be applied to such interpretations. Sexuality is a key area of human conduct. Childhood is the key phase of human biography. The on-going activity of the self may be understood in terms of the operation of scientifically ascertainable mechanisms, of which the two most important are repression and projection. Culture may be understood as the scene of interaction between unconscious motor forces and consciously established norms.[14]

The method guiding this research is necessarily interdisciplinary because relevant information is scattered through the fields of history, psychology, sociology, religion, and theology. Although I have drawn on numerous useful secondary sources, I would especially like to acknowledge Raymond J. Cunningham's "Ministry of Healing" (Johns Hopkins University, 1965) and Robert C. Powell's "Healing and Wholeness" (Duke University, 1974). Both unpublished doctoral dissertations—the one a study of the origins of the psychotherapeutic role of the American churches in the late nineteenth and early twentieth centuries and the other a study of Helen Flanders Dunbar and the extramedical origins of the American psychosomatic movement—exhibit scholarly research and analysis of the highest order.

The vast Religion and Health literature has provided a rich and sometimes bewildering volume of primary materials. From the turn of the century to the present day, thousands of books and articles have been published dealing with the integration of religion and psychology, psychiatry, or psychoanalysis.[15] In addition to primary and secondary written materials, an invaluable source of information and guidance has been the oral testimony of Religion and Health Movement leaders.

This book identifies the beginnings of the Religion and Health Movement, 1906–1945, but it does not tell the whole story. I hope that researchers in years to come will not only fill in the narrative, but come up with a more complete cast of characters.

# Acknowledgments

SOREN KIERKEGAARD wrote at length about "our duty to be in the debt of love to each other." The occasion of completing this study is a natural time to recall those who influenced the course of my dissertation and, finally, the shape of this book. It is a time when I feel in the debt of love—the word is not too strong—to advisers and friends who gave me the gift of their time and themselves.

My mentor, Prof. Sydney Ahlstrom, resisted and even discouraged some of my ideas, for which I am grateful. He caused me to clarify and buttress my arguments. With Sydney's death, historians of American religion—his colleagues and students—have lost the encyclopedic breadth of learning of an incomparable mind.

The interdisciplinary American Studies approach made it possible to arrive at my thesis topic, and I specially thank Yale American Studies professors Kai T. Erikson and Dr. David F. Musto. Yale Divinity professors who helped and encouraged me include James Dittes, Robert Johnson, and Henri Nouwen, who defected to Harvard. Editor and humorist William Zinsser, former master of Branford College at Yale, not only edited some work but made me laugh when I most needed to laugh. I thank my students at Yale and Vassar for asking tough questions that caused me to pause.

Seward Hiltner, professor of theology and personality at

Princeton Theological Seminary until shortly before his death, guided my work from his perspective as a pioneer in the Religion and Health Movement. His generous sharing of New York Psychology Group materials, recollected experience, and wisdom— as well as time and home hospitality—was invaluable. Charles Hall Jr., retired executive director of the Association for Clinical Pastoral Education (ACPE), trusted me with sensitive historical records and introduced me to the ACPE Historical Committee, to which I became a historical consultant. I thank the Committee for including me in their annual meetings in Lexington, Kentucky, and for a travel grant to Sedona, Arizona. There, in September 1978, I met Rosamond Grant Fisher, long-time personal secretary and friend to Flanders Dunbar. The full story of our incredible meeting and its consequences is the stuff of another book.

A research trip to Napa, California, in October 1983 was made possible by Herman Eichorn, chaplain at the Napa State Hospital. Ike's help in supplying Anton Boisen letters and other research materials and hospitality is deeply appreciated.

To Dr. Robert Charles Powell, the psychiatrist-historian whose dissertation initiated all of this, I owe special thanks. With forbearance and kindness he assisted my early work.

I acknowledge Dr. Violet de Laszlo, Helen Nichol Fernald, Rollo May, and Hannah Tillich (who attended meetings of the New York Psychology Group) for risking interviews with me and then for contributing information that I could not have known except for their decisions to share candidly. Harry E. Smith, former executive director of the Society for Values in Higher Education, and David C. Smith, present executive director, provided valuable assistance in my search for information about members of the New York Psychology Group.

For insight into the benefits of psychotherapy I am grateful to Patricia Dunton and Dr. Iago Galdston. For their pastoral counseling, I owe a debt of love to Fr. John Tivenan, the Rev. Gaylord Noyce, and the Rev. Christopher Emerson. For their skillful help I acknowledge Marion Meyer, my editor; Phyllis Seward, my administrative assistant; and Anne Hiltner, my poet friend. For insisting that I learn how to use a word processor, Profs. Dierdre Bair and Mary Carroll Smith can call on me for any favor any time.

To Jerome W.D. Stokes, but for whom I may never have read Freud, studied at Yale, or been prompted to investigate the Religion and Health Movement, I express special thanks. And I lovingly acknowledge our children—Jonathan Jerome and Anne Jennings Stokes—who grew up with this project. Jon does not remember, although I do, the day his tiny voice called from the bookcases in the other room:

"Hey, Mom. Who's this guy Fraud?"

"Who?"

"You know: *Fraud.* F-r-e-u-d."

Their high spirits and good humor have made all the difference.

Recognition and financial assistance have come from the American Association of University Women, the Kanzer Fund for Psychoanalysis and the Humanities at Yale, the Roothbert Scholarship Fund, and the Hattie M. Strong Foundation. The important work of these groups in supporting graduate students at a time of shrinking economic resources is to be especially acknowledged. To complete this book is to give tangible evidence that their hopes for my contribution were not misplaced. Nor, I trust, were the hopes of my parents and grandfather, to whom this work is dedicated.

Poughkeepsie, New York

# MINISTRY AFTER FREUD

# CHAPTER 1

# The Freudian Revolution and American Protestant Liberalism

> A man who inspires new ideas has little
> power to restrict them to the area of his
> original intentions.
>
> —ERIK H. ERIKSON[1]

LONG BEFORE THE Freudian revolution became a documented fact of American life, Protestant ministry had taken steps to accommodate Freud's discoveries. When, in the 1960s and 1970s, social observers proclaimed the advent of psychological man (and woman) and the psychological society, the triumph of the therapeutic, and the Americanization of the unconscious, they were describing an intellectual and cultural revolution that had been preceded by a scientific revolution a half century earlier, a revolution to which ministry had been particularly alert. American religious historians have been slow to appreciate the fact that decades before scientific advances in depth psychology permeated popular consciousness, liberal Protestant pioneers had addressed themselves to the significance of psychoanalysis. Even before Sigmund Freud's historic appearance in 1909 at Clark University, some liberal clergy recognized the import of the new psychology for ministry, and by the late 1920s many agreed with Prof. Harrison Elliott that "the development of psychology probably has more bearing upon religion than has any other scientific advance."[2] Thus it was that ministry was not caught unawares by the psychological revolution that, in its effects, seems to make the original American Revolution pale. (One sociologist explains: "That was a revolution of mere *externa;* this of *interna, ultima, privatissima.* . . . We have added a dimension and there is no more radical act."[3])

Because Sigmund Freud anticipated that psychoanalytic theory would disturb the peace of the world even more than had the theories of Copernicus and Charles Darwin ("Psychological research of the present time . . . seeks to prove to the ego that it is not even master in its own house"[4]), he was more prepared for hostile rejection than he was for friendly acceptance. Initially gratified by the scientific recognition he received in Worcester, Massachusetts, he soon became distressed by the growing American popularity of psychoanalysis—knowledge of it was superficial and uncritical. One of Freud's earliest biographers noted that he was "afraid no less of the manner in which he was being accepted than of the manner in which he had been rejected."[5]

4

Freud—an "incredulous Jew" (self-described) who in his later years militantly sought to expose faith in God as illusory—was similarly unprepared for the cordiality extended psychoanalysis by liberal Protestant clergy, among them his good friend Oskar Pfister (1873–1956). Freud's changing attitude toward ministry's interest in psychoanalysis may be inferred from his letters to Pfister, a Swiss pastor and psychoanalyst. In 1909 Freud conceived psychoanalysis to be an "impartial tool which both priest and layman can use in the service of the sufferer,"[6] but by 1928 he had reversed himself. He then explained to Pfister that just as he wrote *The Question of Lay Analysis* to protect psychoanalysis from the doctors, he wrote *The Future of an Illusion* to protect it from the priests. "I should like to hand it over to a profession which does not yet exist, a profession of *lay* curers of souls who need not be doctors and should not be priests."[7] Although Freud was remarkably tolerant of Pfister's practice, the pastor's use of psychoanalysis in the service of God was disconcerting to him.

Freud seemingly miscalculated the response to his assault on human megalomania, for with Darwinism the history of the warfare of science with theology in Christendom ended. Despite the fact that many Christians are still pressing for the teaching of biblical creationism in the schools, the Scopes trial marked the last of religious presumption in *scientific* matters, as intellectual historian Bruce Mazlish has pointed out. There has been no pitched battle between psychoanalysis and the churches because "the churches have learned, through bitter experience, not to contest science on scientific grounds."[8] By "the churches" Professor Mazlish means the fundamentalist churches. In the battle over issues that science and religious scholarship had raised, particularly the theory of evolution through natural selection and the historicity of the Bible, the Protestant churches had divided into two camps—liberal and fundamentalist. Whereas fundamentalism staunchly defended biblical literalism, liberal theology made the adjustment by accommodating modern science and scholarship. The combat experience of both factions shaped their responses to psychoanalysis. Liberal strategy had been tried, tested, and proved by the time Sigmund Freud enlisted in the fray: his blow would be absorbed, his weapons commandeered.

If fundamentalists did not fight Freudianism as they fought Darwinism, this decision signaled not so much a change of attitude as a change of strategy. Today conservatives do not defy the authority of science as often as they proclaim the sufficiency of scriptural revelation. Consider, for example, *God's Psychiatry*, first published in 1953 and reprinted many times, in which Charles Allen, pastor of the First Methodist Church of Houston, states that the most important psychiatry must be God's psychiatry—restoring of the soul by learning the laws of God. Quite logically, the book is an extended exegesis of scripture—the Twenty-third Psalm, the Ten Commandments, the Lord's Prayer, and the Beatitudes. Scientific psychiatry is not criticized; it is just ignored.

Conflicts between science and religion, according to Harvard Divinity School dean emeritus Krister Stendahl, can be understood very simply: they occur when a religious tradition becomes a defender of outdated scientific views. Conflict is "always just a question of the world and the church being on different timetables, a question of scientific lag in the churches."[9]

One indication of a closing gap between conservative churches and scientific culture was the healing ministry of the late Ruth Carter Stapleton, which received much public attention during Jimmy Carter's 1976 Presidential campaign and after his election. Stapleton preached an unusual blend of born-again Christian faith and depth psychological therapeutics. She believed that Jesus can be an all-knowing psychotherapist who heals painful childhood experience—the psychic damage suffered then is replaced with God's love now. "Inner healing" or "healing of the memories" through Jesus is surer and more swift than years of psychoanalysis because, with the Holy Spirit, one can cut right through to subconscious problems.[10] Because Jesus is Lord of all—"Lord of the subconscious," "Lord of the repressed memory"—Ruth Stapleton prayed for his blessing before helping people to find and expose painful memories.[11] Her ministry signaled the inroads that psychoanalytic ideas have made on conservative, evangelical consciousness.

Early fundamentalist opposition to Freud, especially to Freud's atheism and to the revolution in sexual mores attributed to Freud, must not be understated; however, the focus of this study is not the response of fundamentalists, but the far more vocal and influential effort of liberals to appropriate Freudian discoveries for ministry. Having reasoned that the truth of science and the truth of scripture are not incompatible, but are essentially one truth, liberals were not of a mind to contest psychoanalysis.

## The Liberal Tradition in American Protestantism

One prerequisite to historically locating and evaluating the work of leaders in Religion and Health, who sought to integrate Christian faith and depth psychology in the service of the sufferer, is an understanding of the liberal tradition in American Protestantism. The word liberal derives from the Latin *libre*, to free. The essence of liberal thought—whether theological, philosophical, or political—is free inquiry. Because American Protestant liberalism is characterized by an attitude, its content is not fixed, but changes over time. The liberalism of Channing, Parker, and Emerson, for example, differed distinctly from the liberalism of Rauschenbush, Gladden, and Fosdick. For this reason it is a mistake to identify liberalism with a particular denomination (e.g., Unitarianism)[12] or to find the key to liberalism in its response to a single scientific advance (e.g., evolution by natural selection).[13]

Historians of American Protestant liberalism have many disagreements; however, there is a consensus that the period roughly from 1870 to 1930 marks the "golden age of liberal theology," or the "liberal era," and that from 1930 until the 1960s, liberalism was in disrepute. Accustomed for decades to ascendancy, liberal theology suffered a defeat in the 1930s with both neoorthodoxy's relentless attack and the economic depression. The word liberal became a pejorative adjective, and even today liberals are reluctant to use it to identify themselves. As recently as 1970, Seward Hiltner wrote: "You can call a good guy progressive, up-to-date, imaginative, insightful, attentive to the modern situation, and have his appreciation; but if you say he is a downright liberal, he will wonder if you are trying to cost him his job.[14]

To suggest that after the neoorthodox assault, theological liberalism died would be misleading, even though some pronounced its epitaph. In 1939 Halford Luccock described himself, "With No Apologies to Barth," as an unrepentant liberal, out on a limb in a position badly exposed to the strong tides of crisis theology and apocalypticism but still hanging on. Others shared his tenacity. A collection of essays in honor of liberal theologian Eugene Lyman, edited and published in 1940 by Union Theological Seminary professors David Roberts and Henry Pitney Van Dusen, reaffirmed the vital heritage of liberalism—"chastened" and "tempered" by the influence of Niebuhr et al. Not for another generation, however, would voices for liberalism be heard. In the 1960s several young historians—William Hutchinson, Kenneth Cauthen, and Lloyd Averill—focused their attention on the liberal era and its achievement. All noted the reemergence of liberalism as a force in theology to which their recovery of the past, no doubt, gave impetus. Then in 1979 Peter Berger admitted "without hesitation or embarrassment" his theological location within Protestant theological liberalism, in the line of Schleiermacher, and he observed that "there are quite a few people whose thinking is veering in more or less this direction."[15] Berger's position in *The Heretical Imperative* is that the inductive, liberal approach is the only viable possibility for contemporary religious affirmation.

Given these developments it is both inaccurate and short-sighted of some observers to describe ours as a "post-liberal" era. The liberal attitude, observable in the witness of the first Christians, reasserts itself throughout human history.[16] What is necessary is to distinguish between nineteenth- and early twentieth-century liberalism and contemporary, reconstructed liberalism. It is also necessary to identify a movement within liberalism that is largely responsible for its contemporary, reconstructed look: the Religion and Health Movement pioneered by Elwood Worcester, Anton Boisen, Helen Flanders Dunbar, the team of Smiley Blanton and Norman Vincent Peale, Seward Hiltner, and Paul Tillich.

In an introduction to readings from the classical liberal era, Professor Hutchinson carefully distinguishes the legacy of eighteenth- and nineteenth-century liberal ideas from the ideas charted by post-Civil War culture. Inherited from rationalistic liberalism of the Enlightenment were confidence and optimism about human nature and progress, readiness to distrust religious creeds and institutions, and emphasis on ethics. Inherited from romantic liberalism of the early nineteenth century (the Transcendentalists and Bushnell) was a stress on the immanence, or "indwelling" of God in humanity and nature.[17] What was distinctive about the liberalism of the Gilded Age was its unprecedented widespread success and emergence of what was to be called "modernism." Hutchinson finds few examples before 1870 of the kind of religious liberalism that modernism denotes, mainly the idea that theology must consciously strive to come to terms with secular culture.

The modernist impulse, according to Hutchinson, was central to the liberal movement between 1870 and 1930. Taken as a cluster of beliefs, it was, first, "the conscious, intended adaptation of religious ideas to modern culture"; second, the belief that "God is immanent in human cultural development and revealed through it"; and, finally, that "human society is moving toward realization (even though it may never attain the reality) of the Kingdom of God."[18]

Historian Kenneth Cauthen agrees that the spirit of cultural accommodation was central, but he divides liberalism between 1901 and 1933 into two types that differed in the *way* they related the biblical faith to modern culture. "Evangelical liberalism," Cauthen writes, "represents the attempt of men who were convinced of the truth of historic Christianity to adjust this ancient faith to the modern era."[19] Some evangelical liberals were William Adams Brown, Harry Emerson Fosdick, Walter Rauschenbush, A.C. Knudson, and Eugene W. Lyman. Conversely, "modernistic liberalism represented the attempt of men who were thoroughly immersed in contemporary culture to reinterpret what they felt to be of permanent truth and value in the Christian tradition in terms of the methods and categories of early twentieth-century science and philosophy."[20] Shailer Matthews, D.C. Macintosh, and Henry Nelson Wieman were modernist liberals. Although Hutchinson challenges Cauthen's assumption that the difference between the two types was a difference of fundamental loyalties,[21] the term evangelical liberal, when applied to Religion and Health leaders, is both accurate and useful. The starting point of these persons was in fact the truth of historical Christianity, *not* modern depth psychology. They acted and wrote as pastors and theologians and so differed from the psychologists of religion who, as "modernistic liberals," viewed Christian experience from the perspective of early twentieth-century psychology. This distinction is important and is considered again in chapter 3.

Studies of liberalism's accommodation of modern culture so far have examined a modernity that does not include Sigmund Freud, even though his life's work was essentially complete before the 1930s. The work of avant garde Protestants whose orientation was clearly modernism of the evangelical type but whose focus was dynamic psychology, not evolutionary biology, must be analyzed. It is now time to build on the careful and thorough scholarship of the past, to use the guide that historians have provided to the liberal heritage, in order to chart the early course of this movement in American religious and intellectual history.

My method in studying the Religion and Health Movement and examining its continuity and discontinuity with classic liberalism has been to use the three characteristics of the modernist impulse that Professor Hutchinson has isolated—accommodation of secular culture, a sense of God's immanence, and a belief in progress. Although these ideas are considered extensively in the following chapters, I must say that what impressed me initially was the willingness of theological liberals to see God's purpose in Freud's work. Nowhere is this more apparent than in the warm correspondence between Freud and two of his disciples—the Rev. Oskar Pfister of Zurich and Dr. James Jackson Putnam of Boston. Over the years both men confronted Freud with the religious significance of his life's undertaking. When Freud described himself as "godless" in a letter to Pfister, the reply came back, "He who lives the truth lives in God, and he who strives for the freeing of love 'dwelleth in God.' " Pfister felt that if only Freud raised to his own consciousness his place in God's design, "I should say of you: A better Christian there never was [10/29/18]."[22] The Swiss clergyman, who was the first to work out a psychoanalytic system of pastoral work, appealed to Freud to "cast a benevolent glance at the analytic cure of souls, which is, after all, another of your children. . . . If only men can be made good and happy, with religion or without it, the Lord will assuredly smile approvingly at the work [9/10/26]."[23] In one of his last letters to Freud, Pfister wrote: "Your marvelous life's work and your goodness and gentleness, which are somehow an incarnation of the meaning of existence, lead me to the deepest springs of life. . . . At heart you serve exactly the same purpose as I, and act 'as if' there were a purpose and meaning in life and the universe [2/9/29]."[24]

Unlike Pfister, Dr. Putnam did not believe in a personal God, but in transcendental energy and élan vital; from his youth he had been steeped in a powerful tradition of Unitarian liberalism. For Putnam, the measure of one's life was one's self-improvement and one's contribution to progress (i.e., the community and truth). On October 3, 1915, the occasion of his sixty-ninth birthday, Dr. Putnam sent what was to be his last substantive letter to Freud (their communication was broken by the war and in 1918 Putnam died). The idealist told the determinist:

> We do not and cannot stand so far apart as one might think—and for the simple reason that we are both attempting, by the use of our intelligences and our intuitions, to reach the truth, and there cannot be two sorts of logical process in the world. It is you that have helped to teach me to be "religious" and to believe in the reality of the unseen, and in "free will." Even though our freedom accounts for only 1/1,000,000 of our acts and thought, that smallest fraction is the most valuable part of them. For it is you that have taught me to believe in "truth" and "justice" as in things outside of us yet in us, and to make *voluntary* sacrifices for them, and this *is* religion and the worship of the unseen.[25]

Dr. Putnam's stubborn persistence in raising the question of the higher nature of the human being deeply affected Freud, as Nathan Hale Jr. has shown, and was one of the influences that led Freud to take up the study of religion and conscience.[26]

Years later, when the significance of psychoanalysis for religion became, in retrospect, more apparent than it had been previously, some interpreters implicitly suggested that they saw God's action in contemporary history. God had, it seemed, revealed God's judgment and initiative through an unexpected agency. "We are indebted to a non-Christian thinker, Sigmund Freud, for supplying new resources which have rescued modern theology and ethics from a kind of scholastic dullness and barrenness into which it had fallen," wrote Paul Maves.[27] Paul Tillich observed that theology had to learn from the psychoanalytic method "the meaning

11

of grace, the meaning of forgiveness as acceptance of those who are unacceptable and not of those who are the good people."[28] And Rabbi Joshua Liebman concluded that wise religious teachers were beginning to see "the fallacy of identifying truth with the frozen concepts of the past." Depth psychology's discoveries "are really the most recent syllables of the Divine," a "new revelation of God's working in history."[29]

From the psychoanalytic establishment itself came Erik Erikson's witness to converging truths—the one spiritual, the other psychological. Just as Luther tried to free individual conscience from totalitarian dogma, wrote Erikson in *Young Man Luther,* Freud tried to free the individual's insight from authoritarian conscience. Neither man came on his contribution by professional design; instead, neurotic suffering had precipitated the breakthrough in his creativity. "Both men endeavored to increase the margin of man's inner freedom by introspective means applied to the very center of his conflicts; and this to the end of increased individuality, sanity, and service to men."[30] Erikson's studies of *Homo religiosus*—Luther, Gandhi, Jefferson—as well as his shorter essays (especially "Letter to Gandhi" and "The Golden Rule in the Light of New Insight"[31]) make plain his deeply felt belief that, with Freud, insight joined faith as the therapeutic agent of wholeness in our time.

### The Religious Situation in Late Nineteenth-century America

To comprehend *why* liberals were eager to adapt the insights of depth psychology for ministry, one must take cognizance of the need for healing and wholeness that became urgently felt in late nineteenth-century America. Complex forces—economic, social, and intellectual—converged during the Gilded Age to cause an upheaval in American life. Industrial and urban expansion, scientific and technological discoveries, waves of immigrants, the collapse of "civilized morality" all threatened traditional values, causing Americans to experience disorientation, alienation, fragmentation (Durkheim's *anomie*). Nineteenth-century American nervous and mental disorder and the subsequent quest for health (Christopher Lasch writes of the "religion of health") have recently become popular subjects as historians inquire into the origins of modern therapeutic culture. Neurasthenia, rest cure, mind cure, hypnosis, positive thinking, Christian Science, New Thought, mental hygiene, sexual hygiene, Victorian morality, the beginning of psychoanalysis, psychosomatic medicine—all have come under scrutiny.[32]

Ministry's developing awareness during the Gilded Age of the individual's need for more adequate pastoral care is plainly revealed by an examination of the literature of pastoral theology produced in the sixty-year period from 1847 to 1907.[33] Because the work of the church must constantly be adapted to the circumstance, wrote liberal leader Washington Gladden in *The Christian Pastor and the Working Church* (1898), books on pastoral theology necessarily "reflect the life of the churches out of whose experience they have grown. The flavor of the soil is always in them."[34] Emphasizing that "new occasions teach new duties"[35] (the words were borrowed from James Russell Lowell's "The Present Crisis"), Gladden observed that the practice of ministry in American Protestantism had changed considerably over the nineteenth century. As pastoral theology extended its field, the functions that the minister was called on to perform were quite unlike those he once performed.

> The advent of the nineteenth century strikes the hour of the utilities; and the studies which bear directly upon the activities of the church are exalted to a rank which has not before been given them. Of this tendency Schleiermacher, who is pastor as well as professor, is the protagonist.[36]

It is appropriate that Gladden acknowledged the influence of Friedrich Schleiermacher (1768–1834), for it was Schleiermacher who first argued for religious-cultural accommodation. Although Christianity had throughout history adapted the gospel to the thought and culture of particular eras, not until Schleiermacher was the modernist impulse self-conscious.[37]

Between the Civil War and World War I the effort of religious liberals to relate and apply the Christian ethic of love to modern industrial society gave rise to the Social Gospel, a movement led by Washington Gladden and Walter Rauschenbush. Rampant

13

capitalism, unbridled competition, laissez-faire economy, monopoly, urban dislocation, slums, depression, unemployment—all came under Christian moral judgment.

The most concrete, organized products of the Social Gospel Movement were the institutional church and the religious social settlement, innovative forms of urban ministry that confronted the pastor with new functions of management, organization, and administration. These new functions posed a dilemma as committee meetings, record keeping, fund raising, budgeting, and overseeing limited the pastor's *personal* visitation. Gladden likened the minister's position to that of an American college president who, fifty years before, had been the principal teacher of his college and now had become mainly an organizer and administrator. He lamented: "There are parishes where things are well organized, where there are all sorts of activities and societies, but where there is no proportionate apprehension of, and no provision for, the real wants of men and women."[38]

Institutional church work was not the only obstacle to personal pastoral care in the late nineteenth century. Historian Raymond Cunningham makes it plain that the traditional Protestant conception of ministry—the proclamation of the Word—gave the cure of souls a decidedly minor place. Preaching was the chief function of ministry, and in the United States the national habit of popular oratory and the evangelical character of religious life reinforced this emphasis. Personal pastoral labors were held in particularly low esteem in the last decades of the century, for with Phillips Brooks and Henry Ward Beecher as models, there developed an intense preoccupation with homiletic effectiveness, and the pulpit achieved an unprecedented ascendancy.[39]

Even so, pastoral theology texts of the period bear witness to a growing concern for pastoral care, a "turn to the interpersonal."[40] It was a time when many ministers became convinced that their training for pastoral work had been too much neglected; they felt unprepared to be spiritual counselors. The very years, then, that witnessed the nadir of the Protestant cure of souls in America were the years in which new voices and new attitudes were being heard. One minister, admitting the weakened influence of the church over the loyalties of people, suggested that only a resur-

14

gence of the pastoral ideal could reverse this trend. He predicted that the twentieth century would be the century of the pastor.[41]

Preoccupied as he was with the social context of ministry, even Washington Gladden stressed that the busy pastor must attend to individual needs. He must, for example, extend himself to the doubters in his congregation so that they may find the truth and their way back into the active work of the church. The problem of doubt Gladden knew to be a serious one: the tremendous advance of the physical sciences, the rise of the philosophy of evolution, and the prevalence of the methods of historical criticism, he said, had swept the foundation from beneath the feet of multitudes who had not had time to adjust themselves to these rapid movements of mind. The wise pastor, however, could give relief to burdened minds. By always keeping before him the close relation of "mind and body," he might bring "health and peace" to people suffering from religious despair, melancholy, a troubled conscience, or morbid fear.[42]

The minister's role in promoting health and the close relationship between mind and body were timely concerns. Shortly after the turn of the century, the Rev. Dr. Elwood Worcester (1862–1940), a man utterly frustrated in his social ministry, began a modest experiment in the cure of souls based on the unity of body and soul. Popularly known as Emmanuel, this experiment had an immediate national impact at the time. Today it is notable for signaling the rise of the Religion and Health Movement in American Protestantism.

## CHAPTER 2

# Elwood Worcester and the Emmanuel Movement

*We have taken our stand fairly and squarely on the religion of Christ as that religion is revealed in the New Testament and as it is interpreted by modern scholarship, and we have combined with this the power of genuine science. This we consider a good foundation—the best of all foundations.*

—ELWOOD WORCESTER[1]

The Rev. Dr. Elwood Worcester
*From a painting by Pollak-Ottendorff;*
*courtesy of Emmanuel Church, Boston*

W HEN ELWOOD WORCESTER was graduated from Columbia College in 1886, he knew just how he intended to prepare for the ministry to which God had called him when he,was sixteen. He planned to study under the greatest living teachers, to be thorough, and to devote himself to the subjects he deemed would be most valuable in his future work—the Bible, philosophy, and psychology.[2] With an excellent mind, a phenomenal memory, and grounding in the classics[3] (a Phi Beta Kappa), Worcester thought of Germany for graduate work, but his bishop, Henry C. Potter of New York, vetoed the plan, insisting that he must study in one of the Episcopal Church seminaries, preferably General Seminary of New York.

Stubbornly determined to go to Germany, Worcester began an intensive study of the curriculum of the first two seminary years. Cramming from late May through August, he often reminded himself of a saying of Lao-tzu: "My religion is to think the unthinkable thought, to speak the ineffable word, to do the impossible creed, and to walk the impassable way."[4] He then took the examinations to enter as a senior, passed them, and completed the degree in one year. In his autobiography he recalled that when the "trick" he had played was discovered, it so angered his superiors that they made it forever impossible for the performance to be repeated.[5]

Worcester spent nine peaceful and happy months at General Seminary but complained that he learned nothing which was of any value in his later ministry. He felt that he had seen the school at its worst, "during the extreme old age, one might say the dotage, of a group of ancient teachers who belonged to another generation."[6] In advance of exams before bishops and the clergy, his pastoral theology professor would tell the students what questions he would ask. Then, when they drew questions from a hat, the professor would press into the hand of each student the question he had studied. Worcester often wondered what kind of ministry he would have had if he had followed the instructions of this favorite minister; the problems he later encountered demanded that he work out a technique of his own.[7]

At the University of Leipzig, which ranked second only to

Berlin, Worcester found the challenge he sought. He studied under Franz Delitzsch, orientalist and theologian; Gustav Fechner, founder of physiological psychology; and Wilhelm Wundt, pioneer in experimental psychology. Although Wundt had brought the young American to Leipzig (Worcester attended every course Wundt gave), it was Wundt's teacher, Fechner, who entered "deeply" into Worcester's soul, whose thought accompanied Worcester through life.[8] Then approaching the end of his career, Fechner combined the knowledge and reasoning of a man of science with the imagination of a poet and seer, for which Worcester admired him greatly.

While in Germany a new truth dawned on Worcester that influenced all his subsequent thinking and that is a key to understanding the Emmanuel Movement. He observed:

> In our [American] colleges and in our literature it is generally assumed that science concerns itself only with physical and material things, such as the science of astronomy, of botany, physics, biology, and so forth. I was greatly surprised to find that in the judgment of the great German thinkers science is not so limited, that wherever phenomena are present which can be studied, classified, and reduced to order, material for science is given. In other words, what may be called science consists in a method, not in a given subject-matter. Thus, there may be a science of the immaterial and spiritual as well as of the physical and material.[9]

A *science* of the immaterial and spiritual. Worcester experienced the concept as liberating because it removed false opposition between mind and spirit. He wondered that it was not more generally known and accepted in America.

Another principle that intrigued Worcester, one laid down by Fechner, is that the practical motive is a legitimate motive of faith: "That that which is true cannot help being useful and that the practical value of any belief or theory is a presumption in favor of its truth."[10] When Wundt's American student, William James, developed his philosophy of pragmatism, Worcester called James' attention to his unconscious indebtedness to Fechner.[11]

Worcester returned from Leipzig in 1889 with his doctorate in philosophy (his published doctoral thesis was on *The Religious*

*Opinions of John Locke*). After a brief period at St. Ann's Church in Brooklyn, New York, in the fall of 1890, he accepted the position of Chaplain and Professor of Philosophy and Psychology at Lehigh University, in Bethlehem, Pennsylvania. While there he gave a series of public lectures on the results of the latest biblical criticism and in 1901 published *The Book of Genesis in the Light of Modern Knowledge,* the first of many books in which he related the scientific approach to religion and human problems.

Preferring a more diversified ministry, Worcester moved in 1896 to St. Stephen's Church in Philadelphia, "a parish of liberal tradition which welcomed his scholarly approach to religious problems and warmly supported his charitable enterprises."[12] A parishioner at St. Stephen's made a casual remark that Worcester would later recall and bring to fruition in the Emmanuel enterprise. Suggested Dr. S. Weir Mitchell, an eminent neurologist who was well known for his "rest cures": "Rector, if you and I should get together and establish a work for the sick, basing it on sound religion and sound science, we could put [a local faith healer] out of business."[13]

In 1904 Worcester was called to Emmanuel Church. The largest Episcopal church in Boston, it was regarded as one of the most successful in the city. Before accepting, he made one condition: a promise by the vestry guaranteeing his freedom of thought and action as rector of the parish. This was readily given.[14] A liberal church, Emmanuel had gone further than most others in developing institutional activities to soften the strain of modern economic forces—clubs, classes, camps, gymnasium, hospital work, and a social settlement house in one of the poorer Boston neighborhoods. Although these were extraordinary activities that would have been undreamed of twenty years earlier, Worcester found something lacking. He believed in the importance of the Social Gospel ("so long as the Church is animated by the divine charity of Jesus Christ, it can never fail"); yet he also believed that the church in its social endeavor was not bringing the whole force of the Christian religion to bear on people's lives. People willingly accepted fine parish buildings, libraries, music, trade schools, art classes, and even baths:

> But the best that the Christian Church has to offer men is the
> new life in Christ Jesus, and this all our social endeavors do not

21

seem to make people especially anxious to receive at our hands. We have heard many of the ablest and most conscientious clergymen of our Church confess with sorrow that they are doing this work with a sense of humiliation and despondency because they do not feel that they are giving their people the best they have to give. Of one thing we may be very sure: unless we soon find a way to unite faith to charity, that is, to infuse our social work with a more religious spirit, it will be taken from us and given to others.[15]

For Worcester, the defect of the Social Gospel was that it was not sufficiently personal and spiritual:

It can change the environment, but as yet it seems to have no means of changing the heart. It can help men in the bulk, but it has no direct access to the depth of the individual conscience. We therefore venture to believe that the social movement will soon be supplemented by a psychical movement which speaks in the name of Christ to the soul.[16]

Worcester pointed out a paradoxical fact of the religious situation: first, the church had lost its vital power and influence in the daily lives of Americans, and second, a new wave of spontaneous spiritual activity was occurring outside the churches. A journalist corroborated the distressing facts of the church's lost hold:

With expensive equipment, large funds, an educated clergy, often costly music and other attractions, the church, taken as a whole, no longer leads or even deeply moves the American people. Able young men do not go into the ministry as they once did; in 1907 there were seven hundred fewer students in fifty-eight Protestant theological seminaries than there were twelve years ago. Ministers generally are underpaid and often disheartened with the prevailing apathy and neglect. Many churches, especially in the East, stand empty and deserted.[17]

### The Threat of Christian Science

At the same time Worcester observed "a wholesale defection to strange cults and institutions."[18] He was alarmed by the unexpected power of "errors, illusions and aberrations of every sort"[19]—power that the intelligent could no longer ignore. The rapid growth of faith healing, of New Thought, and, particularly, of Christian Science distressed him. Although Worcester maintained that the Emmanuel Movement was founded neither in protest nor in imitation of Christian Science, although he insisted that Emmanuel would be what it was even had Christian Science never existed, it is clear from Worcester's writings that in fact the threat of Christian Science had a good deal to do with the beginnings of Emmanuel. In *Religion and Medicine, the Moral Control of Nervous Disorders* (1908), written to explain the psychotherapeutic work at Emmanuel Church, Worcester declared:

> The doctrines of Christian Science . . . have been denounced, ridiculed, exploited times without number, apparently with as much effect as throwing pebbles at the sea checks the rising tide. Preachers, physicians, editors of powerful journals, philosophers, humorists, unite in pouring contempt upon this despicable superstition . . . but in spite of them it lives. While most other religious bodies are declining or barely holding their own, it grows by leaps and bounds. All over this country solid and enduring temples are reared by grateful hands and consecrated to the ideal and name of Mrs. Eddy. And this strange phenomenon has occurred in the full light of day, at the end of the nineteenth and at the beginning of the twentieth century, and these extraordinary doctrines have propagated themselves not in obscure corners of the earth, but in the chief centers of American civilization. Such facts may well cause the philosophical student of religion to reflect . . . we must be able to pass beneath the vulgar and repulsive exterior of Christian Science and to find a truth in it, a gift for men, a spiritual power answering to men's needs which the churches at present do not possess.[20]

Recalling Darwin's advice to distinguish between facts and hypotheses that are intended to account for facts, Worcester rejected Christian Science dogma and sought instead the truth of Christian Science's power. It did not disturb him that the essential truth was marked by error and illusion because, he noted, in this

23

form all the older sciences had first presented themselves. What was the great truth Worcester said he found in Christian Science? Its promise of immediate benefits as the result of faith. Christian Science aims at "supplying present strength for present needs,"[21] and "its effects are direct, practical, immediate."[22] For these reasons Christian Science was superior to vague, impractical preaching that dealt with a distant future.

But what were the "present needs" and what was the "present strength" of Christian Science? Worcester cites its efficacy but does not clarify the essential truth that he implied was the basis of a new science. Worcester never explicitly makes the link between Christian Science and the psychosomatic principle; instead, he attributes the new understanding of the unity between mind and body to the teachings of modern psychology and physiology. He does not say, although it can be inferred from what he does say, that it was not just the teachings of modern psychology, but also the healing successes of Christian Science, that made it imperative for the church to consider the whole person. No longer could the church afford to address people as "disembodied spirits."[23]

In the past generation, wrote Worcester, the best thinkers of the world had come to recognize the unity of body and soul as essential to the integrity of human nature. This new conclusion "does not sacrifice the soul to the body like the older materialism. It does not seek to dissipate this compact and marvelous human frame into a mere idea, like Christian Science, nor to represent it as the garment of the soul as does the so-called New Thought."[24] Worcester did not see what scholars today understand, that in familiarizing clergy and their parishioners with the idea of psychosomatic illness, the mind cure movement prepared the way for the new psychology. Historians Gail Parker and Nathan Hale Jr. credit Christian Science and New Thought with contributing to the American acceptance of Freud's teaching that many physical symptoms have psychic origins.[25]

### Recovering Christ's Healing Ministry

Responsive as he was to new conditions, Worcester was one of the first of many twentieth-century liberal pastors to lament that the church had retained Christ's ministry to the soul but had rejected his ministry to the body. For the renewed life of the church, Christ's healing ministry must be recovered. Worcester was convinced that the genius of Christianity is its fidelity to the permanent needs of human nature. To meet the insistent contemporary need for health and wholeness, he worked with an assistant, the Rev. Dr. Samuel McComb, an Irishman whose interests and training were similar. (He had earned his degree at Oxford University and had done graduate work at the University of Berlin.) Worcester and McComb joined with prominent Boston physicians James Jackson Putnam, Richard Cabot, and Isador Coriat in the first American venture between clergy and doctors in the cure of souls.

An accurate source of fact and interpretation of Emmanuel is the account by Progressive journalist Ray Stannard Baker. In 1908 Baker ambitiously began a comprehensive study for the *American* magazine of religious thought and development in America. Religion had been a subject of continuing interest for Baker. Raised as a Presbyterian, he became a sporadic church-goer; for him, as for countless others of his time, the higher criticism had demolished the old fundamental religion, yet he felt a need for faith to give him a sense of unity and wholeness. (Baker's biographer found evidence of his lifelong quest for God and unity scattered throughout his notebooks.[26]) Although Ray Baker's series of articles on American religion (1908–09) fell short of his original undertaking, they did provoke public interest and comment. Baker, who heartily endorsed preachers of the Social Gospel, was most touched by the tribute paid him by Washington Gladden. From his Columbus pulpit, Gladden had called Baker a "prophet" who showed clear proof of "divine anointing:"

> I have been watching his work for years and it always rings true. The evidence of his candor, his carefulness, his freedom from prejudice appears in everything he writes. And he is as tender-hearted as Hosea, as reluctant to give pain, or eager to get the hopeful view. Journalism which is animated by such a spirit is a sacred function.[27]

The editors at the *American,* however, were less sanguine. They worried about Baker's "roasting" of the churches, about his outspoken criticism of religion's failure to provide a vital and

25

purposeful faith.[28] It was no doubt intentional, then, that the initial articles of the survey concerned *constructive* attempts to minister to the needs of society, to meet the current "spiritual unrest." The first article described the Emmanuel Movement. It was later reprinted as Part I of Baker's *New Ideals in Healing* (1909) and again as chapter 5 of his *The Spiritual Unrest* (1910). Clearly, Ray Baker had not a little to do with publicizing the new movement.

The story of Emmanuel can be summarized thus: on a November evening in 1906 Worcester announced at a lecture in the Emmanuel Church that he, McComb, and two psychiatrists would be available for consultation the next day in the parish house. To their astonishment, 198 people appeared. From the beginning, psychotherapeutic work was restricted to those who suffered from functional nervous disorders (for example, neurasthenia, hysteria, hypochondria, morbid fears and worries, alcohol and drug addictions, moral disorders). Carried on in health classes as well as in private conferences, the work flourished over the next few years. Six hundred persons were present in 1909 for the opening health class in October and 5,000 applicants requested treatment.[29] Worcester recalled:

> One thing, however, we had not taken into account, the depth and magnitude of the human need we were about to sound, and I frankly confess that if I had seen in advance the obloquy I must suffer, the incredible amount of work that would devolve on me (7 days a week for 9 months of the year), the burden of guilty and heavy-laden consciences, whose secrets I must guard, the weight of the sin and sorrow of the world I must bear for others—I fear that I would never have undertaken it.[30]

He was, he explained, led and sustained by the spirit of God.[31]

The influence of the movement spread beyond Boston as Worcester and McComb lectured throughout the country and as articles appeared in popular journals like *Good Housekeeping* and *Ladies' Home Journal.* In New York City the Healing Mission of St. Mark's Church opened, and in San Francisco a department of psychotherapy was established at St. Luke's Hospital. In 1909 the movement was reported in operation in Brooklyn, Buffalo, Detroit, Philadelphia, Baltimore, and Seattle, as well as internationally in England, Ireland, Australia, South Africa, and Japan.

The Emmanuel Clinic in Boston remained in the public eye for only about five years, but the work continued there until Worcester resigned his parish in 1929—he had been rector for a quarter of a century. With Courtney Baylor, a layman who had been helped at Emmanuel, Worcester then moved to offices nearby, where the two received patients until Worcester's death, in 1940.[32]

### The Distinctive Influence of Emmanuel

Despite the considerable impact of Emmanuel and its pioneering quality, most historians of American religion have tended to treat the movement as being in the same category as faith healing, mind cure, New Thought, Christian Science, and positive thinking. It is imperative, however, to see the *distinctive* influence of Emmanuel.

First, unlike Christian Science or New Thought, the Emmanuel Movement occurred *within* the mainline Christian churches, or, to use the words of historian Raymond Cunningham, in the "historic" churches. In addition to the Episcopalians, also represented were Baptists, Presbyterians, Congregationalists, Unitarians, and Universalists.[33] To disarm his critics, Worcester emphatically pointed out that "we have taken our stand fairly and squarely on the religion of Christ as that religion is revealed in the New Testament and as it is interpreted by modern scholarship."[34] Worcester aimed his appeal to "the educated, to the scholarly among the friends of Christ who see and deplore the present condition of His Church."[35] Emmanuel was intended as an agent of mainline Christian renewal.

Second, unlike Christian Science, the Emmanuel Movement was not sectarian or exclusive, but inclusive. As may be inferred from the first point, it cut across denominational lines, thereby fostering a spirit of ecumenism. In 1908 the Federal Council of Churches had been organized largely because of the effort of liberals who were seeking to carry on Christ's *social* ministry. With the same liberal attitude, Worcester remarked of Emmanuel's effort to carry on Christ's *healing* ministry:

> Since engaging in our new work, we have been gratified to observe what a powerful solvent this new interest has proved

27

and in what pleasant ties of fellowship it has united Christians formerly estranged. Not only do members of all Protestant churches worship with us freely and constantly, but Roman Catholics and Israelites also take part in our services with the approval of their priests and ministers.[36]

It is noteworthy that Worcester and McComb's chief collaborator in the Emmanuel clinic and in the book *Religion and Medicine* was an "Israelite," prominent Boston psychiatrist Isador Coriat. Unlike Drs. Cabot and Putnam, who became critical of Emmanuel, Coriat supported and defended Worcester for many years.[37]

Third, unlike faith healing, Christian Science, or New Thought, the Emmanuel Movement used the means of modern science (i.e., of modern psychological science). Both Worcester and McComb had a deep respect for "science truly so called,"[38] for the power of "genuine science"[39] (in contradistinction to Christian Science). Writing in *Religion and Medicine* in 1908, they were possibly the first to interpret Jesus' healing miracles in the light of the higher criticism *and* modern psychological knowledge (see "The Healing Wonders of Christ," chapter 19). While acknowledging that the enlightened Christian often finds the healing miracles more of an obstacle than a help to faith, they nevertheless affirmed the historical trustworthiness of the Synoptic Gospels as one of the remarkable results of modern criticism. Jesus' healings and exorcisms cannot be denied; however, by explaining Jesus' methods in terms of psychological science, in terms of suggestive therapeutics, the miracles can be made more intelligible to contemporary people. In their rather daring and potentially controversial scriptural exegesis, Worcester and McComb seemed to strike an exquisite balance between the demands of faith and science.

Fourth, Emmanuel was conceived as a *partnership* between religion and medicine, the joint ministry of Paul and Luke being a model:

There was much in this project which was radically new and original, chiefly that educated men, university scholars and critical students of the Bible had been willing to undertake it and

28

that they had induced scientifically trained physicians to work with them. In the history of Spiritual Healing this had not happened before, at all events, not since the days of St. Paul and St. Luke who had formed the same combination.[40]

From the beginning, the cooperation and advice of physicians were sought. Without the support of men like Cabot and Putnam the work would not have proceeded.[41] No treatment was begun without careful medical diagnosis and without medical assurances that the treatment was likely to be beneficial. Pains were taken to preserve records "without which no treatment can be regarded as scientific or even safe."[42] Record keeping was modeled after that at Massachusetts General Hospital, the teaching hospital of Harvard Medical School.

The collaborative approach to healing was advanced by *Psychotherapy,* a magazine that ran for three volumes (a total of twelve numbers) from 1908 to 1909.[43] It was subtitled "A Course of Reading in Sound Psychology, Sound Medicine, and Sound Religion." A partial list of announced contributors to *Psychotherapy* indicates the exceptional quality of mind, training, and scholarship represented[44]:

- Rev. Loring W. Batten, Ph.D., S.T.D., Rector of St. Mark's Church, New York; Professor of Old Testament, General Theological Seminary
- L.W. Becan, Ph.D., Associate Editor of the *Churchman*
- Richard C. Cabot, A.M., M.D., Instructor in Medicine, Harvard Medical School
- Isador H. Coriat, M.D., Assistant Physician for Nervous Diseases, Boston City Hospital
- Paul Dubois, M.D., Professor of Psychotherapy, University of Bourne, author of *Psychic Treatment of Nervous Disorders*
- Right Rev. Samuel Fallows, LL.D., Presiding Bishop of the Reformed Episcopal Church
- Rev. Curtis Manning Geer, Ph.D., Professor of Church History, Hartford Theological Seminary
- Frederick Peterson, M.D., Professor of Psychiatry, Columbia University

- James Jackson Putnam, A.D., M.D., Professor of Diseases of the Nervous System, Harvard Medical School
- Josiah Royce, Ph.D., LL.D., Professor of Philosophy, Harvard University
- Frederick T. Simpson, M.D., Visiting Physician to the Hartford Hospital; Lecturer, 1907–1908, on Psychotherapy, Hartford Theological Seminary

After Freud's visit to the United States in 1909, several of these men began practicing psychoanalytic psychotherapy; partly through them the Religion and Health Movement would be shaped by Freud's discoveries.

### Emmanuel, a Product of Protestant Liberalism

To examine the Emmanuel effort from the point of view of the modernist liberal impulse is to find all three identifying characteristics—accommodation of secular culture, a sense of God's immanence, and a belief in progress. First, Worcester explicitly stated that as Augustine, Luther, and Schleiermacher had won people to Christ by revealing Christ anew to their contemporaries, just so he sought to return to Jesus, to interpret his purposes in terms of modern life.[45] It must be emphasized that as an evangelical liberal, Worcester's first allegiance was to Christ, not contemporary culture. A religion beset by problems "has only one means of extricating itself, that is, by the rediscovery of its Founder and by a return to Him."[46]

Second, Worcester saw God's healing action in the cure of psychogenic disease by psychotherapeutic means. This perception of God's immanence had far-reaching consequences for American religion and culture, consequences that have not yet been adequately appreciated. In answer to the taunt of faith healers, "If you believe in God's power to cure disease, how dare you place any limit to that power?" Worcester replied, "We believe God has power to cure all disease, but we do not believe God cures all disease by the same means."[47] Scientific psychotherapy as a means for God's cure of souls—the concept was seminal. Some fifty-six years later pastoral counseling specialists had

30

achieved sufficient professional identity to organize and incorporate the American Association of Pastoral Counselors.

There have been two distinct kinds of healing ministry in twentieth-century American Protestantism: the one represented by faith healing, the other by healing that combines the insights of faith and science. Faith healing is based on literal biblical exegesis. Raymond Cunningham has demonstrated that the faith-cure movement of the 1870s and 1880s, led by Charles Cullis and Albert Simpson, was founded theologically on fundamentalism and perfectionism.[48] Healing revivalists who succeeded Cullis and Simpson in the early twentieth century included Alexander Dowie, Fred Bosworth, and Aimee Semple McPherson; later there were William Branham, Oral Roberts, Gordon Linsay, Jack Coe, A.A. Allen, and Kathryn Kuhlman (see David Edwin Harrell Jr., *All Things Are Possible: The Healing and Charismatic Revivals in Modern America*[49]). The fundamentalist approach of these people to a ministry of healing must not be confused with the liberal approach initiated by Worcester and McComb.

Finally, the Emmanuel literature rings with the note of triumphant optimism characteristic of the Progressive Era. The opening announcement in the magazine *Psychotherapy* heralded the new Religion and Health Movement:

> Few movements in the history of mankind probably have been of more vital significance than that now on foot in America to put psychotherapy to effective use. So vast and beneficent have been the results of the union of religion, medicine, and psychology for this purpose that further knowledge and use of it are at once a duty and a privilege. In it leaders in science and in religious thought—two of the greatest forces of civilization— are cooperating to relieve suffering and widen life. It remains to be seen how this cooperation can best be made effective.[50]

The movement had promoted an ecumenism that, to Worcester, indicated "how quickly the superficial differences which separate Protestant Churches will disappear so soon as a new and powerful motive in religion which affects us all equally shall begin to make itself felt."[51] Although the condition of the churches was one of apathy and deadness, "when the light and warmth of a new day begin to animate us, then this coating of ice will melt and the waters will flow and mingle."[52]

Worcester held a sublime vision of a new age in which the church, aided by modern science, would reconcile the world to Christ:

> Armed with the resources of modern science, and more especially of modern psychological science, inspired with the enthusiasms of humanity which is the grand legacy bequeathed her by the Founder of our faith, the Church to-day should be able to outdo the wonders of the Apostolic and post-Apostolic Age, and in a new and grander sense to win the world for Him who came to take its infirmities and to bear its sicknesses.[53]

How his rhetoric captures the bright, American optimism of those pre-world war years.

John Burnham has pointed out that the Progressive effort to reconstruct both society and individuals—based on the Progressive belief that human beings could, to a degree, make and remake their own world—was not limited to politics, economics, and social philosophy, but pervaded all American endeavors, including psychiatry and psychology.[54] Progressive psychiatrists and psychologists undertook to interfere in and change their patients' attitudes and ways of life.

Freud objected to the optimistic social reformism of American psychoanalysts. For example, although he was delighted that James J. Putnam enthusiastically supported psychoanalysis and threw the whole weight of his universally respected personality into the defense of its aims, Freud said that he regretted one thing: Putnam's "inclination to attach psychoanalysis to a particular philosophical system and to make it the servant of moral aims."[55] Moral reform was not the goal of psychoanalysis. In a letter written to Putnam in June 1915, Freud revealed his pessimism about human nature:

> The unworthiness of human beings, including the analysts, always has impressed me deeply, but why should analyzed men and women in fact be better. Analysis makes for integration but does not of itself make for goodness. I do not believe, as do Socrates and Putnam, that all vices originate in a sort of obscurity and ignorance.[56]

Freud's criticism of progressive, liberal optimism would later be taken up by neoorthodoxy.

### Criticism of Emmanuel

The Rev. Dr. Worcester's grand hopes for the Emmanuel Movement were not universal. From the start it was the center of a storm of controversy. Many judged the undertaking to be "fanatical, sensational, or dangerous."[57] Criticism and objections came from all quarters. At the Yale Divinity School, the Rev. George B. Cutten told students in a course on pastoral functions that Emmanuel was a passing fad: "Of course we know that the churches in America are not very different from the church in Athens, in being attracted by 'some new thing.' Churches will adopt Mental Healing because they think it is new."[58] Cutten expected that once the excitement and novelty evaporated, the church would be satisfied to delegate to physicians the work that legitimately belongs to them. Cutten sarcastically advised students that in order for them to take up therapeutic work:

> after finishing your seminary course this year, you will need four years in a medical school, two years, at least, in post-graduate study in psychology, and at least one year in clinical work. If this is done, there will be no use of the churches demanding young ministers, for there will not be any, i.e., any trained ones.[59]

In Cutten's opinion, Emmanuel and Christian Science did have value in *prompting physicians* to take up mental healing, but the direct work of ministers was the moral and religious development of humankind.

Dr. James Jackson Putnam agreed. He soon withdrew his original endorsement of the Emmanuel clergy when he perceived them as acting as leaders of a new medical movement.[60] Putnam believed that boundaries needed to be drawn between physicians and clergy, who represent two coordinate, but different, professions. "Their permanent distinction should be safeguarded," he wrote in an article for the *Harvard Theological Review.*[61] Only the physician has the training and experience to meet the needs of the nervous invalid; only the physician can carefully search out all

33

bodily and mental causes of his or her problem.[62] The task of the clergy consists "mainly in the development of character and motives."[63]

Others shared Putnam's position. The Rev. Charles Reynolds Brown, pastor of the First Congregational Church in Oakland, California, published a study in 1910 of *Faith and Health*,[64] which included chapter-length critiques of Christian Science and the Emmanuel Movement. Brown wrote that because he had studied the subject for twenty-three years, and because he had wide experience with people in his congregation who were suffering from nervous disorders, he was as qualified as the average pastor to use the methods of Emmanuel—"but I should shrink utterly from such a responsibility."[65] Dr. Worcester and Dr. McComb were "exceptional men" with "exceptional training in psychology."[66] It would not be wise to try to emulate them, for to do so would mean a widespread practice of medicine by the untrained: "Do we want to confuse the work of the physician . . . with the work of the minister of religion? I do not believe that we do; I believe it would be bad for the physician and still worse for the minister and worst of all for the community."[67] To give support to his argument, Brown quoted a comment Freud made about Emmanuel when he visited Clark University: "When I think that there are many physicians who have been studying psychotherapy for decades who yet practice it with the greatest caution, this introduction of a few men without medical, or with only superficial medical, training, seems to be of questionable good."[68] A year after *Faith and Health* was published, Charles Reynolds Brown became dean of the Yale Divinity School, a position he held until 1928. When, in 1923, Dean Brown updated his study, he added a chapter on "The Method of Coué" but did not revise his opinion of the clergy's practice of psychotherapy.

Critics charged that, in the Emmanuel Movement, religion became captive to culture and that clergy outstepped their proper role. Dr. Putnam further imputed the movement—it placed individual welfare before community welfare:

> On one side, it is urged, stands the community with its sorrows, on the other stands a band of men knowing themselves equipped with weapons for rescue and capable of utter devotion in the use of them. Why should they not rush in, thrust aside

customs and conventions, constitute themselves as *posse comitatus,* and do what they can, as men for men? There are many generous-minded persons who regard these facts and arguments as covering the case, and say that when the house is in flames it is no time to inquire too carefully into the credentials of those who pass the water-buckets. From this standpoint it would obviously be of little consequence whether the performance of the volunteer fire-brigade was in all respects up to the best technical standard, or whether or not it exactly squared with their intentions as at first asserted.[69]

To Putnam's mind, however, those who have the best interests of the community at heart are those who leave the problem of nervous invalidism to physicians. Clergy, physicians, teachers, social workers, and laymen—all may profitably work in common *if* there is tacit agreement "that every one should recognize the importance of promoting the steady growth in expert skill of special groups of workers, the gain in strength and public confidence of professions and of systems."[70] Putnam believed that maintenance of professional expertise was in the best interest of the community as a whole. In 1925 his colleague, Dr. Richard Cabot, would be instrumental in launching a revolutionary program in professional education for ministry: clinical pastoral education.

These early criticisms of Emmanuel—its captivity to culture, its inappropriate intrusion into the medical sphere, its emphasis on the individual at the expense of the community—raised issues that were to surface again in the Religion and Health Movement.

### Pre-Freudian Limitations of Emmanuel

When, in 1930, Elwood Worcester reviewed his life's work, he acknowledged that the suggestion therapy he and McComb had practiced was outdated by Freud's discoveries. He pointed out that psychoanalysis was practically unknown to America when they wrote *Religion and Medicine,* in 1909. At that time the best helps available were in the older psychology of hypnotism and suggestion represented by Charcot, Janet, Bernheim, Forel, Morton Prince, Moll, and others. Since then, however, the world had seen "the most important development that psychology has known since the days of Plato and Aristotle."[71]

Freud himself had begun with hypnotic therapy, sometimes practiced by Worcester and his colleagues, but had abandoned it because even the most brilliant results were liable to be suddenly wiped away if his personal relation with the patient became disturbed.[72] In *An Autobiographical Study* he related how his use of hypnosis had screened from view the phenomena of resistance, repression, conflict, and the unconscious. With these forces in sight he was able to formulate a theory of repression, which became the foundation for understanding the neuroses: "Its aim was no longer to 'abreact' an affect which had got on to the wrong lines but to uncover repressions and replace them by acts of judgment."[73] The result was that he no longer called his method "catharsis," but instead "psychoanalysis." Psychoanalytical investigations showed that psychological phenomena were the result of dynamic factors: mental conflict and repression.[74]

In his later years Worcester was to pay tribute to Freud:

> In his unearthly power of describing the unseen, in the fearlessness with which he proclaimed and continues to proclaim truths most humiliating to man, in the extraordinary tenacity of his logic, and in his uncanny art of coining names and phrases which stick, he is one of those geniuses who appear on earth once or twice in a century.[75]

Knowing that the psychology of *Religion and Medicine* had been antiquated by Freud, Worcester and McComb published *Body, Mind and Spirit* in 1931. (The book was received so favorably by the religious, medical, and secular press that Worcester's son offered—for a sum—to write a searching, slashing criticism of it for the *New York Times.*[76]) Worcester wrote that he felt a deep obligation to Freud "for a new and incomparable method, an instrument of precision whose employment in the investigation of the mind has enabled us to discover the secret springs and motives of human conduct unknown before him and possibly unknowable but for his genius."[77] These reflections help make it clear that the work of Emmanuel was limited by its pre-Freudian origins. Before the Religion and Health Movement could grow (as it did in the 1920s and 1930s), a more adequate psychology was needed. This Sigmund Freud, "a wicked pagan,"[78] supplied.

# CHAPTER 3

# Anton Boisen and the Council for the Clinical Training of Theological Students

*About the middle of December, while talking with one of my physicians, I remarked that while I recognized the grotesque character of the ideas I had had during the disturbed period, I still felt that in the experience there had been some purpose. It was not all a mistake. He shook his head solemnly and said I was entirely wrong.*

—Anton Boisen[1]

The Rev. Anton T. Boisen

LATE IN THE evening on Saturday, October 9, 1920, six police-men escorted the Rev. Anton T. Boisen to Boston Psychopathic Hospital. He had suffered an acute psychotic disturbance while working intensively on a statement of religious belief, and his mother and sister were frightened. Doctors diagnosed the condition of the forty-three-year-old bachelor minister as catatonic schizophrenia and said that there was no hope of recovery. Years later Boisen was to observe that being plunged as a patient into a hospital for the insane may be a tragedy or it may be an opportunity.[2] For him, it was an opportunity. How he dealt with this opportunity has affected the course of American religious history.

During the period of violent delirium Boisen endured that October, he was overcome by terrifying fears of a coming world catastrophe and mysterious forces of evil. These were followed by notions that he was more important than he ever dreamed: "My idea . . . was that I had broken down the walls between religion and medicine. With these ideas I seemed to have nothing to do. They came surging in with such power and were so utterly different from anything I had previously thought or dreamed that they seemed to carry authority."[3]

After one week Boisen was transferred to the Westboro State Hospital. Two weeks after that he snapped out of the delirium much as if he had wakened from a bad dream. In November he was transferred to a convalescent ward. Interested in finding out what had happened to him, he began by observing fellow patients. He soon concluded that most were in good physical condition but were rather discouraged. It appeared that what had happened to him had also happened to them—their inner world had come crashing down:

> It came over me like a flash that if inner conflicts like that which Paul describes in the famous passage in the seventh chapter of Romans can have happy solutions, as the church has always believed, there must also be unhappy solutions which thus far the church has ignored. It came to me that what I was being faced with in the hospital were the unhappy solutions. Most of the patients whom I saw around me would then be in the hospital because of spiritual or religious difficulties.[4]

Boisen tried to talk with the doctors about his illness but with little success; they did not believe in talking with patients about their symptoms. The hospital took the common, somatic point of view that symptoms are rooted in some as-yet-undiscovered organic difficulty. Boisen recalled that the longest time he was ever granted was fifteen minutes with a young doctor, who pointed out that "one must not hold the reins too tight in dealing with the sex instinct."[5]

During the time Boisen was attempting to understand his experience, he corresponded with the Rev. Fred Eastman, a friend from seminary days at Union in New York. Eastman sent a copy of Freud's *Introductory Lectures.* This was Boisen's first introduction to Freud, and he was excited to find much in the book that supported his independently-arrived-at ideas. On December 11 he wrote his friend a long letter of appreciation that began:

> Dear Fred:
> Let me thank you heartily for your fine letter and for the book on psychoanalysis. I have been reading it with intense interest and, in fact, excitement. Freud's conclusions are so strikingly in line with those which I had already formed that it makes me believe in myself a little bit once more. . . . He asserts in the first place that neuroses—i.e., abnormal, or insane conditions— have a *purpose.* They are due to deep-seated conflict between great subconscious forces and *the cure is to be found not in the suppression of the symptoms but in the solution of the conflict.* That is just what I tried to say in my last letter.[6]

Another important Freudian concept that helped Boisen was transference. Attachment to the physician is a source of healing that is to be accepted and used as part of the process of treatment. The transference relationship must be resolved before the cure is complete. For Boisen, this explained his experience—he was working out his transference to the person he regarded as his "healer," one Alice Batchelder.[7] His crisis had its roots in an unrequited love; his long-time dependence on Alice had to be resolved before his cure could be complete. The psychotic episode was a healthy, problem-solving experience.

For four and a half months Boisen tried to convince his friends and physicians that he was as well as he had ever been. (He had lost thirty pounds during the disturbed period but regained them afterward.[8]) About the middle of December he told a doctor "that while I recognized the grotesque character of the ideas I had had during the disturbed period, I still felt that in the experience there had been some purpose. It was not all a mistake."[9] The doctor replied that he was entirely wrong, and the remark cost Boisen a long-anticipated visit to Long Island to see Fred Eastman and his family. The hospital superintendent wrote to Eastman:

> I beg to inform you that I do not consider Mr. Boisen well enough to visit you at your home during the coming week-end. He still has many false ideas and although his conduct is not greatly disturbed, it is easy to see that his mind is far from right. He still believes that the experience through which he has been passing is part of a plan which has been laid out for him and that he has not suffered from any mental disease. This mistaken idea is sufficient to tell us that he is still in need of hospital treatment.[10]

By saying that he had not suffered from any mental illness, Boisen meant to distinguish between cerebral disease and mental disorder: he had no cerebral disease. The effect of the attitude at the hospital was to increase Boisen's fears and sense of helplessness.

Eastman had suggested to Boisen early on that he transfer to Bloomingdale Hospital in White Plains, New York, where he could undergo psychoanalysis. Boisen's initial reaction had been positive; he would like to go there to watch the results of the Freudian method. He did, however, have some subsequent doubts: "I don't like to be dissected as a pathological subject. I don't want to say more than is necessary and then only to those I trust absolutely."[11] Nevertheless, he pressed for a transfer, and after three months of negotiations it was arranged. He was to be moved on March 25, 1921. As the time drew near he became apprehensive. Having been forcibly hospitalized, he dreaded a treatment by people he did not know. On March 24 he suffered a relapse, becoming severely disturbed once again, this time for a duration of ten weeks.

As before, this began abruptly and ended suddenly. "On coming out of it, I changed my tactics and said nothing about release.

Instead I looked around for something to do."[12] He found a job doing photographic work for the hospital, work that gave him an opportunity to study the hospital inside and out. So doing, he found a new purpose: the service of the unfortunates with whom he was surrounded.

Boisen continued to write letters to Eastman and to the Rev. Norman Nash, a friend from World War I days in France who was then teaching at the Episcopal Theological School in Cambridge, Massachusetts. Nash discussed the possibility of consulting Dr. Elwood Worcester of the Emmanuel Church. Boisen's letters to both Eastman and Nash were turned over to Worcester to supply him with the information he wanted about Boisen before their first meeting, which took place in early November 1921; their consultations continued until May or June 1922.[13] At the close of the interviews Worcester returned all Boisen's letters to him. Boisen made limited use of them in his first book, *The Exploration of the Inner World,* published in 1936. However, when he wrote *Out of the Depths,* an autobiography published just a few years before his death, in 1965, he drew extensively on these letters in telling his story. Unless otherwise noted, I have consulted the autobiography for facts of Boisen's life.

### Boisen's Student Years

Anton Boisen's determination to come to a rational understanding of his experience of the irrational may be explained in part by his strong intellectual and educational background. Born in 1876 in Bloomington, Indiana, he grew up in the academic milieu of Indiana University. His father, a German immigrant, was a professor of modern languages; his maternal grandfather was a professor of pure mathematics; and his mother was one of the first women to enroll at Indiana University. Another relative had been the school's first president. Boisen did both undergraduate and graduate work at Indiana University and became an instructor there in romance languages.

In addition to academics, many clergy were in Boisen's ancestry. At no time did he have any intellectual difficulty with religion, for as he said, "The faith of my fathers was for me at one with the

42

authority of science."[14] His father, who died when Boisen was only seven, was a "thorough-going liberal" and his mother had accepted the liberal position early in life. As a teenager he attended and joined the Presbyterian church in Bloomington. Boisen's intellectual interests and development were deeply influenced by William Lowe Bryan, a professor of philosophy and psychology at Indiana University and later its president. Under him Boisen took a course in ethics and read William James' *Principles of Psychology*. He also attended Bryan's Bible class at the Presbyterian church. During a near psychotic episode on Easter 1898, he turned to Bryan for counseling. With his teacher's help he was able to see the event as bringing him to a higher level of functioning, an idea that formed the core of his later thinking about mental disorder and religious experience.[15]

In 1902, on the Bloomington campus, Boisen met the love of his life, Alice L. Batchelder. A native of Portsmouth, New Hampshire, and a graduate of Smith College, she had become Secretary of the YWCA at Indiana University. The story of their friendship is a complex one, told in bittersweet detail by Boisen in his autobiography. Over decades he courted her. Over decades she would not yield. In 1935 Alice Batchelder died—unmarried.

When he was twenty-six Boisen decided to give up his career as a teacher of languages and embark on the study of forestry. From 1903 to 1905 he attended the Yale Forestry School, where he met Raphael Zon, a U.S. Forest Service scientist. In an interview shortly before his death, Boisen told F. Henri Nouwen that Zon most influenced his scientific thinking. Nouwen writes:

> In Raphael Zon he found a scientist who not only strengthened Boisen's "clinical sensitivity" but trained him in the systematic survey. . . . The educational background of Boisen in which the emphasis was always on the empirical approach, using surveys, questionnaires and statistical analysis, has determined a great deal of his own contribution to the field of the psychology of religion. His own hospitalization certainly was the deciding factor in the choice of his subject for investigation, but the empirical approach to this subject had its roots long before the climax of his illness.[16]

In April 1905, while walking down New Haven's Chapel Street, Boisen felt called to the ministry, a call he associated with his love for Alice. The next day his decision was confirmed, when he heard Henry Sloane Coffin preach at Battell Chapel on the Call to Ministry. Boisen did not heed his call immediately but spent three years in the U.S. Forest Service. Then in 1908, when he was thirty-two years old, he entered Union Theological Seminary in New York:

> Although Union was one of the most forward-looking theological schools in the country, there was no provision in its curriculum for the consideration of the subject in which I was especially interested, the psychology of religion as interpreted by William James. That was true of our theological schools generally at the time. The study of psychology of religion had arisen during the eighteen-nineties in the secular educational institutions, but even in 1908, six years after the appearance of James' great *Varieties of Religious Experience,* it had as yet found little place within the structure of theological education.[17]

### The Psychology of Religion, and Religion and Health

Boisen's second year at Union was chiefly memorable for the arrival of George Albert Coe as professor of religious education and psychology. Boisen took all the courses he offered. As Nouwen explains: "His own problems were and remained central, and his main criterion in the selection of his subjects was their relevance for the clarification of his own problems."[18] Years later, when Boisen was an inmate in Westboro Hospital, he remembered Coe's inspiring guidance and support and wrote to him, hoping that, as a specialist in the psychology of religion, he would be able to help. Although Boisen received many kind letters, Coe had no suggestions for him; he held that the psychology of religion had nothing to do with the pathological.[19] Furthermore, like many leading psychologists of the time, Coe took an organic view of mental illness. He wrote to Boisen at Westboro in September 1921:

> If the attacks from which you have suffered, are, as appear, rather severe, then your physicians are probably right in assuming a physiological root, even though the process whereby a

44

given content arrives is that of suggestion. The fact that the specific physiological root has not been discovered hardly decreases the probability that there is one. I speak thus freely because you are so cool and objective yourself. I am glad that you have the disposition to face all the facts and that nothing needs to be concealed.[20]

When Coe died, in 1951, Boisen wrote a tribute to him that appeared in *Pastoral Psychology*. He praised Coe as one of the three foremost pioneers in the psychology of religion (along with James and Starbuck). Coe had ardently championed the empirical approach to the study of religious experience. But Boisen had to admit that on many vital issues they never could agree: "As a student of his I was never introduced to the domain of psychopathology. I doubt if he ever fully gave up his conviction that psychotic experiences can be explained by organic factors."[21] Boisen concluded his article by observing that Coe's passionate faith in social redemption and his antipathy to the mystical and the pathological had much to do with the direction taken by the science of the psychology of religion. "Its main drive seems to have been directed into other channels."[22] Coe himself gave increasing attention to religious education, and others to the philosophy of religion.

Properly to understand the origins of the Religion and Health Movement, it is important to underscore Boisen's comments about the direction taken by the psychology of religion. Although Coe was a friend who supported Boisen in times of crisis and despair, Coe could not accept the dynamic psychological view that Boisen came to espouse at Westboro and later to explain in *Exploration of the Inner World*. Dynamic thinking, an experiential discovery of Boisen's that was confirmed for him by reading Freud, was long neglected by the discipline. As Boisen said, its main drive was directed in other channels; the path to which he pointed was not followed. Dr. Paul Pruyser, who published a ground-breaking *Dynamic Psychology of Religion* in 1968, comments:

With psychoanalysis the psychology of religion should have undergone a change in concepts, in orientation, and in attitude toward the material studied. Instead, it underwent a change in personnel. For psychoanalysis is also a branch of psychiatry and, through it, of medicine. Within psychology its impact was felt mostly in the specialization of clinical psychology, which has had relatively little contact with the psychology of religion—the latter has remained more closely in the fold of academic psychology and educational psychology. The psychoanalytic impact on psychiatry is great. Its impact is also felt keenly in pastoral education, and in pastoral theology. I believe that this selective spread of the influence of psychoanalysis has altered the status of scientific concern with religion in a major way.[23]

Brooks Holifield has written that it is hard to imagine clinical pastoral education without the interest in the psychology of religion.[24] This may be so *if* one is speaking of the *initial* interest Boisen, Worcester, Dunbar, and Hiltner took in the psychology of religion. All, however, moved beyond the narrowness and limitations of the psychology of religion of their time and adapted a dynamic (i.e., clinical and essentially Freudian) point of view. Only much later would the psychology of religion catch up.[25]

Another point that must be made is that although pioneers in Religion and Health were interested in the *psychology* of religion, they differed from pioneer *psychologists* of religion. These men, as Peter Homans indicates, were by and large either psychologists or educators, and "thus they were not professionally concerned with institutional forms of Christianity or with theology, except as these were understood to be the proper subject of psychological analysis."[26] Religion and Health leaders, however, were Christian ministers; their primary concern was with the vitality of the church and its theology.

### Decade of the Teens: A Time of Crisis for Boisen and for American Protestantism

Anton Boisen had occasion to learn a good deal about the position of the church in America after his graduation from Union in 1911. Alice Batchelder had made it clear that she would not marry him, and he concluded that a pastorate without her help was unthinkable. He therefore accepted a job with the Presbyterian Board of Home Missions doing rural survey work, first in Missouri and then in Tennessee. He later supplemented his findings with studies in Kansas and Maine. A prolific writer throughout his life, Boisen published the results—"Factors in the Decline of the Country Church"—in the *American Journal of Sociology* in 1916. He found that

> the influence of the church, as measured by church attendance, varies inversely with the degree of liberalization of popular religious opinion. Thus, in western Tennessee, where extreme conservatism held sway, only 20 per cent of the heads of families were classed by their neighbors as nonchurchgoers. In Missouri, 28 per cent of all those over twelve years of age were so classed. In Kansas, 42 per cent of those over twelve were classed as nonchurchgoers, and in liberalized Maine, 65 per cent.[27]

These facts were to influence his later thinking about Protestant liberalism.

Boisen did, after all, become a country pastor, albeit an unsuccessful one. Over a period of five years he served Congregational churches in Ames, Iowa; Wabaunsee, Kansas; and North Anson, Maine. Then, after two years during World War I with the YMCA in France and Germany, he accepted a job with the Interchurch World Movement (IWM). This movement was organized in late 1918 by American church leaders who, as Boisen said, "were dreaming great dreams."[28] Prof. Sydney Ahlstrom describes the IWM:

> What they attempted was a grand peacetime crusade which would unite all the benevolent and missionary agencies of American Protestantism into a single campaign for money, men and spiritual revival. Included in its scope were every phase of church work, domestic and foreign. . . . A lavish prospectus, expensive offices, and elaborate promotional plans featured in the movement's launching.[29]

The first step was to analyze worldwide need by making a worldwide survey. In July 1919 Boisen became director of the North Dakota Rural Survey. Within a short time he could see that things had not been going well with the IWM and that it was going to fold.[30] Ahlstrom explains that the IWM became "a victim of its dreams and its overhead."[31]

The failure of the movement coincided with Boisen's sense of personal failure.[32] In June 1920 he met Alice for the first time in nine years; she remained adamant in her refusal of his persistent love. Having spent years wandering, he was uncertain of his real vocation; his "rambling life in the ministry had not yet given him the sense of meaningfulness he was looking for."[33] At midlife, it was a time of crisis. Remarkably, Boisen's sense of pending catastrophe came at a period when the church's position in American life was itself threatened[34]:

> It was a time of crisis for both the Protestant Establishment and the historic evangelicalism which undergirded it. It was the critical epoch when the Puritan heritage lost its hold on the leaders of public life, and when the mainstream denominations grew increasingly out of touch with the classic Protestant witness.[35]

Overwhelmed by ominous personal fears, Boisen was taken to the hospital by six policemen. Fifteen months later, in January 1922, he was released. In the interim he had found a true vocation in ministering to the mentally ill.

On leaving Westboro, Boisen took residence in the Episcopal Theological School in Cambridge. For the next two and a half years he studied the problems that had become central for him. As a special student at Andover Theological Seminary he took seminars at Andover, Harvard, and the Boston Psychopathic Hospital. He studied social ethics and the preparation of case records with Dr. Richard C. Cabot; abnormal psychology and the theories of mind and body with Prof. William McDougall; the psychology of belief with Dr. Macfie Campbell. Boisen became better acquainted with Freud and delved into Jung, Janet, and Meyer as well. His most time-consuming task was the formation of a research project for the study of the interrelationship of religious experience and mental illness.

### Fundamental Conflict with Dr. Richard Cabot

Of the many persons who played a role in Boisen's life at the time, Dr. Richard Cabot was one of the most important. Cabot's seminar at Harvard on the preparation of case records for teaching purposes was one of the best Boisen had ever taken, and it led him to develop the case method in theological education.[36] When Boisen's research proposal on religious experience and mental illness was rejected by the Institute for Social Research,[37] Dr. Cabot offered to back it himself. This became unnecessary, however, when Dr. William A. Bryan offered Boisen a job as Chaplain at Worcester State Hospital. (It had been Cabot who first heard of the new opening and suggested Boisen.) He began work on July 1, 1924.

Believing that there was great need among neglected mental sufferers, Dr. Richard Cabot was much interested in Boisen's story and supported his work with the mentally ill. Nevertheless, he did not feel "that a religious worker could do anything beyond giving comfort and consolation."[38] Cabot did not accept the psychogenic explanation of mental disorder. One of his brothers from the age of eighteen had recurrent attacks of manic-depressive psychosis, and Cabot was sure that this was of chemical origin. In a letter to his wife, Ella Lyman Cabot, he wrote that he "should rejoice doubly over progress in understanding the chemistry of depression . . . because it would help discredit the Freudians who now explain depression, like everything else, by their familiar absurdities."[39]

The origin of mental illness was an issue that came up again and again between Boisen and Cabot. Boisen reports an incident that occurred at the Week of Work of the National Council for Religion in Higher Education (NCRHE) in 1929. (The circumstance is notable since it was at the NCRHE Week of Work in 1941 that the idea originated for the New York Psychology Group, described in chapter 6.) When the interest group with which Boisen had been meeting made its report, it embodied one of Boisen's "pet doctrines," that the sense of guilt is a major factor in mental disorder and that it is essentially a social judgment that the individual pronounces on himself or herself. Boisen remembered that when the paper was read "Dr. Cabot stood up straight as a ramrod and stated that he thought it his duty to say that he did not believe there was a word of truth in that report."[40]

When in November 1930 Boisen suffered a second acute psychotic episode, it was Cabot who saw to it that he was hospitalized. He recovered after three weeks, but Cabot, who had always opposed his psychogenic views, now found them "abhorrent."[41]

In 1934 Cabot gave a lecture at the Chicago Theological Seminary on "The Wisdom of the Body" in which he described the marvelous devices of the body in maintaining and restoring health. Talking afterward with him privately, Boisen suggested that he wondered about the analogous processes in the human mind: "Dr. Cabot shook his head emphatically and replied that he believed thoroughly in the wisdom of the body, but not in that of the mind."[42] Cabot wrote Boisen a letter in 1936 that made his position clear: "The facts of recovery in manic depressives and in some schizophrenics certainly prove God's/nature's power to heal in the psychoses. I never doubted *that*. What I doubt is man's power to help God's work in this field save by physical and environmental hygiene."[43]

In September 1925 Dr. Cabot published an article, "A Plea for a Clinical Year in the Course of Theological Study," that is often cited as heralding the clinical training movement. In assessing the import of this article and Cabot's leadership in the clinical training movement, one must keep firmly in mind his rigid, somatic position. Even though the movement could hardly have gotten under way without his "powerful support" (as Boisen remarked at the Silver Anniversary in 1950[44]), Cabot was basically at odds with the wisdom and intention of its founding father, "Pappy Boisen."[45]

Cabot's "Plea" was significant for drawing national attention to the needs of theological students to develop skill and ability in helping troubled people, but his vision was limited. The task of these students, he thought, was to learn by practice "to encourage, to console, to steady human souls."[46] A clinical year would be a year in "applied theology." Students would learn to look after "the minds, the emotions, the wills, the souls"[47] of inmates in hospitals and asylums. Cabot's insistence on a division of labor between doctors and ministers—his drawing of a strict boundary between the professional functions of the two—is reminiscent of the thinking of his colleague, Dr. J.J. Putnam.

Within four months of the publication of Cabot's plea, Boisen countered with one of his own—"The Challenge to Our Seminaries." Boisen criticized Cabot for stopping short of the "crucially important proposition that in mental disorders we are dealing with a problem which is essentially spiritual."[48] Boisen cited an IWM survey of 1919 that showed that 381 hospitals in the United States were supported and controlled by Protestant churches. Only three were especially concerned with problems of mental disorder:

> We have therefore this truly remarkable situation—a Church which has always been interested in the care of the sick confining her efforts to the types of cases in which religion has least concern and least to contribute, while in those types in which it is impossible to tell where the domain of the medical worker leaves off and that of the religious worker begins, there the Church is doing nothing.[49]

Where they existed, the church's efforts to deal with conflicts were "without scientific basis or intelligent direction."[50] Boisen maintained that whereas fundamentalists supply treatment (i.e., promise of salvation) without diagnosis, liberals supply neither treatment nor diagnosis. He placed a share of the blame on the seminaries, for they teach about human personality neither in sickness nor in health:

> When we remember that what we know today about the human body has come very largely through the study of diseased conditions, is it any wonder that a Church which has so completely ignored the problem of the soul that is sick, is able to speak with so little spiritual authority concerning the laws of the spiritual world.[51]

These, Boisen said, were *his* reasons for approving Cabot's suggestions of a clinical year for theological students. To carry the suggestion further, he viewed the ordinary parish as "the laboratory of a new religious psychotherapy," providing opportunity for study and research *after seminary.*[52]

## Origins of Clinical Pastoral Education

The clinical training of theological students—known today as clinical pastoral education, or simply CPE—began in June 1925.[53]

Four students enrolled for a summer of study with Chaplain Boisen at Worcester State Hospital, an institution for 2,200 patients.[54] During the day they worked on the wards as attendants, conducting recreational and social programs, writing letters for patients, walking and singing with them, observing them, and keeping records. During the evening they read books on psychology, psychiatry, and religion and held seminars with Boisen and the medical staff. One of the students was Helen Flanders Dunbar, who at the time was working on her B.D. at Union and her Ph.D. at Columbia. Within a few years Dunbar would have a pivotal role in the Religion and Health Movement.

In the summer of 1926 four more students came; in 1927, seven; in 1928, eleven; in 1929, fifteen.[55] Later all the early leaders in the field of CPE could claim some direct or indirect relationship with the beginnings under Boisen.[56]

Financing clinical training constituted one of Boisen's major problems. Fortuitously, one of his early students, Philip Guiles, volunteered to help secure funds. Guiles was able to raise a substantial contribution from his father-in-law, provided that a corporate body to promote the work was formed. So it happened that on January 21, 1930, the Council for Clinical Training of Theological Students—referred to by Dunbar as "the Cs and the Ts"[57]—was incorporated. Cabot agreed to have his house at 101 Brattle Street in Cambridge (across the street from the Episcopal Theological School) listed as headquarters.[58] Guiles became field secretary and Dunbar, who dropped the "Helen" and became known as Dr. Flanders Dunbar after she earned her M.D., was appointed medical director.

Dissention soon split the Council. Prof. Edward E. Thornton, historian of the movement, writes that "the relationship between Guiles and Dunbar became so bitter by 1932 that Dunbar simply declared the headquarters to be New York City rather than Boston."[59] Although the initial schism was a conflict of personalities, an ideological polarization gradually took place between the Boston group and the New York group, which gathered around Dunbar, Boisen, and later Hiltner.[60] After Boisen's second hospitalization, in November 1930, Dr. Cabot terminated his support of Boisen's program at Worcester. When Carroll Wise became chaplain there, Cabot told Wise that Cabot's "continued support of the

Worcester program was conditioned upon a decision by Wise to renounce the views of Boisen, particularly psychogenic theories about mental illness."[61] When Wise could not do this, Cabot invested his support in the program at Massachusetts General Hospital. The appropriateness of *mental* hospitals as training centers then became an issue between Boston and New York.

In 1932 Boisen, who had been teaching fall semesters at Chicago Theological Seminary since 1926, left New England to organize an independent clinical training program at Elgin State (Mental) Hospital, an institution for 3,600 patients near Chicago.[62] He remained in residence at Elgin until his death.

As the reader may expect, Cabot's attitude toward psychodynamic thinking was a major factor in the split between the Boston and the New York groups. Reviewing the situation in 1970, Thornton wrote that the mainstream of CPE has been "more fully congruent with Cabot's vision of the goals" than of Boisen's. He maintained that the central purpose of CPE is defined by Cabot's vision of "pastoral competence in ministry."[63] Although I am indebted to Professor Thornton for many observations about CPE, particularly its roots in scientific thinking and evangelical liberalism, I cannot agree with him on this point. Boisen's deeper vision of pastoral competence *through* clinical, psychodynamic insight is, as I understand it, the controlling ideal of clinical pastoral education. It is Boisen, not Cabot, whom pioneering leaders—including Hiltner, Wise, and Oates—honor and revere as the founding father. Not Cabot's, but Boisen's original aims and goals are cited when the movement seems to move off course, away from theological reflection on the basis of empirical observation.

Like Elwood Worcester, Boisen made a distinction between two methods of mental healing.[64] The one seeks to impose suggestions by relying on the personal influence of the healer. It is clear that Dr. Cabot used this method:

> Cabot said that people are sick from functional illnesses because they do not know how to behave themselves—for example, poor scheduling, compulsive overactivity, and the like. He advocated a didactic approach to treatment such as helping patients make a realistic schedule. He believed in "work cures"

more than in "rest cures," and most of all in a kind of positive thinking that discriminates fear of pain from fear of death, worry from thinking, and the like.[65]

The other healing method calls for the application of scientific understanding to the source of the problem. Boisen wrote: "It hardly seems necessary to say that the hope of genuine progress lies with the latter. . . . *It is equally clear that for those techniques which call for understanding, the training can hardly be too thorough* [italics added]."[66]

The essential part of the clinical training of theology students, said Boisen, is that they should be introduced under guidance to "living human documents" and that they should learn to recognize and understand the pathological. Boisen believed that unless the clergy understand "those experiences in which men are grappling with the issues of spiritual life and death,"[67] they will not be able to speak with authority regarding the way to salvation—individual or social. Pastoral competence comes with insight.

### *Anton Boisen's Psychodynamic Orientation*

My point—that Boisen based psychological insight on a clinical, psychodynamic, essentially Freudian model—will meet with objections. Thornton has stated flatly that "the first steps toward clinical pastoral education were not informed by Freudian psychoanalysis."[68] He writes that the founding fathers—Dr. William Keller,[69] Dr. Richard Cabot, and Anton Boisen—were "akin in their detachment from psychoanalytic theory."[70] And historian Brooks Holifield maintains that Boisen found Freud "useful but shortsighted," whereas Boisen's "intellectual heirs felt more at home with the new depth psychologies."[71]

Have these scholars interpreted Boisen's thought accurately? The question is not merely academic. How one interprets the meaning and intentions of the founder of clinical training will determine how one assesses the movement's development and where it stands today. Holifield concludes, for example, that "we are still the children of the progressives."[72] To the extent that CPE leaders are Boisen's intellectual heirs, as they interpret themselves to be, it is impossible to see them as kin to the progressive reformers. Boisen's ideas derived from evangelical liberalism and scientific psychology, not the progressive movement. Cabot may have been a progressive, but his influence in clinical training did not endure.[73]

During his long lifetime Anton Boisen observed abuses in the CPE movement that were attributed to Freudian, psychotherapeutic influence. These were particularly apparent in the Council in the 1940s. When he spoke out against these abuses, he was incorrectly perceived to be at odds with psychoanalytic theory. The following brief analysis of Boisen's basic criticisms is an attempt to set the record straight.

First, Boisen criticized the Freudian emphasis of clinical training supervisors. The psychotherapeutic milieu had focused increasing importance on the relationship between the supervisor and the student, with a consequent shift of attention from the patient to the student. This development was contrary to Boisen's original aims for clinical training, and he said so. He insisted that it was as important to have students trained in *research* and in *religious* insights, as it was for them to be analyzed and trained in Freudian doctrine.[74] What is notable is that Boisen did not condemn Freudian method or theory, but the weight that supervisors gave it. He was protesting a secular trend in CPE. An evangelical liberal, he put ministry first. As a patient he had been shocked to learn that the mentally ill received no special pastoral care; he had worked hard to cure the situation; and he had even compiled a special hymnbook for hospital inmates to use.[75] For him, the purpose of clinical training was *not* psychotherapy for the theological student.[76]

Evidence that Boisen's criticism of psychotherapeutic influence did not imply a criticism of psychodynamic thinking itself is his opposition to another development. Boisen complained about the growing emphasis on the analysis of verbatim reports, a teaching technique pioneered by Russell Dicks, because of their *lack* of psychodynamics.[77]

A second criticism Boisen made was that in CPE in the 1940s

"there was a tendency to accept Freudian doctrine on authority without scrutinizing it closely."[78] Boisen objected to dogmatic and simplistic psychoanalytic thinking.[79] In the spirit of Freud, who continuously revised his own theories throughout his career, Boisen insisted on open-minded inquiry. He was a *liberal* thinker who did not endorse Freud's ideas uncritically, but felt free to reject what was unacceptable, especially Freud's positivistic views about religion. Boisen also had reservations about the crucial importance Freud placed on infant/childhood experiences.

A third criticism Boisen made was that under the influence of Freud, some supervisors in the 1940s tried to help patients who were torn between the demands of conscience and of erotic impulses by lowering the conscience threshold.[80] Boisen knew that Freud would, "to an extent," let down bars and remove the inhibitions when conflict had to do with the sex drive.[81] This solution Boisen found unacceptable; he aimed at high moral achievement. Nonetheless, Boisen had learned from Freud that when instinctual cravings or wishes are denied natural expression, they may become split off from the conscious self and then manifest themselves in psychopathic symptoms. The cure was to be brought about, as Freud taught,

> by uncovering the source of the difficulty and enabling the patient to incorporate the disowned or "repressed" tendency into the structure of the self. The truly satisfactory solution is found when the repressed tendency is able to find expression in socially acceptable and constructive fashion.[82]

If Boisen did not advocate lowering the conscience threshold, neither did he advocate *repressing* instinctual desires.

For Boisen, instinctual cravings were to be managed by "frankness" and "socialization." One needs to face difficulties honestly and to be ready to acknowledge them both to oneself and to others. This is a precondition of socialization and assimilation. New levels of development cannot be reached unless one assimilates one's experiences—particularly sexual ones.

Boisen disagreed with Freudians that the sex "complex" is unconscious:

It seems to me to be rather clamoring insistently for attention, giving the unhappy individual no peace until it is taken care of, while all the time he is trying to escape from it by forcing it back into the region of shadow and darkness, or incorporate it into his mental structure by means of some formulation which will enable it to get by in disguise. *The root evil is a craving or tendency which the individual is unable either to control or to acknowledge to those whom he loves, and by the same token to himself* [italics added].[83]

Boisen agreed with Freudians that one could be free and well only by bringing into the open and being clearly aware of whatever it is that causes inner dichotomy: "The individual not only recognizes it himself but he is ready also to acknowledge it to those whose love is necessary to him. He is not afraid to tell."[84]

Anton Boisen was a participant-observer in mental illness: he knew whereof he spoke. At age eighty-five he published what Ernest Becker calls a "courageously frank" autobiography[85]—he was not afraid to tell. Commenting that the patient's reconstructions of his or her experiences are the least reliable of all, Becker claims that Boisen completely overlooks the failure of his relationship with Alice as a possible contribution to his breakdown.[86] On the contrary, Boisen explicitly connects his interpersonal failure and his sexual problems with psychotic episodes. His meticulous reporting of the unsatisfactory relationship with Alice as well as his sexual reactions and difficulties are indications of his awareness—however dim or clear—of the sexual etiology of his disorder.[87] If "throughout his life he patrolled his own internal walls like a prison guard and punished every deviant desire," as Holifield observes,[88] Boisen seems to have recognized the price he paid for this.

Becker claims that Boisen saw his breakdown only in cosmic religious terms.[89] Although he did, indeed, interpret his experience in terms of religious faith, his autobiography witnesses to his own consciousness that feelings of failure, guilt, and sexual conflict were contributing factors in his illness. The following letter supports this interpretation:

Dr. Elwood Worcester
Emmanuel Church
Boston, Mass.

Dear Dr. Worcester,

In the interview of last Monday the following ground was covered, if I remember correctly:

1. The precise nature of the original trouble.
2. The character of the first abnormal condition.
3. Some facts regarding the love affair around which the whole thing centers.
4. Your advice that I take up some outdoor work.


I hope that the following facts have been established:

1. The original trouble was primarily a mental one. There was no habit of masturbation and no perversions, as I understand those terms. There was difficulty in controlling the wayward sex interests.
2. The first abnormal condition, while containing many morbid elements, was a clear-cut conversion experience, with effects which were wholly beneficial.
3. The love affair was not rooted in friendly association but rather in inner struggle and in what might be called quite accurately the need of salvation. The motive power has been the deep feeling that this was for me the right course, the only one I could follow and be true to my best self.
4. The danger that I may underestimate the gravity of these abnormal conditions and the necessity of avoiding future recurrences. This danger I recognize. The horror of the recent catastrophe is with me still. It has been terrible beyond the power of words to express. And yet I do not regard these experiences as "breakdowns." If I am right in believing that through them difficult problems have been solved for me and solved right, and if through them help and strength have come to me, am I not justified in such a view?[90]

Psychologist Paul Pruyser draws our attention to Boisen's remarkable power of assimilation. He *lived* the depth psychological principles that he taught:

> Boisen felt reborn, regenerated, and converted by his great psychic upheaval, despite several relapses afterward and despite his candor of accepting for these episodes the classical psychiatric label of "acute schizophrenia, catatonic type." He did not disown his disorganized periods. His sense of identity as continuity through time remained firm, as his autobiography shows, and he did not disclaim his past, nightmarish as it was. . . . Boisen could have dissociated himself from his old premorbid self, and he could have repressed the memories of his nightmarish episodes. The fact that he did not is to the credit of his integrative and synthesizing capacities.[91]

Boisen supported efforts of clinical training supervisors to help persons to find psychic freedom through frankness, integration, and socialization of instinctual drives. He also encouraged moral striving and aspiration. For Boisen, "the liberation of the self through insight into depth of the personality" was not itself an ethical ideal, as some supervisors took it to be,[92] but a *means* to an ethical ideal: depth psychological insight freed one to choose Christian moral behavior. Had he used the words, Boisen might have spoken of "freedom" for "formation." Freud put the matter this way:

> Our art consists of making it possible for people to be moral and deal with their wishes philosophically. Sublimation, that is striving toward higher goals, is of course one of the best means of overcoming the urgency of our drives. But one can consider doing this only after psychoanalytic work has lifted the repressions.[93]

If there was a period in the clinical training movement, as it seems clear there was in the 1940s, when supervisors justified libertine attitudes and behavior on the basis of pop psychoanalysis, their "Freudian" orientation must not be confused with the genuine Freudian insights that informed Boisen's thought and life.

It is worth summarizing Boisen's fear of CPE misuse of Freudian psychology because these tendencies loom even today as threats to the integrity of the movement. To be guarded against are:

1. shift of attention away from the theological exploration based on empirical research toward secular psychotherapy and doctrine;
2. uncritical, dogmatic acceptance of Freudian theories, or simplistic interpretation of Freud;
3. a lowering of ethical behavioral standards as a consequence of secular psychotherapy.

Boisen's critique of popular Freudian influence seems gentle and mild-mannered compared with 0. Hobart Mowrer's devastating assault in the late 1950s and early 1960s. In a series of lectures and articles, collected under the title *The Crisis in Psychiatry and Religion,*[94] Mowrer charged that liberal Protestantism had fallen for, or been infiltrated by, Freudianism.[95] He wrote that "present-day Protestantism and Freudian analysis are so blended and inter-digitated that it is hard to tell when one ends and the other begins."[96] Many theologians, he said, "preach and write as if Freudian theory and practice were the Alpha and Omega."[97] In Mowrer's opinion, Freud is not the prophet that theologians tried to make of him, but rather "the Pied Piper who beguiled us into serious misconceptions and practices."[98]

For Mowrer, Anton T. Boisen is the true prophet. An admirer of Boisen's work, Mowrer entitled one of his articles after Boisen's—"The New Challenge to Our Churches and Seminaries." He began, "Has evangelical religion sold its birthright for a mess of psychological pottage?" and as a psychologist and churchman, he answered yes. Mowrer wrote that under Boisen the pastoral counseling movement got a promising start in the right direction, but it was then "deflected and distorted" by psychoanalytic theory.[99] Interestingly, for Mowrer, the "primal psychoanalytic premise" is that "conscience is a real monster which complains and tortures the individual without just cause."[100] The pastoral counseling movement, said Mowrer, was gradually permeated and possessed by the

> basic assumption of Freudian psychoanalysis—namely, that psychoneurosis arises, not from moral weakness or failure, but

60

from an excessive and irrational severity (or "disease") of the superego or conscience. . . . One of the earliest and most transparent indications of this victory of the Freudian view, *as opposed to that advocated by Boisen,* was the appearance in 1943 of Harry Emerson Fosdick's book, *On Being A Real Person.* [italics added][101]

Clearly, Mowrer sees the "Freud-Fosdick position"[102] as quite different from Boisen's.

According to Mowrer, the pastoral counseling movement had four stages. The first was a growing awareness of the failure of religion to meet people's psychological needs. The second was the beginning of pastoral counseling, which was given a conceptual framework by Boisen. The third and fourth stages he described as follows:

> (3) the blighting of this aim by the intrusion of the Freudian doctrine that human beings sicken in mind and soul, not from sin, but from their very excess of piety (or "moralism")
> (4) current developments in the sciences and secular professions which are casting grave doubt upon the validity of the Freudian view and thus placing many contemporary clergymen and seminarians in the awkward position of having "sold their birthright."[103]

Mowrer faulted the "Freudian formula" for making human beings not only helpless, but also blameless.[104] A moralist whose views are reminiscent of Dr. Richard Cabot's, Mowrer wrote that personality disorder is caused by "real guilt," not "imaginary guilt." His discussion of "Psychopathology and the Problem of Guilt, Confession, and Expiation"[105] forms the nucleus of his thinking. In this chapter he makes a conjecture that Boisen's own hospitalization was *"dynamically necessitated by the confession."*[106] Subsequent publication of Boisen's *Out of the Depths* proved this guess totally inaccurate; not feelings of guilt, but feelings of failure and conflict precipitated Boisen's illness. Even though Professor Mowrer was acquainted with Boisen, admired his work, and quoted it frequently, it is clear that Mowrer neither understood nor appreciated Boisen's indebtedness to Freud. Had Mowrer had the benefit of reading *Out of the Depths,* he might not have made the following "historical" statement:

Today there are literally thousands of ministers who are under the spell of Tillich, Fosdick, and the other Freudian apologists. And what is the basis on which ministers accept the leadership of such men? Is it because psychoanalysis has been empirically validated? Not in the least. It is rather because theology, by becoming bookish and unredemptive, had lost its true center of gravity, its contact with basic human realities, and its leaders bob about like loose corks in a choppy sea. They turn to Freud because they have lost their own integrity and anchorage. If religious leaders had been deeply involved in the care and redemption of seriously disturbed persons for the past century, instead of systematically "referring" such persons, there would have been no Freud and no necessity for a Tillich or a Fosdick to try to legitimize him.[107]

As his autobiography makes apparent, Anton Boisen accepted Freud's dynamic psychological theories *because* his own experience empirically validated them. Boisen did not turn to Freud because he had lost his own integrity and anchorage. Nor, as we have seen, did Worcester. Anchored firmly in evangelical faith, Worcester turned to Freud for psychological insight only after years of work with disturbed persons. American Protestantism had sorely neglected the care of souls, as both Worcester and Boisen took every opportunity to tell the world, but this was not because ministers were busy systematically referring disturbed persons elsewhere.

In this chapter I have endeavored to show that Boisen's thought was essentially Freudian inasmuch as he took a scientific (or clinical), dynamic approach that was consistent with the spirit and therapeutic purpose of Freud himself. Throughout this study I quote excerpts from Freud's writings, particularly his letters, to distinguish his position from that attributed to him. Mowrer, however, is not concerned if what he intends by the word Freudianism does not correspond precisely to what Freud said, for what Mowrer is speaking of throughout his critique is "Freudianism" *as popularly understood.*[108] Given his working definition, I cannot argue against Mowrer that Boisen's thought was "Freudian." Religion and Health leaders did not build a movement, as Mowrer implies, on popular, distorted conceptions of Freud.[109]

Mowrer's familiar charge that Freudian psychoanalysis is a pseudoscience is a separate issue, an issue considered in chapter 8.

Just as we examined the Emmanuel Movement in the light of modernist Protestant liberalism, it is necessary now to examine the clinical pastoral education movement from that perspective. Were the three distinguishing characteristics—accommodation of secular culture, a sense of God's immanence, and a belief in progress—evident in the thrust of the founder's thought and work? It is not difficult to demonstrate that they were, for Boisen made explicit his liberal attitude.

In 1925 he published an article in the *American Review*, "In Defense of Mr. Bryan, A Personal Confession by a Liberal Clergyman."[110] Boisen's original intention was to sign himself not "a liberal clergyman," but rather "a disciple of Dr. Fosdick." This proved impossible when, after reviewing the article, Fosdick retorted that if it were published under that title, "it would have to be over his dead body."[111]

Boisen admitted that it was unusual for a liberal member of the clergy to venture a defense of Mr. Bryan. Historian Hugh Hammett reminds us of the ambience of the time—"the old doggedly determined to stay alive and the new kicking and squalling to be born":

> The sultry July of 1925 found William Jennings Bryan in the drowsy village of Dayton, Tennessee, defending Jonah's big fish and Joshua's immobile sun while Clarence Darrow thundered ominously, "With flying banners and beating drums we are marching backward into the glorious age of the sixteenth century, when bigots lighted fagots to burn the men who dared to bring any intelligence and enlightenment and culture to the human mind."[112]

Strange as it may seem, Boisen came to Bryan's defense. To remember Boisen's sociological surveys for the Presbyterian Church is to remember that he had come to the "disturbing conclusion that wherever the liberal influence is strongest, the influence of the church tends to be weakest."[113] Boisen's statistical studies had showed him that Mr. Bryan was not wrong in believing that the breakdown of traditional authority destroys popular faith; nor was he wrong in believing that the church must have an

63

authoritative message. Boisen could not, however, agree with the fundamentalist that the church must go back to the traditional authority. The forces "of the truth which sets men free" had made that beyond the church's control to do.[114] The solution was to be found not in retreat, but in advance: the liberal church "has not yet gone far enough," Boisen said. "It has merely surrendered the authority of the tradition without freeing itself from the traditional point of view."[115]

The authority Boisen sought was not a return to tradition and the written word, but "a return to the experience and the central interest of Him who came to seek and to save the lost"—the saving of souls.

> In the light of all that modern psychology and psychiatry and sociology have to offer I would study the living human person-ality in health and in disease, in prosperity and in disaster, seek-ing patiently and systematically and reverently to discover the dynamic factors and the mechanisms which are involved and to formulate the laws which govern them.[116]

Like Elwood Worcester, Boisen reiterated that he had no new gospel to proclaim, only a new approach. He wanted to call atten-tion away from liberal preoccupation with social reform and reli-gious education and back to the central task of the church: soul cure. The attempt to apply methods of science to this unexplored field was a radical departure, "but our findings are in line with the insights of Jesus and of Paul, of Augustine and of Luther."[117]

Boisen was an empiricist who believed that theology, "erst-while Queen of the Sciences," truly deserves a place among the sciences.[118] He based his theological thinking on "living human documents," on the authority of *experience*. As a pastor working with hospitalized patients who thought they were prophets, he said he never tried to "shake their faith in themselves or the value of their experience," but rather to help them "to take the next step of freeing the divine from their idea of themselves."[119] What continued to strike Boisen throughout his life was that liberals attempt to deal with the central problems of the Christian faith while making little effort to attack these problems empirically.[120]

Boisen cautioned that authority grounded in experience would not come all at once, but through cooperative effort and with the growing certainty "of the life of God in the soul of man." Boisen was convinced of God's *immanence,* of the purposive nature of personal experience. In the epilogue to *Out of the Depths,* entitled "The Guiding Hand," he wrote that it was painful to think of his own failure that cost him his marriage to Alice, and yet he had no regret. If they had married, if he had become a successful minister with her help,

> there would have been no new light upon the interrelatedness of mental disorder and religious experience. Neither would there have been for me any clinical training movement. . . . I would surely be a man of little faith if I did not recognize in this story the guiding hand of an Intelligence beyond our own.[121]

Boisen cannot be accused of a delusive, visionary optimism typical of some Social Gospel liberals. He knew that even if his voice were heeded, "no miracle need be looked for": "The problem of the human personality and of the laws and forces which are concerned therein is entirely too baffling."[122] Nevertheless, he did believe that theology could make *progress* in formulating what he called "the laws of the spiritual life." By the study of present experience, "the Church may once more come into its own and speak no longer as the scribes and Pharisees and interpreters of traditions but with *the authority of the knowledge of the laws of the life that is eternal* [italics added]."[123]

The parallels between the aims and thinking of Worcester and Boisen are striking. Emmanuel was a precursor of CPE; out of the failure of the former, the more durable structure of the latter was built.[124] Both movements may be seen to contribute to the more encompassing Religion and Health Movement. This arose in a society that found itself "increasingly dislocated by the incredible velocity of modernity."[125] Put in the simplest terms, Religion and Health was a search for ways of effective ministry to individuals under stress. Professor Thornton has summarized the situation dramatically and vividly:

> We might interpret the rise of clinical pastoral education in the twenties in terms of the contest between Elijah and the prophets

65

of Baal. Using the biblical account as a paradigm of contemporary events, we could say that the scientific community threw down the challenge: "The God who answers by healing, he is God." Medicine invoked science; theology invoked religion. The people hesitated, then turned to medicine. For it was the god Science who answered with healing. The great temples of America became her medical centers devoted to the god of health. The high priests became physicians and psychiatrists. Clinical pastoral education may be said to be an effort by the religious community to secure the fire of healing for the altars of church and synagogue. Most clinical pastoral educators have been convinced that without effectively meeting the needs of people for psychic wholeness, the altar fires will go out and the houses of worship will go dead.[126]

In my reading of the events, this metaphorical analysis is strikingly accurate.

Anton Boisen lived to be eighty-nine years old, long enough to see clinical pastoral education securely established as a feature of the theological seminary curriculum. Two years after his death the rivalry between the New York-based Council for Clinical Training and the Boston-based Institute of Pastoral Care ended when the two merged as the Association for Clinical Pastoral Education (1967). Also involved in the merger were Lutheran and Southern Baptist groups, which in 1949 and 1957, respectively, had established their own clinical pastoral education programs.

In 1975 the Association for Clinical Pastoral Education celebrated the fiftieth anniversary of its beginnings. At that time as many as 4,799 men and women were enrolled in basic, advanced, or supervisory training programs:[127]

|  | Men | Women |
| --- | --- | --- |
| Seminary students | 1,507 | 282 |
| Parish clergy | 1,102 | 54 |
| Institutional clergy | 340 | 35 |
| Military chaplains | 191 | |
| Missionaries | 67 | 13 |
| Graduate students | 269 | 69 |
| Foreign students | 107 | 20 |

| Nuns  |     | 457 |
|-------|-----|-----|
| Other | 188 | 98  |

Among those who became prominent leaders in clinical training were Donald Beatty, John Billinsky, Thomas Bigham, Robert Brinkman, Ernest Bruder, James Burns, Henry Cassler, Lennart Cedarleaf, Russell Dicks, Herman Eichorn, Rollin Fairbanks, Joseph Fletcher, Charles Hall Jr., Seward Hiltner, Reuel Howe, Charles Jaekle, Paul Johnson, Obert Kempson, Thomas Klink, Frederick Kuether, Wayne Oates, William Oglesby, Robert Preston, Otis Rice, Samuel Southard, John Thomas, Edward Thornton, Granger Westberg, and Carroll Wise. To list even as many as these is to risk excluding others who are equally deserving of mention. When Westberg was appointed to the School of Medicine and Federated Theology Faculty of the University of Chicago in 1956, he gained the distinction of being named the first associate professor of religion and health in the United States.

## CHAPTER 4

# Flanders Dunbar and the Joint Committee on Religion and Medicine

*The clergyman is coming to realize the danger of seeing the personality committed to his charge in terms of spirit only, just as the physician is awakening to the fallacy of thinking merely in terms of diseased lungs and livers.*

—DR. FLANDERS DUNBAR[1]

Dr. (Helen) Flanders Dunbar
*Courtesy of Marcia Dunbar-Soule*

Perhaps the most remarkable of the early leaders in Religion and Health—without a doubt the most fascinating—was Flanders Dunbar, psychiatrist and pioneer in psychosomatic medicine. But who today has heard of her? "There seem to be operative in Dunbar's case more than the usual mechanisms for swallowing up a woman's work and relegating it to oblivion," a diligent student of her life and thought has observed.[2] To understand the story of the Religion and Health Movement in the United States is to recognize the pivotal contribution of this brilliant woman. Through her ground-breaking articles and books, written for professional colleagues in the early years and the general public later, she provided a link between the worlds of medicine, theology, and popular culture. Her concern for the whole person—psyche and soma, mind and body—helped pave the way for holistic health care.

### Dunbar's Early Training

As we have learned, when Anton Boisen began clinical training with four theological students at Worcester State Hospital, in the summer of 1925, Helen Dunbar was one of them. Boisen had met her in April at Union Theological Seminary while recruiting students for his new program. A graduate of the Brearley School in New York City (1919) and of Bryn Mawr College (1923), she was then a middler at Union and a Ph.D. candidate in comparative literature at Columbia. She was studying with Prof. Jefferson B. Fletcher, who introduced her to Dante's central argument that through symbolism, religion and science are not antagonistic, but complementary.[3] Her dissertation on "Symbolism in Medieval Thought and Its Consummation in the *Divine Comedy*" much interested Boisen, who kept in his room a picture of Dante, as a sort of patron saint.

Boisen found Dunbar "a young woman of extraordinary ability and charm" who shared other things in common with him: "At the age of twenty-two she was conversant with some fifteen languages and dialects. Most important was the fact that she was planning to study psychiatry."[4] Even though Dunbar stayed at Worcester for only one month that summer, she did outstanding research work and was quick to understand the significance of Boisen's clinical training project.

In the fall of 1926, while still a student at both Union and Columbia, Dunbar moved to New Haven to begin medical studies at Yale, one of five women in a class of more than forty persons. Her second husband later wrote:

> It is not strange that one who had studied Dante should wish to know more about religion, or that one interested in symbolism should be attracted by dynamic psychology. To understand religious thought she went to Union. . . . To penetrate depth psychology she earned her M.D. at Yale.[5]

Classmates called her "pocket Minerva." One historian has said that she was an "intellectual amazon."[6] Certainly she was no ordinary student: to help her keep up with classes and research, she employed two secretaries, Mary Anita Ewer and Rosamond Grant.

In the spring of 1927 Dunbar earned her B.D. degree and completed her Ph.D. dissertation. She was graduated magna cum laude from Union, winning a traveling fellowship, which the school held for her until she could use it. When her doctoral dissertation was published by the Yale University Press two years later, she gained a lasting reputation as a Dante scholar. (The book, which became difficult to obtain and was carefully guarded by libraries, was reprinted in 1961.)

Busy as she was, Dunbar maintained her association with Boisen. He writes in his autobiography:

> All her leisure time she was using in the study of symbolism, and she wanted to include symbolism which was not medieval. She therefore turned to Worcester. She wanted to know what sort of symbolism we were finding in our acutely disturbed patients, and under what conditions it occurred. She made several trips to the hospital and worked out a questionnaire on schizophrenic thinking.[7]

Boisen, like so many of her associates, was impressed with "her swift intelligence, her keen understanding, and her enormous capacity for work." He said that he saw in her "an instrument of the finest precision sent to help in the new undertaking."[8]

In July 1929 Dunbar sailed for Europe with her secretary and friend Rosamond Grant for her final year of medical school. Dr. Robert Powell reports that while living in Vienna she used her intentionally ambiguous signature, "Dr. H. Flanders Dunbar," to become a member of the American Medical Association of Vienna—the only member not actually an M.D.—and to enroll as hospitant in the General and Psychiatric-Neurological Hospitals of the University of Vienna.[9] Eventually, Dunbar was to drop the "H." altogether in a deliberate attempt to mislead readers of her published articles and books into assuming the author was a man.[10]

From Vienna, Dunbar wrote to a friend at Worcester: "All the Freudian school here seem to want me as a subject. It is really quite a delicate situation but very amusing, too amusing for a letter."[11] She entered psychotherapy—not a standard psychoanalysis—with Dr. Helene Deutsch, who was trained by Freud and worked closely with him for years. Deutsch was to use Dunbar's story (disguised) in her celebrated two-volume study *The Psychology of Women* published in 1944.[12]

Dunbar participated in hospital rounds in the department of Deutsch's husband, Dr. Felix Deutsch, a researcher who sought to bridge the gap between psychoanalysis and medicine.[13] On the occasion of Freud's one hundredth birthday, Felix Deutsch wrote a paper on "the mysterious leap from the mind to the body," a phrase used by Freud. In tribute Deutsch remarked that the mind-body riddle would have remained an insoluble one "if the magic key of the unconscious" had not been discovered by Freud.[14] Dunbar's subsequent work in psychosomatic medicine was surely influenced by Deutsch's work.

In January, Dunbar moved to Zurich where she became an assistant in the Burgholzli Clinic.[15] She had exchanged books with Dr. Carl Jung at Christmas and had a number of meetings with him.[16] It is no surprise that she found his views on religion more acceptable than Freud's. Before returning home in March to complete her medical thesis, "The Optic Mechanisms and Cerebellum of the Telescope Fish," she visited the shrine at Lourdes to begin a study of the healing there.

73

While Dunbar was in Europe there were some important developments at home. Austin Philip Guiles, a student of Boisen's at Worcester in 1928 and a protégé of Dr. Richard Cabot's, had decided to devote himself to clinical training. Cabot offered financial backing. In January the Council for the Clinical Training of Theological Students (CCTTS) was incorporated in Boston with Phil Guiles as field secretary and interim director. After Dunbar returned from Europe and was graduated from medical school, Guiles proposed that she take over as director, which she did in September 1930. Her "precocious professional achievements" and "the very special regard" of Boisen had won her the post.[17]

## Boisen and Dunbar

Despite his unrequited love for Alice Batchelder—or because of it—Boisen's feelings for Helen Dunbar went deeper than professional admiration. This fact, so carefully guarded by Boisen, has been revealed by the research of psychiatrist/historian Robert C. Powell. In an original, unpublished version of his autobiography, Boisen writes that, soon after his first meeting with Dunbar, he told her of his belief that she had been sent to help him. He also told her about Alice, and Alice about her, although Alice continued to refuse to see him.[18] (Since 1902, the year of Dunbar's birth, he had met with Alice only five times: once in 1904, 1907, 1910, 1911, and 1920.[19]) Boisen felt drawn to Dunbar, who reminded him of his mother. He noted that Dunbar "responded" to his advances and called him by his middle name, Theophilus ("lover of God").[20]

Then, in June of 1928, Alice consented, for the first time in eight years, to see Boisen. (She may have felt jealousy, but it is more likely that she felt relief as he decided to change his policy, stop writing daily, and rest his case.) She wrote: "It won't be easy for either of us and we may not 'have a good time,' but we are neither of us children, and I hope we can adjust to the demands of the situation."[21] They met at Marshall Field's in Chicago and then had lunch at the Palmer House. After this meeting they got together "as often as circumstances and Chicago's vast distances would permit," at least every other week, for lunch, a play, or the opera. On Thanksgiving Day in 1929, while Dunbar was in Europe, Boisen and Alice "knelt together before the altar in Hilton Chapel and entered into a covenant of friendship." Alice closed a letter to him that day saying, "For the first time in all these twenty-seven years I feel that I can with safety and with entire honesty sign myself—with real affection, Alice."[22]

In his published autobiography Boisen discloses that "the shadow of another, younger woman" lay between him and Alice. He does not name Dunbar, twenty-six years his junior:

> It was a gracious shadow. . . . This other woman knew about Alice, and Alice knew about her. . . . She was even included in our covenant of friendship. There was no disloyalty to either one. I discussed the situation with Alice, and always I found her wise and helpful. But it was hard to see the way, and I was greatly troubled.[23]

Finding a "right solution" to his unresolved conflict became an "urgent problem" for Boisen. He proposed that the three meet. When Dunbar returned from Europe in March 1930, she traveled to Chicago for the meeting. Then Boisen accompanied her to Washington, DC, for the International Mental Hygiene Conference, and to New York, where they worked on a translation of Eugene Kahn's *Psychopathic Personalities*.[24]

What was Dunbar's behavior toward Boisen? Whether it was "more than just friendly," as Powell surmises, is unclear. It is known that the months abroad transformed her. A petite person—only four feet eleven inches tall—as a young woman she was intensely unhappy about her short, fat appearance. Friends called her "Little Dunbar" and she felt shunned. Returning from abroad she was slender, strikingly pretty, and adept at using her feminine charm. Whether or not she used it on Boisen may never be known; however, her effect on him was to cause a deep disturbance, the seriousness of which, by his own account, she could not ignore.[25]

In June 1930 Boisen's beloved mother died. In July or August Boisen wrote to Alice:

> While there has been in my mind no question as to my love for Helen and while I believe in her as God's message to me, there has been a very real question as to the role which should be

75

mine. . . . Helen's help seems to me most necessary in the carrying through of this undertaking and marriage would permit the closest possible co-operation and understanding.[26]

Boisen was confused: was he to ask Helen Dunbar to be the helpmate Alice declined to be, or was he to give her up?

Late in November Boisen suffered an acute psychotic episode. After a period of intense absorption and prayer, he broke into uncontrollable sobbing. "It seemed that something which ought to have been, was not to be. I had failed, and the world was in danger."[27] Deeply agitated, Boisen started out in his car, frenetically called on a number of people, and finally went to see Dr. Richard Cabot. When Boisen inquired about himself in the third person, Cabot saw to it that he was hospitalized immediately. As mentioned in chapter 3, this psychotic breakdown aroused Cabot, who insisted that Boisen was to have nothing more to do with clinical training. Never hinting at Dunbar's role in all of this, Boisen writes, "Dr. Dunbar stood by me and saved the day so far as I was concerned."[28] In fact, she took over management of the Council.

In retrospect Boisen was clear about the causative factors in his breakdown: the complications in his relationship with Alice. He concluded that the disturbed condition, which lasted only three weeks, "solved the problem which had occasioned it" but was not creative. It merely saved him "from a situation which should not have arisen."[29] Ousted by Guiles and Cabot, Boisen shifted his base of operations from Worcester to Elgin State Hospital, in Illinois, and his undivided loyalty to Alice Batchelder, whom he continued to see in Chicago about once a month.

As for Dr. Dunbar, her life was no less hectic than when she was in graduate and professional schools:

> There were times when those close to her felt as if she were driven by some Fury to carry on beyond the point of exhaustion. Although she knew that human beings are limited in time and space, she could not seem emotionally or practically to admit it, or to limit her own obligations to those she could fulfill without strain. When she was involved in one of her many projects she drove herself and those with her almost beyond the limits of endurance.[30]

A friend once wrote to her, "You should have been at least three people."

In addition to being Director of the CCTTS, in April 1931 Dunbar agreed to be Director of the Joint Committee on Religion and Medicine. The Joint Committee was a combined effort of a religious group (the Federal Council of Churches) and a medical group (the New York Academy of Medicine), which, under Dunbar's leadership, was to play a pivotal role in the promotion of psychosomatic understanding in the United States. While the area of Religion and Health was predominantly the territory of men (clergy and physicians), two interested and wealthy women—Ethel Phelps Stokes Hoyt and Kate Everit Macy Ladd—were instrumental in the success of the Joint Committee and of Dunbar.

### The Joint Committee Founded by Ethel Phelps Stokes Hoyt

On March 8, 1923, a small group of distinguished physicians and clergy met in the Park Avenue home of Ethel and John Sherman Hoyt to discuss the relation of religion and medicine in healing and health. The doctors present were William Darrach, Ransom Hooker (brother-in-law of Ethel Hoyt), James Miller, and Thomas Salmon. Ministers were Russell Bowie, Henry Sloane Coffin, and Harry Emerson Fosdick. Minutes taken by Ethel Hoyt indicate that these professionals talked about their common aims and about the need and value of cooperation.

Echoing the words of Elwood Worcester almost twenty years earlier, Fosdick reported: "Not finding healing in the churches, people are seeking to have their problems solved by spiritual and psychological means, and strange cults, quacks, and bogus psychologists have been flourishing." But gains were being made. Fosdick explained to the doctors:

> Now, modern ministers are approaching their problem in a scientific manner, trying to interpret spiritual laws with the same scientific spirit with which you doctors are working to interpret physical laws. We must work scientifically from both sides until the tunnel joins.[31]

When, in 1927, the Federal Council of Churches and the New York Academy of Medicine formally organized the Joint Committee on Religion and Health, its beginnings could be traced back to this informal gathering called by Ethel Phelps Stokes Hoyt. She was responsible not only for founding the committee, but also for generously supporting and sustaining it through the 1940s with her time and money.

Ethel P.S. Hoyt (1877–1952) came from a family known for its business enterprise, wealth, and religious, civic, and philanthropic interests. Her great-grandfather Anson Greene Phelps Dodge founded the mercantile house of Phelps, Dodge & Company and the city of Ansonia, Connecticut. Her father, Anson Phelps Stokes, a man of "pronounced piety," was a New York banker and merchant. He helped to found the first tuberculosis sanitarium in the United States, at Saranac Lake, New York, and the Metropolitan Museum of Art. Ethel was the sixth of Anson's nine children (there were four boys and five girls). Her brother the Rev. Dr. Anson Phelps Stokes Jr. served for many years as secretary of Yale University and as canon of Washington Cathedral. He also authored the three-volume *Church and State in the United States* (Harper & Brothers, 1950). Brother James Graham Phelps Stokes was active in the settlement house movement and lived for a time at a settlement on the East Side. He married Jewish radical Rose Pastor, and together they actively supported the Socialist party before their divorce. Another brother, Isaac Newton Phelps Stokes, an architect, designed Yale University's Woodbridge Hall, which was donated by Ethel's unmarried aunts, Olivia Egleston Phelps Stokes and Caroline Phelps Stokes.[32]

In 1895 Ethel married New York manufacturer John Sherman Hoyt (1869–1954), who was one of the founders of the Boy Scouts of America. He also acted from 1912 until his death as a trustee of the Phelps Stokes Fund, a public educational trust, and from 1902 to 1928 served as president of The Babies Hospital of the City of New York. As a young man Hoyt was an elder and trustee of the Madison Avenue Presbyterian Church, later a trustee of the Rowayton (Connecticut) Methodist Church, and at the time of his death a deacon of the Congregational Church of New Canaan, Connecticut.[33]

Although data on John Sherman Hoyt and the many Stokeses are readily available in biographical dictionaries, the life and unique contribution of Ethel P.S. Hoyt in the field of Religion and Health has generally gone unnoted.[34] In 1921 she published a study in the relation of religion to health called *Spirit.* Dr. Richard Cabot introduced it with a foreword: "This little book seems to me to embody a great deal of important truth. I believe that it contains no errors in statement of fact, and that the advice given in it will be found to stand the tests of time and experience."[35] We can be sure that *Spirit,* published when she was forty-four, grew out of Ethel P.S. Hoyt's personal faith and life experience. As the mother of five children (a sixth had died in infancy), she knew something about the nervous problems she warned about: worry, anxiety, hurry, anger, and fear.

Ethel Hoyt began her book by noting that, according to recent medical estimates, more than half the cases of illness in the United States are of nervous origin. Through a series of charts she demonstrated the psychosomatic truth that nervous disorders can lead to functional disease. Following the charts was a discussion of the health-giving power of the indwelling Spirit of God, amply documented with quotations from scripture. A chart on the last page served as a kind of summary:

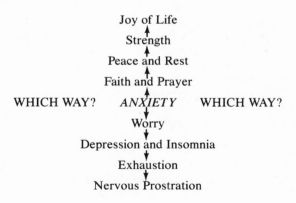

Hoyt's patient and persistent behind-the-scenes lobbying to promote understanding of the influence of spiritual states on physical illness can be understood in the light of these thoughts.

In the years between the meeting in the Hoyt home in 1923 and the establishment of the Joint Committee in 1927, research was quietly carried out. After an initial investigation of faith healing movements by E.H. Lewinski Corwin, Ph.D., a subcommittee of the New York Academy of Medicine engaged Alice E. Paulsen to make a survey of religious healing in and near New York. (Ethel Hoyt raised $500 for Dr. Paulsen's preliminary work and was prepared to raise as much as $10,000 for further study.[36]) A psychologist at St. Luke's Hospital at the time, Paulsen had an A.B. from Mount Holyoke College (1913) and M.A. and Ph.D. degrees in psychology from Columbia University (1915, 1924). She said that she felt qualified to make the study because she had "no prejudices to color facts." Although she was a member of the Congregational Church, she attended services irregularly.[37]

As part of her important initial survey of religious healing, Alice Paulsen interviewed many ministers and doctors. Most were interested and cooperative, but not all. Her notes of a meeting with one surgeon reveal a testiness that is almost comic:

> Inclined to be annoyed. Unwilling to listen to explanation. Said his opinion would be of no value. Surgery able to cure all regardless of creed. People will come to doctor when really ill, meanwhile are entitled to be as foolish as they like. These cults always have existed and always will. Catholic religion only one worthwhile and is effective because it puts fear of God into people. Talking of healing will do church no good. They must find a teaching that will enable worthwhile leaders to enter the seminaries. Thinks law is sufficient to protect medicine and Academy foolish to mix in with religious inquiry of any sort. Hurried, going from one room to another, very abrupt. Interview extremely unsatisfactory and cut as short as possible. No experience specially responsible for his attitudes.[38]

Paulsen's preliminary report was printed in the *Journal of the American Medical Association* in March 1926 and reprinted in *Mental Hygiene* in July. Because this report showed the magnitude of the field and the great need of study and coordination between physicians and clergy, it gave impetus to the formation of the Joint Committee on Religion and Health. (The name was changed to the Joint Committee on Religion and Medicine in 1931.)

# A Coming Together of Lives: Dr. Frederick Peterson, Worcester, Hoyt, and Dunbar

Dr. Frederick Peterson, neurologist and psychiatrist, was selected to be Chairman of the Joint Committee. Almost seventy at the time, he had had a long and distinguished career. Peterson, a native of Minnesota, earned a medical degree from the University of Buffalo before spending three years studying at the universities in Göttingen, Vienna, Strasbourg, and Zurich. As the first resident physician at the Hudson River State Hospital for the Insane (now Hudson River Psychiatric Center), in Poughkeepsie, New York, from 1884 to 1887, he found his calling: the treatment and care of those suffering from mental disorders and the education of others for this work.[39] Peterson went to the Columbia University College of Physicians and Surgeons in 1888, and from 1903 to 1915 he held the first full professorship in clinical psychiatry there.

Peterson's contributions to the mental health field are many. He helped to establish the first colony for epileptics in the United States, at Sonyea, New York, and served as president of the New York State Commission on Lunacy (1901–04). Largely through his efforts, "hospital" replaced "asylum," underscoring the modern attitude that mental disorder is treatable.

A man whose lifetime (1859–1938) spanned roughly the same years as Freud's (1856–1939), Peterson showed an early interest in psychotherapy and welcomed the work of Freud and of Jung. In 1907 (the year he and his friend A.A. Brill went to Zurich), Peterson published an article in *Harper's* calling attention to the significance of dreams. He also contributed a personal column, "The Nerve Specialist to His Patients," to *Collier's* magazine.[40] Psychoanalysis reinforced Peterson's belief that the mind, particularly the emotions, affects physical functions. A textbook that he coauthored with Archibald Church, *Nervous and Mental Diseases* (1899), was perhaps more favorably disposed to psychotherapy and psychopathology than any other major text.[41]

Peterson knew and admired the work of the Rev. Drs. Samuel McComb and Elwood Worcester at the Emmanuel Church in Boston.[42] Under Peterson's leadership, in 1927, the Joint Committee authorized McComb, who was serving as rector of the American Episcopal Church in Nice, France, to make an inquiry into the subject of religious healing. McComb made a report, which was published in *Mental Hygiene* (October 1928). "The time has come," he wrote, "to utilize the forces which our modern knowledge of psychology and the religious instinct and impulse give us, with a view to right guidance of public opinion on these matters."[43]

In 1928 the Rev. Dr. F. Ernest Johnson, acting on behalf of the Joint Committee, formulated a plan for study of religious healing to be presented to the Rockefeller Foundation for funding. He wrote: "What we desire ultimately to do is to canvass the whole field of the Relation of Religion to Health in order that a useful cooperation may be worked out." The two requirements for this investigation were "(1) that the conditions of religious ministry and experience shall be maintained and (2) that the conditions of scientific observation, testing and measurement shall also be established and maintained."[44] In January 1929 the Rockefeller Foundation turned down the proposal.

In June, Ethel P.S. Hoyt went to see Dr. Peterson to discuss Helen Dunbar.[45] Hoyt had known Dunbar from the time she was a teenager at the Brearley School with Hoyt's daughter. Dunbar was about to leave for her year in Europe, and Hoyt wanted her to meet Peterson before she left so that the Joint Committee could endorse her study and appropriate funds. In August, Hoyt wrote to Dunbar in Paris to say that they were enthusiastic about aiding her: "It is with great pleasure that I send you five hundred dollars from the Committee." Dunbar replied, saying that she hoped to have time to get to Lourdes in the spring.[46]

In February 1930 Dunbar wrote to Hoyt from Zurich, asking for a letter of recommendation. In response Hoyt wrote to the executive vice-president of Presbyterian Hospital:

> My young friend, Dr. Helen Dunbar, has asked me to be one of the non-medical sponsors for her application for internship at Presbyterian Hospital. It is a special pleasure to write for Dr. Dunbar as I consider her a young woman of unusual power, ability and strength of character, and of most charming personality.[47]

At about this time Elwood Worcester began commuting weekly, Wednesday through Friday, from Boston to New York to carry on his healing ministry at Grace Church on Broadway, where the Rev. Dr. Russell Bowie was rector. (Bowie was active in the Joint Committee. Dunbar listed him on her Union Seminary application as her pastor.) While in Manhattan, Worcester stayed with the Petersons: "This weekly contact with one of the greatest neurologists and psychiatrists has been a liberal education to me, while his and Mrs. Peterson's broad, general culture and knowledge of art, religion, and philosophy have refreshed my soul."[48] (An indication of Peterson's broad, general culture was his collection of more than 825 Chinese paintings, one dating back to A.D. 1204.[49]) In April, Hoyt and Peterson consulted Elwood Worcester about a director for a center in New York where the relation of religion to healing and health could be scientifically studied.[50]

Dunbar returned from Europe and, as mentioned earlier, in September became director of the Council for Clinical Training of Theological Students. She also got an appointment at Presbyterian Hospital as assistant in medicine. In November a meeting was held in Dr. Peterson's office to discuss the appointment of Dr. Dunbar as director of the Joint Committee's project. Finding someone to do research had not been easy, and her training and qualifications made her particularly suitable. On April 17, 1931, Dunbar became director. Her secretary/friend Rosamond Grant became executive assistant; Peterson, chairman; Howard Robbins, vice-chairman; E.H. Lewinski Corwin, secretary; and Ethel P.S. Hoyt, treasurer.


### Dunbar's Achievement as Director and Kate Everit Macy Ladd's Supporting Role

Research was Dr. Dunbar's focus as director of the Joint Committee. Education was her focus as director of the Council on Clinical Training. Because historians have written much more about the development of clinical pastoral education than about the development of her psychosomatic research, the latter is my particular interest here.

Between 1931 and 1932 Dr. Dunbar supervised a combined study by physicians and clergy at Presbyterian Hospital and Vanderbilt Clinic. Sixty-two patients given the usual medical treatment were contrasted with sixty-two patients treated "with the

83

aid of a clergyman's ministrations." The results were inconclusive, and the project was given up as "too complex for the status of our knowledge."[51]

In November 1932 Dunbar reported to the Joint Committee that her attention had turned to a study of the effect of emotions on the body, which was suggested to her by Dr. Walter B. Cannon, leader in psychosomatic medicine. She said that a preliminary investigation of the literature on the subject was being undertaken through a grant made by the Josiah Macy Jr. Foundation.[52]

The grant was a notable development because behind this foundation was a woman—Kate Everit Macy Ladd (1863–1945). Kate Ladd and Ethel Hoyt were friends. Together they founded the Cosmopolitan Club in New York City in 1909, of which Dunbar became a member much later.[53] Unlike Hoyt, Ladd never had children. From the time she was in her late fifties until her death at eighty-two years of age, she was confined to a bed or a wheelchair.[54] Her personal physician was Dr. Charles L. Dana, professor of neurology at Cornell University Medical College and a founder of the Joint Committee.[55] She was a Presbyterian.

Kate Macy Ladd established the Josiah Macy Jr. Foundation in memory of her father in 1930 with an initial gift of $5 million. The income was to be used to promote effective methods for the prevention and cure of disease and to help relieve suffering. Ladd believed "that health is more than freedom from sickness, that it resides in the wholesome unity of mind and body." She also believed that private philanthropy serves human welfare best "by investigating, testing and demonstrating the value of newer organized ideas"; consequently, she hoped the foundation would take more interest "in the architecture of ideas than in the architecture of buildings and laboratories."[56]

That Ladd aided Dunbar's work through the Macy Foundation is significant. One cannot tell Dr. Dunbar's story without reference to the stories of the many women, like Ladd and Hoyt, who assisted and supported her. Dunbar was a "magnetic, charismatic woman,"[57] a person who had a way of "drawing people in" to do things.[58] This compelling quality had great importance for the growth of the Religion and Health Movement.

The project that Dunbar undertook with the help of the Macy Foundation was compiling a massive bibliography containing some 2,200 abstracts of studies indicating unity of mind and body. The bibliography was published in 1935 as *Emotions and Bodily Changes, A Survey of Literature on Psychosomatic Interrelationship, 1910–1933*. It became a standard reference work that she was to update several times.

In the introduction Dunbar explains in her clear, direct style the rationale behind the work. "We know more than we think we know" because available scientific information from several specialities "has never been gathered together, correlated, and evaluated."[59] Her aim was to bridge the specialities and "bring together all the fragments of knowledge we possess." The genius of Dunbar not only in this book, but in all her endeavors, was to cross narrow boundaries, to make connections, to find wholeness. In an epigraph she quotes Descartes: "If, therefore, anyone wishes to search out the truth of things in serious earnest, he ought not to select one special science, for all the sciences are conjoined with each other and interdependent." Dunbar's many achievements can be attributed, in part, to her creative, cross-disciplinary, unifying vision.

Pulling together an annotated bibliography on *Emotions and Bodily Changes* may seem to be an arduous, dull, dry project: not for Dunbar. The passion she brought to the work is evident in an article written at the time. In all the history of the development of the human race, she said, there has been *no more important happening* than the application of the scientific method to the study of human behavior, especially emotions. Emotion makes us think, emotion makes us act, a fact science has been slow to comprehend:

> Science has brought us far, but science in setting the standard of pure thought, eliminating emotion, has constructed a grand, powerful Pompeii at the side of Vesuvius. If we fail to realize this, it is only because we are too busy to step out from the traffic of the lighted streets to see the smoke rising from the volcano, be it to ponder on the havoc of another war, or on the chaos of blind feeling seething behind many of the fine trained minds of our college youth.[60]

This woman who brought passion to her work made little effort to separate her work from her personal life. In her acknowledgments in *Emotions and Bodily Changes,* Dunbar mentions that the bulk of the material was prepared by Dr. Theodore P. Wolfe, Josiah Macy Jr. Foundation Fellow in Medicine at Presbyterian Hospital. What she fails to mention is that Wolfe was her husband.

Dr. Theodor Peter Wolfensberger (1902–54) was a Swiss psychiatrist whom Dunbar had met in Zurich. He came to America in 1932 on an appointment to the Phipps Psychiatric Clinic in Baltimore, where a friend of his, psychobiologist Adolf Meyer, was director.[61] Married in October 1932, Dunbar and Ted Wolfe collaborated on books and articles; in fact, careful investigation by Powell reveals that chapter 9 of *Emotions and Bodily Changes* later appeared verbatim as Wolfe's thesis for the doctorate of medical science degree at Columbia.[62] Wolfe is remembered today for bringing orgone therapist Wilhelm Reich to America and for translating his work into English. Through Wolfe, Reichian analysis was powerfully to influence Dunbar's successor as director of the CCTTS, the Rev. Robert E. Brinkman.[63]

Dunbar and Wolfe had no children and were divorced in 1939. Within six months Dr. Dunbar married liberal economist George Henry Soule Jr., an editor of *The New Republic,* who was fifteen years her senior. In 1941, when she was almost forty, Dunbar gave birth to her only child, a daughter, Marcia Dunbar-Soule. In both her marriages Dunbar maintained her own name by law, an action so uncommon as to be noted in several news stories about her.

The year after *Emotions and Bodily Changes* was published, the Joint Committee was dissolved; apparently, Dunbar felt that its aims could be approached more efficiently if the Academy and the Federal Council each had its own committee. Dr. Peterson became chairman of the Academy's Committee on Emotions and Health, and the Rev. Howard Chandler Robbins became chairman of the Federal Council's Commission on Religion and Health.

The list of charter members of the Commission on Religion and Health contains the names of many people included in this study: Ethel P.S. Hoyt, Robert Brinkman, Harry Bone, Smiley Blanton, Norman Vincent Peale, Russell Dicks, A. Philip Guiles, Otis Rice, Henry P. Van Dusen. In 1938 Seward Hiltner was chosen executive secretary, a position he held for more than ten years.

Earlier, Hiltner had worked under Dunbar's supervision for three years as field secretary for the Council for Clinical Training and as her executive assistant at an annual salary of $1,500. During the first year his office was in Dunbar's apartment at 730 Park Avenue. (It was a former maid's room separated from the living quarters.) Then the clinical training headquarters moved to an office in the New York Academy of Medicine at 2 East 103d Street, bordering Central Park. Hiltner, who had no typing or secretarial assistance, remembers using a hand-crank duplicating machine and later sharing the small space with Brinkman.

Of his working relationship with Flanders Dunbar, Hiltner was later to recall that she paid close attention to detail and so reviewed and often edited the letters he wrote. Because their writing styles were different, he felt compelled to curb his tendency to be expansive in order to conform to her own more reserved and formal style. Their brief meetings, usually three or four a week, were conducted over a carefully organized agenda. She asked him to write out all reports, plans, and ideas before discussing them with her. This, he observed, not only saved her time, but also proved to be good discipline for him.

In reviewing the story of Religion and Health, it is clear that Flanders Dunbar played a pivotal role. She provided a link between the early work of Elwood Worcester and Anton Boisen, who promoted her career, and the later work of Seward Hiltner, whose career she promoted.

### Dunbar's Later Publications and Death

The next book Dr. Dunbar wrote, *Psychosomatic Diagnosis* (1943), contained research results that shape our thinking today. In the 1930s she conducted with others a study of 1,600 unselected, consecutive patients admitted to Columbia-Presbyterian Hospital, suffering from such illnesses as asthma, coronary heart disease, diabetes, and high blood pressure. Examining these patients as whole persons—their emotional makeup as well as their environments and personal medical histories—she discovered distinctive personality profiles that were characteristic of each disease. Quite unexpectedly, she also identified an

87

accident-prone personality. Self-injury, she learned, is often an outlet for emotional disturbances.

In his tribute at the time of her death Dr. Franz Alexander called her hospital study a "classical contribution" and said that no single person was more effective than Dunbar "in the organization of the psychosomatic approach in modern medicine." He pointed out that although, under the influence of other researchers' findings, she modified her view of global personality traits, her discovery of the accident-prone personality is impressive and enduring.[64]

Because Flanders Dunbar was convinced that her work had value for *preventive* medicine and mental health, she popularized her findings in 1947 in a best-selling book called *Mind and Body* (Random House). It was the August 1948 selection of the Book Find Club, appearing the month after Norman Mailer's *The Naked and the Dead,* and a selection of the Book-of-the-Month Club, appearing on the list with Joshua Loth Liebman's excellent contribution in Religion and Health, *Peace of Mind.* (One confused reader wrote Random House asking for *Peace of Body,* a story that made newspapers across the country.)

*Time* magazine reviewed *Mind and Body* in an article, "Mostly in the Mind," and ran pictures of John Keats, Elizabeth Barrett, and William Gladstone, people whom Dunbar had cited for having psychosomatic symptoms. *Time* called her book "fascinating," written by "a top-rank woman practitioner." (Even so, several newspaper reviewers referred to "Flanders Dunbar . . . he.") *Time* also included a footnote:

> Psychosomatic medicine superficially resembles, but is not to be confused with, Christian Science's mental healing. Christian Science's Founder Mary Baker Eddy, unlike the psychosomatists, held that illness is unreal, and disappears when the mind, stripped of error and evil, discovers God's reality.[65]

The *New York Times* called *Mind and Body* "a serious, sensible, eminently interesting and highly entertaining discussion of medicine's newest and most important field."[66]

Dunbar's later articles and books tended to parallel the development of her daughter, Marcia. *Your Child's Mind and Body* appeared in 1949. *Your Pre-Teenager's Mind and Body* and *Your Teenager's Mind and Body* were published posthumously.

Dunbar's later life was filled with emotional pain. Estranged from husband George Soule for some years, she lived with a lover, a Greenwich, Connecticut, physician, who committed suicide. Newspapers erroneously reported that he was her third husband. She also struggled with alcoholism, the devastating effects of an automobile accident that damaged her beauty and health, and a lawsuit brought by a former patient, a Maytag heiress.

Late one afternoon in August 1959 her daughter found her drowned in the basement swimming pool of their estate in South Kent, Connecticut. (She was in the habit of taking a swim before dinner.) Dunbar was fifty-seven years old. Although her death was listed as an accident, her own research showed that, in 80 percent of accidents, there is an emotional state in the victim that seems to find outlet only through unconscious self-injury. The circumstances of her last years indicate that this may have been so for Dr. Dunbar herself, a tragic end for a woman who gave so much.

Dunbar's direct contribution to the Religion and Health Movement was through the Council for Clinical Training. Her psychosomatic research and writing was an indirect contribution but equally as important. The fact that one's state of mind is a large factor in causing most illness has been called the biggest step in understanding disease since the discovery of germs. The implications for ministry of the psychosomatic unity of mind and body are still being explored.

# CHAPTER 5

# Norman Vincent Peale, Smiley Blanton, and the Religio-Psychiatric Clinic

*Remember that God does nothing except by law.*

—NORMAN VINCENT PEALE[1]

*Since a great many people in mental distress go to ministers, the ministers should be taught the ABC's of human behavior.*

—SMILEY BLANTON[2]

Dr. Smiley Blanton (left) and the Rev. Dr. Norman Vincent Peale
*Courtesy of Foundation for Christian Living, Pawling, New York*

O<small>N A MISTY NIGHT</small> in October 1932 the Rev. Norman Vincent Peale was installed as pastor of the Marble Collegiate Church, located on Fifth Avenue in New York City. The thirty-four-year-old Methodist minister had chosen this pulpit over one in Los Angeles and so became the leader of a Dutch Reformed congregation whose membership had once included Peter Stuyvesant, the first colonial governor of New York, and Peter Minuit, who purchased the island of Manhattan from the Indians.

The year before Peale's installation, New York had celebrated the completion of the Empire State Building, the Waldorf-Astoria Hotel, and the George Washington Bridge—three great monuments to technical achievement, beauty, and elegance; even so, it was the Depression and things were grim. One of Peale's biographers writes:

> In less than three years, the suicide rate for male Americans had risen thirty per cent. It was a bleak city and a bleak church that the Peales found waiting for them. Men were selling apples on street corners. Women were wearing out shoe leather looking for jobs that didn't exist. Heart attacks and nervous breakdowns were daily occurrences. Fear and anxiety were everywhere.[3]

Peale was optimistic that he could fill the church's empty pews, that he could help people to regain faith in God and in themselves. Rejecting an orthodoxy that stressed human sin and shortcomings, he was determined to use the pulpit to remind people of their goodness, to relieve them of their fear and discouragement.

But by the end of two years Peale himself felt discouraged and drained. He had not lost confidence in his message, but he had lost confidence in his ability to get it across. His congregation was not responding. The church was not united. Furthermore, he felt deeply frustrated by his limitations in counseling, his ineffectiveness in helping many of the people who came to him. Close to exhaustion (today we would call it burnout), he decided that perhaps he had made a mistake in coming to New York; the pulpit was evidently too large for him; maybe he should give it up to someone who was more qualified.

Then, during his summer vacation in England, Norman Peale had an experience of conversation and prayer with his wife, Ruth, that proved to be a dramatic turning point. Peale's spiritual depression lifted. Shortly afterward Ruth, a behind-the-scenes pillar of support and advice throughout his ministry, made a suggestion that provided a solution to the pastoral counseling problem: the minister decided to seek assistance from a Christian psychiatrist.

Peale turned first to his personal physician, Dr. Clarence W. Lieb. Lieb talked to him about the effect on health of spiritual and psychiatric problems. Peale remembers: "Through his wise guidance I began to see that fear and guilt, hate and resentment, problems with which I was dealing, were often closely connected with problems of health and physical well-being."[4] Dr. Lieb suggeted that Peale see Dr. Iago Galdston (1895-    ), an analyst at the New York Academy of Medicine. At a lunch at the Harvard Club, Galdston in turn introduced him to Dr. Smiley Blanton, a man who had been analyzed in Vienna by Freud himself. After listening to the minister's proposal that the two collaborate, Blanton asked him:

> "Do you believe in the power of prayer?"
> "Prayer? Of course I do! Why do you ask?"
> "Because I've been praying for years that some minister would see that psychiatry and religion not only might but should work together. And now here you are!"[5]

Writing years later about their "Pioneering Partnership," Blanton recalled:

> Dr. Peale felt that the knowledge of a psychiatrist would help him in working with disturbed and unhappy people, and I agreed. The skeptics immediately declared that religion and psychiatry could never work together because they had nothing in common, but we ignored them.[6]

That Peale perceived a natural partnership between religion and medicine and sought help from a doctor was not remarkable, given his family background. Peale's great grandfather Robert Fulton (a descendant of the inventor of the steamboat) had been both a Methodist preacher and a doctor. He was as likely to prescribe prayer for a patient as medicine, for he believed that most illness was in people's minds.[7] Norman Peale's father, Charles Clifford Peale, had earned a medical degree and practiced in Milwaukee before giving up medicine to become a Methodist clergyman. Norman Peale proudly explains: "When I was born [1898] in the little town of Bowersville, Ohio, population 300, where my father was the minister, he, with his extensive medical knowledge, was not about to let the local doctor deliver me when the birth was imminent."[8]

Personal experience had confirmed Norman Peale's belief in the close relationship between religion and medicine in healing. Early in his ministry at the University Methodist Church in Syracuse, New York, where he had served before becoming pastor at Marble Collegiate, Peale was summoned by a doctor whose patient was not responding to treatment. At the bedside together they recalled scripture passages and prayed. After some time the restless, half-conscious patient fell into a quiet sleep. The crisis has passed, the doctor declared: the woman would recover. This made a vivid and lasting impression on Peale, who later remembered the doctor's words:

> I think that religion and medicine ought to be used together far more often than they are. The early Christians were familiar with spiritual healing. They used it all the time. Why should the power have disappeared? Human beings haven't changed. The relationship between mind and body is just as close now as it was then. I think we've got a lot to learn in this whole area.[9]

Norman Peale's encounter with the physician in Syracuse was not unlike Elwood Worcester's encounter with Silas Weir Mitchell in Philadelphia, and Peale's subsequent effort to enlist the aid of a psychiatrist in healing may be compared with Worcester's. There were, however, remarkable differences between the two men. Whereas Worcester was an intellectual and a scholar, Peale never pretended to be. He had earned degrees at Ohio Wesleyan (B.A., 1920) and Boston University Seminary (S.T.B. and M.A., 1924), but his several doctorates are honorary degrees.[10] And although in those early years Peale considered himself a religious liberal, often in opposition to the status quo, he was politically conservative—against the repeal of Prohibition and against Roosevelt's New Deal.[11]

Who was the man that Peale approached to be his colleague? What do we know about Smiley Blanton?

## *Dr. Smiley Blanton, Psychiatrist*

Born in 1882 in Unionville, Tennessee, only seventeen years after the end of the Civil War, as a boy Smiley Blanton looked for bullets instead of four-leaf clovers and as an adult he knew "the War" by heart. Blanton grew up the only child among seven adults in a rigid Presbyterian household. Because Sunday reading was limited to the Bible or Shakespeare, and because he read avidly from an early age, Blanton memorized much of Shakespeare and twice went through the Bible from cover to cover.

He earned his undergraduate degree at Vanderbilt University in 1904 and then did graduate work in English at Harvard. There he became interested in speech defects. His wife later wrote: "He was too perceptive to accept stuttering as a defect of speech in itself and found himself aiming at a medical degree and psychiatry."[12]

To save money Blanton spent several years teaching speech and dramatics at Cornell University. In 1910 he and Margaret Gray of Nashville married, and in 1911 they moved to New York City so that he could study at Cornell Medical School. After his graduation in 1914 the couple went to the University of Wisconsin, where he established a speech and mental hygiene clinic, and later to Phipps Psychiatric Clinic at Johns Hopkins University, where he studied with Dr. Adolph Meyer. During World War I, Blanton went to France with the army as the head of a special medical section of psychiatrists. After the war the Blantons moved to London for work and study before going to Minneapolis in 1924. There he started a child guidance clinic in the public schools.

Margaret Blanton may have been known for many years as "Smiley's Margaret," but the woman was an ardent feminist who maintained her own career and professional interests during their many moves. (The couple never had children.) In Baltimore she did research for Dr. John Watson, "The Behavior of the Human Infant During the First 30 Days of Life"; in London she worked in phonetics under Dr. Daniel Jones; and in Minneapolis she coauthored with Smiley a book for parents and teachers called *Child Guidance*. (Other books they wrote together are *Speech Training for Children* and *For Stutterers*.) Despite her own accomplishments she could not change her husband's mind about the place of women in Western society: "I spent hours trying to convince him that one of the basic troubles with society today is man's inability to believe in the equality of the sexes and his need to downgrade the sex of his mother. I never succeeded, but I never gave up trying."[13]

In 1927 Smiley and Margaret Blanton moved to Poughkeepsie, New York. Vassar College had hired him to head the new nursery school it was opening. When the position was not everything he had anticipated (he felt the program was "narrow"),[14] he made up his mind to give up teaching to become a psychoanalyst. In the fall of 1929, only weeks before the stock market crash, he took a leave from Vassar to begin a training analysis in Vienna with Freud. That winter Blanton described to Freud dreams about the Vassar campus, and they discussed his proposed career change.

The Blantons resided in Vienna from September 1929 until June 1930 as both were analyzed after twenty years of marriage. While Smiley worked with Freud, Margaret started with Clara Thompson, student of Sandor Ferenczi, and then worked with Dr. Ruth Mack Brunswick, a devoted friend of Freud. The Blantons were part of a large colony of Americans in Vienna—musicians, journalists, and medical people—many of whom were studying analysis. Margaret later remembered: "In a curious fashion, the whole of the foreign colony seemed to revolve around Freud. . . . But Freud did not seem conscious of the excitement he was creating, and his poise remained unshaken."[15] When her husband resumed his responsibilities at Vassar during the next school year, 1930–31, Margaret continued her analysis in Vienna with Brunswick.

Asked to comment about the effect of Blanton's analysis on him, Margaret mentions her own analysis and explains that "it is hard to untangle the changes in two people and assess them."[16] But she observes:

Professor Freud became his beloved father figure, and his grandmother and I, who had been identified with his grandmother, were dethroned. His necessity to accept everything that I said as gospel truth was dispelled, and he became very negative. Of course it is probable that changes in me that I cannot see were factors also. But I do know that thereafter my role became entirely different. We had to quit writing books and articles together.[17]

The initial period of Blanton's analysis was followed by three subsequent periods, of two weeks each, during summers. He saw Freud in Vienna in 1935, in 1937, and, finally, in London in 1938, when Freud was eighty-two years old. (Freud died in September 1939.) Smiley Blanton kept a diary of his sessions, including his observations of Freud's method, which he planned one day to publish for its scientific interest, but he died in 1966, leaving the project incomplete. Fortunately, Margaret Blanton published the book, adding explanatory comments and also an introduction by Dr. Iago Galdston. For historians of Religion and Health, the document is of great value.

At age forty-nine Blanton began a new professional career. He opened a private practice as a psychiatrist and psychoanalyst in New York City. His first patient was referred to him by Galdston, who later sent Peale to him because he was a Christian psychiatrist.

### Blanton's Christian Faith

What were Blanton's religious convictions? Like Freud, he believed that "worship of God has always been a projection of the parent-child relationship, the worship of 'God the Father.' "[18] Unlike Freud he did not conclude from this psychological fact of life that God's existence is an illusion. For Blanton, the highest form of faith is faith in God. If there is lack of faith, then a person must look into herself or himself and past experiences for self-knowledge: because our idea of God is, to a great extent, derived from our attitude toward our parents, an inadequate relationship to our parents frequently obstructs mature faith.

Blanton believed that the "capacity for faith springs from the capacity for love."[19] In his book *Love or Perish* he wrote:

98

Love is a very complex emotion, requiring a richness of personality and a great variety of talents. It is first of all the strong feeling of attachment and dependence that one feels for one's parents. This feeling grows, widens, and changes until it develops, correctly, into the many-faceted desires and strong relationships with human beings of any age or sex. It develops also into the abstract feeling for things and ideas, for beauty and learning, and, finally, into a feeling for the Supreme Being.[20]

It is quite true that far from questioning the perpetuation of transference and projection into adulthood, Blanton encouraged it. Thus he "perpetrated one of his rare corruptions of his master," complains Donald Meyer. The critic continues: "When it came to religion, and his collaboration with Peale, he found himself assuming an ego-weakness which original Freudianism had not had in view."[21] There is nothing in Blanton's writings to suggest that he passively assumed anything; rather, he deliberately chose to subordinate the ego to a Higher Power—a classic spiritual attitude that should not be attributed to Peale's influence. Meyer's declaration that Blanton was "sucked back into the cradle of mind-cure religiosity (if only because of his collaboration with Peale)"[22] is unsupported. Peale had as little to do with Blanton's formulation of faith as Blanton had to do with Peale's grasp of depth psychology.

It is true that Blanton "offered no justification for such faith beyond the nakedly psycho-pragmatic plaint that men needed it."[23] Indeed, the psychiatrist observed: "Each of us feels the need of some sustaining power beyond and above ourselves. Life is too complex and unpredictable, too difficult and too severe, for us to face it with only our own feeble powers."[24] Claims that such a Sustaining Power actually exists *cannot* be justified *except* by faith, which, Blanton reminds us, is "the substance of things hoped for: the evidence of things not seen."[25]

Introducing the subject of faith in one of his sessions with Freud in 1937, Blanton explained his own position that "one could believe what one wished—as, for example, in God or in the Virgin Mary—*as long as science did not disprove it* [italics added]." Freud objected: "You have no right to believe because of ignorance. Of course, if people believe this or that in their private lives, I would not fine or punish them. But scientifically they have no right."[26]

Just twelve days earlier Blanton had implied a rather different position when he told Freud: "My religion is about like yours, as expressed in *The Future of an Illusion*. But I feel that average people cannot have such a bleak religion. Their minds are not well enough furnished. They must have an idealized father to depend on."[27]

What can we make of this startling statement that flies in the face of everything that Blanton professed in print and person? Probably no more than that he told Freud, his "beloved father figure," what he thought Freud would be pleased to hear. The context of the conversation is significant: it was their first meeting after two years, and Blanton was explaining that he and Margaret were soon to set off for the Roman Catholic healing shrine at Lourdes. Knowing Freud's prejudice and skepticism about the place, Blanton may have wanted to establish his own scientific detachment and psychoanalytic orthodoxy. This interpretation is supported by Blanton's record of their conversation later in the hour: "Referring again to Lourdes, I said, 'You must not think I am becoming "religious." Margaret is even more coldly scientific. She will be with me at Lourdes.' 'Well,' said Freud, 'She will keep you from becoming too much so [religious].' "[28]

Blanton was neither a closet atheist nor a hypocrite who cynically deceived "average people" about his own convictions. One may sooner suspect Blanton's failure of courage in witnessing to his religious faith before his disbelieving analyst than question his sincerity in coauthoring *Faith Is the Answer* with Peale. Clearly, Blanton was thinking of himself when he quoted a Harvard physician:

> The medical man . . . will need the support of a true religion. . . . The believing physician often can bring into perfection a cure not otherwise attainable. There is no place in the profession of medicine for the agnostic, the atheist. Man needs a religion, and particularly when he is sick. Religion is not a matter of form but of simple faith.[29]

The thousands of sick people who journeyed to Lourdes each year in search of healing, and the miracle cures reported there aroused the curiosity of Smiley and Margaret Blanton, as it had

Flanders Dunbar's. In the summer of 1937 they set off to visit the shrine, which they felt was the best place for research because of the existence there of a medical board, established in 1882 to examine all claims for cures. The Blantons' inquiring, open attitude toward faith healing was summed up by Margaret in her biography *Bernadette of Lourdes:* "As a student of human behavior one would not be justified in repudiating without examination, any belief long held by the race to be true."[30]

As for Smiley Blanton's particular denominational affiliation, he had none from the age of eight, when his pretty sixteen-year-old Sunday school teacher made a sexual advance (to the shock and horror of his family), until the age of about sixty. Then he associated himself with the Protestant Episcopal Church.[31]

Blanton often told friends that he had no religion—this, his wife explains, because "the ideas evolved by the church doctors meant nothing." He never accepted any statement of faith, or creed, which he called "the quibbles."[32] For him, Jesus' injunction to "Love thy neighbor as thyself" covered it all. Blanton continually marveled that Christianity has survived in the face of violations of Christ's teachings.


## A Pioneering Partnership

In a spirit of adventure and daring the Rev. Norman Vincent Peale and Dr. Smiley Blanton formed, at first, an informal partnership. Peale devoted his energies to counseling and sent parishioners he could not help to Blanton. The two men were in complete agreement that the purpose of their work was to clear psychological obstacles to faith. Peale had learned that conflicts deep within a person could inhibit the message that he preached. Blanton put the matter this way:

> There are those who maintain that if a person is truly devout and carries out his religious duties, says his prayers, goes to church and partakes of the sacraments, this is sufficient to do away with anxiety and feelings of depression. Obviously this is not so. . . . If being devout and truly religious were sufficient, we would not have so many nervous breakdowns, anxiety

states, depressions and actual mental breakdowns. Something more is needed than religion alone, and psychiatry is the natural hand-maiden and helper of religion. Its function is not to take the place of religion but to remove the barriers in the unconscious mind that prevent many people from having a normal life, which includes a normal religious life.[33]

Peale often repeated what he said was one of the psychiatrist's favorite comments in reference to patients: "Norman, I've opened him up. Now you just get in there and give him the good old Gospel."[34]

When mounting appeals for help made it necessary for Blanton and Peale to organize in 1937, they established a clinic in two basement rooms of the Marble Collegiate Church. The Religio-Psychiatric Clinic, as they called it, became a free service of the church.[35]

In one of his final therapy sessions with Freud, Blanton talked about his alliance with Peale:

I then spoke of my work at the Marble Collegiate Church, of how I saw patients who were referred to me by the minister, and of my plan to write a book with Dr. Peale—to write the psychiatric aspect of each subject (anxiety, alcoholism, etc.) and the minister to present his side.

"Do you think you can do it?" asked Freud. (He meant whether I could collaborate in a satisfactory way with a minister.)

I explained again that we would each take a topic and treat it according to our own viewpoint.

"Oh, yes," said Freud, "that seems quite possible."

I also said, "I see no reason why I should not do this church work without impairing my psychiatric standing and psychoanalytic standards." Freud replied, "I don't see why not."[36]

The book that Blanton spoke of was published in 1940 under the title *Faith Is the Answer.* Each chapter was divided into two sections, with Part I by the psychiatrist and Part II by the minister. Chapters included "The Hidden Energies of the Mind," "Conscience and the Sense of Guilt," "Self-criticism, Failure, and Success," and "The Faith That Heals."

The Blanton-Peale team brought out a sequel in 1950, *The Art of Real Happiness.* From then on the men did not collaborate, although Blanton dedicated *Love or Perish* (1955) to Norman Vincent Peale and Peale wrote a foreword to Blanton's *The Healing Power of Poetry* (1960). It appears that the respect the two had for each other never diminished.

A critic might say that the "use" the two had for each other never failed. Although one cannot doubt the genuine commitment each felt toward their joint mission, one cannot help but notice that the partnership was mutually profitable. The minister got much mileage out of his association with the respected psychiatrist. That this is so can be illustrated, for example, by the copy on the dustjacket to Peale's *A Guide to Confident Living* (1948):

> Here is a book by one of America's most famous ministers that sets forth appealingly the confident attitude toward life. . . . It shows how to meet your troubles and put them to flight. The method is a fusion of psychiatry and religion, and Dr. Peale is a pioneer in the use of this method.[37]

A biographical sketch about the author on the back mentions his collaboration "with the well-known psychologist, Dr. Smiley Blanton" and adds: "It is from his long experience as a religious counsellor working with a staff of psychiatrists that Dr. Peale has forged many of his keys to confident living." The partnership was not without its benefits to Blanton. Even though he received no payment for his consultations, his association with the minister earned him a reputation, as Freud pointed out to him "in a tone of approbation."[38] Through their alliance Peale's popular ministry gained in status and Blanton's private practice gained in renown.

The Religio-Psychiatric Clinic grew phenomenally as the world learned about it. Soon letters and even people from across the United States were arriving at the church. In 1948 *Newsweek* reported that more than 10,000 persons had come for help. By then Blanton headed a staff of six psychiatrists and psychologists, all of whom served without fee, and the clinic had expanded into five consultation rooms in the Marble Church parish house.[39] These rooms, Blanton and Peale explained in an article in the *American Magazine,* were furnished like those of an attractive home; the clinic did not look like a clinic with white-garbed nurses.

Whom a visitor saw first, minister or psychiatrist, depended on chance.[40] Looking back after the first ten years, Blanton observed that more than half the people who came in to consult a minister had problems that could be solved only through the cooperation of *both* a minister and a psychiatrist.[41]

It was not long before the arrangement began to strain the church's budget, and further changes seemed desirable. Blanton recalled:

> Dr. Peale and I worked together at the Marble Collegiate Church for fifteen years and then we decided that the work should have a broader base than could be provided by a single church. We applied to the State of New York for permission to form a foundation that would treat patients with a combination of religion and psychiatry and allow us to be an educational institution for training doctors, ministers, social workers, psychologists and others.[42]

The American Foundation of Religion and Psychiatry was incorporated in 1951. Although it continued to provide clinical services for the Marble Collegiate Church, it became interdenominational and pursued a policy of treating people without regard to race, creed, or color. Begun as a tentative, offbeat arrangement between two professional helpers, both Protestant, within twenty-five years it blossomed to become a model institution—the American Foundation of Religion and Psychiatry—with a staff of seventy Protestant, Catholic, and Jewish clergy, psychiatrists, psychologists, and psychiatric social workers. At the time of Dr. Smiley Blanton's death, in 1966, the Foundation ran the second largest outpatient mental health clinic in Manhattan and occupied two floors of an office building.[43]

In 1972 the American Foundation of Religion and Psychiatry merged with the Academy of Religion and Mental Health, an educational organization that conducted national symposia and seminars for clergy, psychiatrists, and mental health workers. The new enterprise is the Institutes of Religion and Health, an interfaith network of clinical service, educational and research programs supporting churches, synagogues and communities in New York and across the United States. Its training arm is the Blanton-Peale Graduate Institute. A grant of more than half a million dollars from the National Institute of Mental Health in 1975 guaranteed the mainstream legitimacy of the Institutes of Religion and Health.

## Blanton, Peale, and Religion and Health

There is no doubt whatsoever about the success of the Blanton-Peale partnership. The question is, was it a factor in the growth of the Religion and Health Movement? If the Rev. Norman Vincent Peale is properly placed in the company of positive thinkers from Mary Baker Eddy to Oral Roberts, as I think he is, how can he be counted one of the leaders of Religion and Health?

Answers to these questions reveal an irony. Although the Blanton-Peale partnership is an important chapter in the story of Freud's impact on American Protestantism, a genuine comprehension of Freudian concepts eluded Peale. As Meyer says, Peale's understanding of the new depth psychology was incoherent and confused. This can be illustrated by just one paragraph from *The Power of Positive Thinking*. In a prescription of how to use faith in healing, Peale directed his reader:

> Form a picture in your mind of the loved one as being well. Visualize him in perfect health. Picture him as radiant with the love and goodness of God. The conscious mind may suggest sickness, even death, but nine tenths of your mind is in the subconscious. Let the picture of health sink into the subconscious and this powerful part of your mind will send forth radiant health energy. What we believe in the subconscious we usually get. Unless your faith controls the subconscious, you will never get any good thing, for the subconscious gives back only that which your real thought is. If the real thought is negative, the results will also be negative. If the real thought is positive, you will get positive and healing results.[44]

By supposing that the "subconscious" could be controlled by conscious will, Peale missed the point entirely. How could he have learned so little from his association with a psychiatrist? Meyer concludes that Blanton was partly to blame: "Blanton was not a sophisticated analyst; he evidently knew nothing of the later

Freud, or of the 'ego-psychology' which had already begun to be developed in the twenties, and the psychology Peale learned from him was therefore unsophisticated."[45]

The assertion that Blanton did not know the later Freud is not true. The charge that Blanton was not a sophisticated analyst is unsubstantiated, and in fact, Meyer contradicts himself by making repeated references to Blanton's psychoanalytic orthodoxy. He gives *Love or Perish* high marks as "one of the best postwar popularizations of Freudian psychology."[46] For an opinion about Blanton's psychoanalytic capability, we can rely on Freud himself; just a year before he died he assured Blanton that he was competent to do training analysis.[47] There could be no higher credential.

If Peale was not aware of how badly he distorted depth psychology, Blanton surely was. Why did Blanton let his colleague go unchallenged? uncorrected? Although we may never know the answer to this question, I suspect that it was because Blanton did not want in any way to jeopardize the work of the clinic. After *The Power of Positive Thinking* was published in 1952, Peale's attention turned to radio programs, lectures, and writing; he spent little time at the clinic. He exercised invaluable leadership, however, as its president by ensuring the financial stability of the enterprise. Money for its support came from wealthy business leaders who were friendly to him. If Peale's positive thinking was an embarrassment to some of the sophisticated professionals who were hired by the Foundation in later years, they nevertheless were indebted to him.

Norman Vincent Peale never boasted of great intellect; in fact, when he explained in 1960 that he had made a mistake in joining a group that opposed John F. Kennedy's election on religious grounds, he quipped that he had "never been too bright anyhow."[48] Although outdistanced intellectually by Worcester, Boisen, Dunbar, and Blanton, he shared their religious liberalism. Peale worked intentionally to accommodate the gospel message to modern culture, he trusted in God's immanent action in daily life, and he believed in progress through "faith with a scientific approach." When, in 1984, he published his autobiography, *The True Joy of Positive Living,* he included an epigraph by George Bernard Shaw that is telling: "This is the true joy in life, the being used for a purpose recognized by yourself as a mighty one." Boisen, of course, had expressed a similar sentiment.

Whatever confusions Peale may have propagated, he contributed to the rise of the Religion and Health Movement as he consistently preached one clear message: the close relationship of mental states to bodily health. Peale knew of Dunbar's work and occasionally quoted her; he served as an ally in popularizing the psychosomatic principle. Again and again he told people: "I believe in the combination of God and the doctor. This viewpoint takes advantage of medical science and the science of faith, and both are elements in the healing process."[49]

Peale used the word science loosely, in a different way than other Religion and Health pioneers used it. For Peale, "science" stands for the predictable, the lawful. Christian faith is "scientific" because its principles are predictable, lawful. He explains:

> Men discover laws and formulas and harness power to do remarkable things. Spiritual power also follows laws. Mastery of these laws works wonders in an area more complicated than any form of mechanics, namely, human nature. It is one thing to make a machine work right. To make human nature work right is something else. It requires greater skill, but it can be done.[50]

In his own fashion Peale articulated a philosophical assumption made by Freud and all Religion and Health pioneers: mental phenomena obey laws.

Blanton's restrained optimism about human progress also reflected the religious liberalism of Religion and Health. In his introduction to *Love or Perish* he made a poignant personal observation:

> In my own life I have lived through part of the Reconstruction period in the South; I have experienced the horror of war in World War I, lived through World War II, and have seen the development of atomic warfare. All this during one lifetime. Nevertheless, I am firmly convinced that the world is actually a better place than it was in my youth. People are kinder, there is less prejudice, less hatred, and there is a deeper realization that we must love our neighbor as ourselves.[51]

107

To promote love in the world the psychiatrist joined the minister to work, in Freud's words, "in the service of the suffering." Blanton and Peale believed that this "modern brand of faith" that they modeled could revitalize the church and provide "such a rejuvenation as it has not known for generations."[52]

# CHAPTER 6

# Seward Hiltner, Paul Tillich, and the New York Psychology Group

*When Jesus asks the disciples to heal and to cast out demons he does not distinguish bodily, mental and spiritual diseases. But every page of the gospels shows that he means all three of them, and many stories show that he sees their unity. We see this unity today more clearly than many generations before us did.*

—Paul Tillich[1]

*Pastoral care and counseling of individuals is here to stay . . . the rise of however many therapeutic professions will not succeed in depriving the pastor of some therapeutic obligation to his people. But the rise of these other groups means that his results are judged by standards never before available. Hence, good intentions without study and knowledge become increasingly impossible.*

—Seward Hiltner[2]

The Rev. Dr. Paul Tillich
*Photograph by Lucas and Monroe
Studio, New York; courtesy of the
Andover-Harvard Theological
Library*

The Rev. Dr. Seward Hiltner
*Photograph by Clearose Studio,
Princeton; courtesy of Princeton
Theological Seminary*

THE GROUP THAT gathered in a New York City, Central Park West apartment on Friday evening, December 5, came not for a holiday party, but to make earnest plans for ongoing discussions about the relationship between religion and mental health. Among those present were theologians, psychiatrists, and psychotherapists, both Freudian and Jungian. Most were Americans; some were European emigrants. Two days later came the news that the Japanese had bombed Pearl Harbor: America was at war.

The New York Psychology Group (NYPG) continued to meet monthly for the duration of the war. Because many members were academics, either teaching or studying at Union Theological Seminary or Columbia University, an academic calendar determined the meetings: from spring semester 1942 through spring semester 1945, with intervening summer breaks. In total there were twenty-nine meetings. Over the years as many as forty persons participated; however, about two dozen individuals constituted a core group. They were:

Ruth Benedict, Ph.D.
Martha H. Biehle
Thomas J. Bigham, M.S., S.T.B., S.T.M.
Harry Bone, Ph.D.
Gotthard Booth, M.D.
Violet de Laszlo, M.D.
Grace Loucks Elliott, M.A., Ph.D.
Harrison Elliott, B.D., M.A., Ph.D.
E. McClung Fleming, Ph.D.
Greta F. Frankley, M.D.
Erich Fromm, Ph.D.
Martha Jaeger Glickman, Ph.D.
Seward Hiltner, B.D., Ph.D.
Daphne Hughes
Elined Kotschnig
Rollo May, B.D., Ph.D.
Helen Nichol, M.A., B.D.
Otis Rice, B.D.

111

David E. Roberts, B.D., Ph.D.
Carl Rogers, Ph.D.
Elizabeth Rohrbach, M.A.
Anna Hartoch Schachtel
Ernst Schachtel
Paul Tillich, Licentiate in Theology, Ph.D.
Hannah Tillich
Frances G. Wickes

Search as one may for information about the NYPG, one is unlikely to find it. For example, neither Hannah Tillich nor Rollo May, themselves members, mentioned Paul Tillich's participation in the group in their biographies of him.[3] Although Tillich attended conscientiously and delivered three papers, Wilhelm and Marion Pauck cite the group only in a brief footnote in their definitive biography.[4] What scanty facts the Paucks have are drawn from Seward Hiltner's 1974 review essay, "Tillich the Person." Here Hiltner describes his early acquaintance with Tillich through the group, gives some skeletal details about it, and concludes, "I still have the summarized notes of those meetings."[5]

When I asked Professor Hiltner, chairman of the NYPG, for more recollections, he generously loaned me these notes, a "historical treasure."[6] They have been invaluable in reconstructing the story of the NYPG and its living members, many of whom Hiltner helped me to locate. Another source of fact has been the historical files of the National Council on Religion in Higher Education, under whose auspices the seminar convened. This organization, now headquartered in New Haven, Connecticut, became the Society for Values in Higher Education in 1975.[7] In addition, I have used materials published by and about individual members. Because many are or were eminent personalities, learning about them has often been as easy as consulting *Who's Who* or the *New York Times.*

Analysis of the NYPG attendance figures indicates that most members must have put high priority on being present. Of the twenty-nine meetings held over a three-and-a-half-year period, several people missed only *two* meetings—Harry Bone, Gotthard Booth, and Seward Hiltner. Thomas Bigham missed only five;

112

Martha Jaeger Glickman and Erich Fromm, only six; Greta Frankley, seven; and Grace Elliott, David Roberts, and Paul Tillich, eight. Rollo May was forced to give up participation when he entered a sanitarium for the treatment of tuberculosis, but of the first fourteen seminars, he missed just three.

Given the stature of NYPG members, their remarkable record of involvement, and the longevity of the group itself, it is puzzling that its existence has been unknown. Is this because knowledge of it was deliberately protected both at the time and in the following years? Partly. There was, remembers Hiltner, an agreement among members that they would not discuss the group's conversations or work outside the group; however, there was no attempt to keep the meetings a secret.[8] An explanation for the group's obscurity has been offered by Rollo May. The significance of the seminar, he says, has become apparent *only in retrospect.* "The Intellectuals Take Aim" would be an appropriate heading to describe what occurred then, the importance of which we see only now.[9] Not until we identify the Religion and Health Movement as a movement can we appreciate the crucial significance of this wartime seminar.

The NYPG essentially functioned not to break new conceptual ground, but to encourage and reinforce members in their own efforts to explore the interrelation of Religion and Health by providing a forum for intellectual exchange and fellowship. At the time of the meetings many members were engaged in Religion and Health work. Some had written articles or books in the field of psychology and/or theology, and after 1945 they would publish many more.

Evidence of the participants' influence is apparent in a 1973 survey made of theological schools to identify the most frequently used books in pastoral care and counseling.[10] Of the ten books most often listed, five were authored by NYPG members:

1. Howard Clinebell Jr., *Basic Types of Pastoral Counseling,* 1966.
*2. Carl Rogers, *Client-Centered Therapy,* 1951.
*3. Seward Hiltner, *Pastoral Counseling,* 1949.
*4. Carl Rogers, *On Becoming a Person,* 1961.
5. Erik Erikson, *Childhood and Society,* 1950, 1963.

113

6. Elisabeth Kübler-Ross, *On Death and Dying,* 1969.
7. Virginia Satir, *Conjoint Family Therapy,* 1964, 1967.
*8. Seward Hiltner, *Preface to Pastoral Theology,* 1958.
*9. David Roberts, *Psychotherapy and a Christian View of Man,* 1950.
10. Carroll Wise, *Pastoral Counseling: Its Theory and Practice,* 1951.

Of the total number of books listed (eighty-one), almost 25 percent (nineteen) were written by Boisen, Freud, Fromm, Hiltner, May, Roberts, Rogers, or Tillich.

During their three and a half years together, NYPG members studied theoretical issues from the perspective of theology and psychology that would illuminate and support practical efforts in the field. Each year a different theme focused the discussion: the Psychology of Faith (1942), the Psychology of Love (1942–43), the Psychology of Conscience (1943–44), and the Psychology of Helping (1944–45).

The idea for the NYPG originated with Seward Hiltner and Erich Fromm. The two met on the campus of Keuka College, Keuka, New York, in late August 1941. The occasion was the annual Week of Work of the National Council on Religion in Higher Education (NCRHE). Fromm was a consultant for a group studying unconscious motivations of group behavior. On two evenings he addressed the 150 Week of Work participants on the topics "How Unconscious Factors Affect Conscious Thought and Convictions" and "A Psychological Analysis of Democratic and Authoritarian Ideologies."[11] Discussions of these subjects proved so interesting that Hiltner and Fromm proposed that they be continued in Manhattan during the coming year. A select group of graduate students who had been awarded Kent Fellowships by the NCRHE participated in the Week of Work and then in the NYPG meetings.

The coming together of these promising students with established theologians, psychologists, and psychoanalysts in constituting the NYPG, achieved a remarkable mix of generations. A breakdown of the membership by age in 1942 will illustrate the point:

114

| Sixties | | Fifties | |
|---------|---|---------|---|
| Wickes | 67 | P. Tillich | 56 |
| H. Elliott | 60 | Benedict | 55 |
| | | Frankley | 53 |
| | | G. Elliott | 51 |

| Forties | | Thirties | |
|---------|---|----------|---|
| Glickman | 48 | E. Schachtel | 39 |
| Kotschnig | 47 | Biehle | 36 |
| H. Tillich | 46 | Rice | 36 |
| Nichol | 44 | Fleming | 33 |
| Bone | 43 | Hiltner | 33 |
| Booth | 43 | May | 33 |
| de Laszlo | 42 | Bigham | 31 |
| Fromm | 42 | Roberts | 31 |
| Rohrbach | 42 | | |

A Program Committee handled NYPG planning and membership. The Committee consisted of Seward Hiltner, who acted as chairperson; Martha Biehle, executive director of the NCRHE, who acted as secretary; and Erich Fromm, Harry Bone, and Martha Jaeger Glickman, in whose Central Park West apartment the meetings were initially held. In consultation with the entire group, the Program Committee worked out a membership policy. They limited attendance and participation—"by invitation only"—to thirty new members, who were suggested at periodic intervals. Requirements were (a) professional competence and (b) contribution to the group from a special field that would enlarge group resources.[12] This policy was necessary because there were others who were "keenly interested" in joining the group; membership had to be cut off.

That these particular individuals met at this particular historical moment is a fact of incalculable importance for the growth of Religion and Health. What had been a small movement before the war blossomed beyond expectation in the postwar era, partly as a result of their intellectual effort and influence.

## The Chairperson of the NYPG

*Seward Hiltner* (1909–84) was more instrumental than any other person in the growth and development of the Religion and Health Movement.[13] Born in Pennsylvania and graduated from Lafayette College (1931), Hiltner met Anton Boisen during his first year at the University of Chicago Divinity School. Boisen, who by that time had moved from Worcester to Elgin State Hospital and was essentially a public relations specialist for the clinical pastoral education (CPE) movement, explained the clinical training program to Hiltner, who found it just the experience he had been looking for. During the next two summers he worked with Donald Beatty at a center outside Pittsburgh, and during his third year, with Carroll Wise at Worcester.

Hiltner entered the Ph.D. program at Chicago and completed his course work before leaving for New York to take the first full-time executive position in the CPE movement: he became executive secretary of the Council for Clinical Training for Theological Students and worked under the direct supervision of Dr. Flanders Dunbar. From 1935 to 1938 Hiltner worked for the Council, making contacts with some forty to fifty seminaries and also laying the foundation for future CPE centers.[14] He left to become executive secretary of the Commission on Religion and Health of the Federal Council of Churches, of which Otis Rice was the director. (This later became the Department of Pastoral Services.) Hiltner held the position until 1950, when he returned to Chicago to complete his Ph.D. dissertation and become professor of pastoral theology.

When Seward Hiltner's first book, *Religion and Health,* was published in 1943, Paul Tillich studied it carefully and acknowledged appreciation for the practical matters he said he learned from it.[15] The many references Tillich made to the book in a lengthy historical and theoretical paper presented to the Religion and Health Seminar at Columbia University in 1945 suggest that it made a deep impression on him.[16]

Hiltner's record of publication, dating back to the 1930s, is prodigious. It includes many books and more than four hundred articles for professional journals.[17] Of particular interest in the context of this study is his "Freud for the Pastor," which derived

116

from his course at the University of Chicago in 1953 entitled "Freud and Religion."[18] This was the first seminary course to concentrate on evaluating Freud's general theory on the basis of religious perspectives. Hiltner concluded that, like the student, the pastor who wishes to understand Freud needs to read Freud himself or herself, not accept the judgment of others; therefore, the main purpose of his articles is to offer some suggestions on *how* to read Freud. Hiltner also makes known his own point of view, that Freud was "unintentionally a greater contributor to religious understanding than one could possibly guess merely from an examination of his negative views on the truth and validity of religion as he understood it."[19] Hiltner found ten of Freud's discoveries to have positive significance for understanding religion.

Seward Hiltner said that the NYPG played an important role in his intellectual life; certainly as its organizer and chairperson he was crucial to the group. Rollo May remembers Hiltner as its "balance wheel"—"he had a capacity to know where the discussion was going."[20]

### Membership Contingent on World War II

The world war was ever a part of the group's consciousness. For one thing, the NYPG would not have been constituted as it was but for the upheaval in Europe. Nine members were emigrants: the Tillichs, Fromm, Booth, Kotschnig, de Laszlo, Frankley, and the Schachtels. (All but the Tillichs were psychotherapists.) Their experience of disruption and displacement intensified the group's awareness of global warfare and strengthened the predominant sense that intelligent and informed discussion of the relationship between depth psychology and theology was urgent.

Systematic theologian *Paul Tillich* (1886–1965) was proud of the fact that he had been the first non-Jewish professor to be dismissed from a German university after Hitler came to power.[21] Tillich moved to New York in 1933 with his wife, *Hannah Tillich* (1896–    ), and their two children. Union Theological Seminary appointed him visiting professor of philosophy of religion and

117

systematic theology and later promoted him to associate professor and then professor of philosophical theology. In 1955 he retired from Union and became a university professor at Harvard.

Long before making the acquaintance of NYPG therapists, Tillich had acquired a sophisticated understanding of psychoanalysis and had drawn some brilliant conclusions about Freud's contribution to theology, as a close reading of *The Religious Situation* (1925) and the autobiographical *On the Boundary* (1936) clearly indicates. However, an intensified interest, knowledge, sensitivity, and commitment to issues of religion and health, pastoral psychology, and theology and counseling can be discerned in Tillich's post-NYPG publications.

Dr. Earl A. Loomis Jr., first director of the Program in Psychiatry and Religion at Union, has written of Tillich:

> As late as 1933 to 1937 he was groping for the place of psychoanalysis in his philosophical system, and for him it still remained somewhat isolated and peripheral. . . . The effort to assimilate and accommodate himself to psychoanalysis was a difficult one for Tillich, as for many others of his time. Persisting, his curiosity eventually was rewarded and the interchange that grew out of his close alliance with analysis and analytic thought was enduring. In time he came to speak and write as one who had seen the problems and the conflicts, one who had experienced the drives and the defenses, one who had struggled with the resistances and the transference. Eventually the familiarity became deep and lasting.[22]

Tillich frequently said that he learned more from conversations, discussion, and debates than from books.[23] One can hypothesize that in dialogue with NYPG clinicians—Freudians, neo-Freudian revisionists, and Jungians—he gained a more experiential understanding of psychotherapeutic healing than he had previously gained from analytically informed intellectuals in Germany.

Of course, Tillich's experiential understanding *could* have come from a personal analysis sometime in the 1940s. However, the evidence indicates that this did not occur. We should probably take Hannah Tillich's word for it that her husband was never psychoanalyzed. (Psychoanalytic therapy, she reports having once been told, would have been destructive for him.)[24]

In association not only with clinicians, but also with Seward Hiltner, Rollo May, David Roberts, and other Christian thinkers of the group who were finding ways to reconcile psychotherapy and a Christian view of humankind in their professional lives, Paul Tillich was nudged toward a more personal, less theoretical understanding.

As a German philosopher, he reveled in theoretical and abstract debate; as a member of the NYPG, however, he was inevitably pulled in the direction of the concrete by practical Americans. A few years after the group disbanded Tillich wrote: "The interdependence of theory and practice in Anglo-Saxon culture, religious as well as secular, has freed me from the fascination of that kind of abstract idealism which enjoys the system for the system's sake."[25]

As a member of the NYPG, Paul Tillich presented three papers: "The Concept of Faith in the Jewish Christian Tradition" (April 1942), "Fragments of an Ontology of Love" (May 1943), and "Conscience—Historical and Typological Remarks" (November 1943). The last was revised and published as "The Transmoral Conscience" in *The Protestant Era*.

Psychoanalyst and social philosopher *Erich Fromm* (1900–80), an old friend of Tillich's from Frankfurt, visited the United States in 1933, when he was invited to lecture at the Chicago Institute for Psychoanalysis. In 1934 he left his Nazi-dominated homeland permanently, having decided to become an American citizen.[26] Just a few months before the NYPG was organized, in July 1941, Fromm published a book that members referred to frequently: *Escape from Freedom*. In it Fromm analyzes the psychological factors operating in the totalitarian flight from freedom." His premise is that

> the basic entity of the social process is the individual, his desires and fears, his passions and reason, his propensities for good and for evil. To understand the dynamics of the social process we must understand the dynamics of the psychological processes operating within the individual, just as to understand

119

the individual we must see him in the context of the culture which molds him.[27]

From 1940 to 1941 Fromm was guest lecturer at Columbia University, and from 1941 to 1950 he was a member of the faculty at Bennington College in Bennington, Vermont. He was also one of the founders, in 1943, of the William Alanson White Institute for Psychiatry, Psychoanalysis and Psychology in New York, and he worked there continuously until 1950.

Fromm and Tillich are remembered today by NYPG members as having been the natural leaders of the group. Fromm addressed the seminar more often than anyone else. Although he spoke on five occasions, he gave his address a formal title only once: "Psychology and Ethics" (October 8, 1943). He claimed that he was a secular humanist, but Fromm had trained to be a rabbi and, according to May, constantly had to be "on guard against his own belief."[28] Helen Nichol Fernald recalls that he sometimes referred to a well-worn edition of the Hebrew scriptures that he carried in his jacket pocket.[29] Minutes of NYPG meetings indicate that Fromm persistently demanded *why* all discussion had to be in reference to a transcendent God, a devil's advocate position that Tillich found useful.[30]

Another German emigrant member of the NYPG was *Dr. Gotthard Booth* (1899–1975). A psychiatrist and specialist in psychosomatic medicine, Booth earned his medical degree from the University of Munich in 1923 and came to the United States in 1934. An Episcopalian, his family roots were Lutheran, Anglican, Quaker, Jewish, Roman Catholic, and Old Catholic.[31] Thomas Bigham Jr. later wrote: "Dr. Booth's psychiatric position was that of a Kierkegaardian Catholic and his theological position that of a psychoanalytic care for the concrete manifestations of the transcendent.[32]

In New York, Booth learned of the Commission on Religion and Health of the Federal Council of Churches from its chairman, Otis Rice (another NYPG member); Booth then took a considerable part in its work. He also served as the psychiatric consultant of the General Theological Seminary and developed its program of psychological testing. When Union began its program on religion and psychiatry in 1958, Booth became an adviser.

Speaking from his expertise in psychosomatic medicine, Dr. Booth addressed the NYPG twice: "Love and the Physiology of Sex" (January 8, 1943) and "Disease and Guilt" (April 12, 1944). He missed only two meetings.

In recognition of Booth's contributions to the understanding of the relationship between personality and illness, a nonprofit society in his name was incorporated in Ontario in 1977. A descriptive pamphlet from the Gotthard Booth Society for Holistic Health states:

> Throughout his long life, Booth was a pioneering figure who through his many articles championed the conviction that we must approach questions of wellness and illness by situating these states of being in the context of a person's life history. For Booth, a psychosomatic approach to medicine meant that we had to come to see that all illness and wellness grows out of the total relationship between a person and his or her biological, familial, social, cultural and spiritual environment. Hence he struggled to overcome the splits between mind and body, illness and health, in a unified vision of the human person.[33]

*Elined Prys Kotschnig* (1895–1983), a native of Wales, and her husband, Walter Kotschnig, an Austrian, were both involved in student service work before their emigration to the United States in 1936.[34] After graduation from the University of Wales in 1918, Elined Prys served as student secretary of the World Student Christian Federation in Rumania and the British Student Christian Movement. In 1924 she married Walter Kotschnig, Ph.D., who from 1925 to 1934 was secretary general of the International Student Service in Geneva. Elined worked with him, and in 1932 they edited a symposium, *The University in a Changing World.*[35]

From 1934 to 1936 Walter Kotschnig served as director of the High Commission for Refugees Coming from Germany, which had been established by the League of Nations.[36] In 1936 the Kotschnigs moved to Northampton, Massachusetts, where she went into private practice as an analytical (Jungian) psychologist and he became a professor of comparative education at Smith and Mount Holyoke Colleges.

Despite the fact that she was the mother of three children, was working, and had to commute from Northampton to NYPG meetings,[37] Elined Kotschnig was a faithful group member. She was present at the organizational session, delivered a paper at the second meeting, and then attended regularly through November 1943. In 1944 the Kotschnig family moved to Washington, DC, where Walter Kotschnig went to work for the Department of State and Elined Kotschnig continued her analytical practice. She returned to New York for a meeting once.

Elined Kotschnig was active in the Society of Friends. From 1943 to 1946 she chaired the Friends' Conference on Religion and Psychology; in 1946 she became a member of the Executive Committee of the Friends' Conference on Religion and Psychology; and in 1950 she began as editor of the Friends' publication *Inward Light*. Teresina Rowell Havens, a Kent Fellow who visited the NYPG once in 1942 and who served on the Friends' Executive Committee with Elined, comments on the Jungian/Quaker connection:

> An interesting point for me is the mix of "professional" analysts or therapists with solid Quaker types, trained by the Inner Guide and a life-long immersion in the Quaker milieu, e.g., serving on Ministry and Counsel Committees. . . . Some of the members were professional analysts, like Elined, as well as what one might call lay-counsellors in the Society of Friends. Women were predominant in the leadership of the Friends' Conference on Religion and Psychology.[38]

Another prominent emigrant member of the NYPG—also a woman Jungian analyst—was *Dr. Violet de Laszlo* (1900–    ). Born in Switzerland, Violet Staub earned her M.D. at the University of Zurich in 1926. From 1927 to 1930 she lived in the United States with her husband, Henry de Laszlo. While he studied at MIT she did research at Massachusetts General Hospital. In 1930 they moved to England, his homeland. Between 1930 and 1932 de Laszlo commuted from London to Zurich for seminars with Dr. Carl Jung and analysis with his associate H.G. Baynes. In the 1930s she was active in the Society of Analytical Psychology in London, which was in the process of planning an institute when the war broke out.

Dr. de Laszlo's departure from London in 1940 was an abrupt and frightening one. Her brother-in-law had witnessed the chaotic exodus of civilians from Paris with the German invasion of France and had shared his fears for England with her and her husband. When France capitulated to Hitler in June, an ad hoc committee of Americans and English hastily organized what was to be a large-scale evacuation of children from England by boat convoy. De Laszlo's husband urged her to take their young son and flee. Because friends in America agreed to receive them, this was possible—they had the requisite sponsor abroad. Hurriedly one July night, during a blackout, they left from an unnamed railroad station for an unnamed seaport (all identifying signs had been removed) to board ship. She remembers that only one boatload of 1,000 children got through; another was torpedoed.[39]

After debarking at St. John's, Newfoundland, and taking a detour through Virginia, Violet de Laszlo settled in New York City and set up private practice. She learned of the NYPG through Dr. Gotthard Booth (his wife was a friend from Switzerland) and attended its meeting faithfully. In December 1943 she spoke to the group about "Conscience and the Transcendent Function." In the late 1950s Violet de Laszlo's name became nationally known when she edited and introduced two volumes of Carl Jung's work with Dr. Jung's help: *Psyche and Symbol* and the Modern Library's *Basic Writings of C.G. Jung.*[40]

Four Americans joined with Kotschnig and de Laszlo to form a Jungian subgroup within the NYPG. These people—Frances Wickes, Martha Jaeger Glickman, Elizabeth Rohrbach, and E. McClung Fleming—are mentioned later, since our focus here is emigrant members.

*Dr. Greta F. Frankley* (1889–1976) changed her name from "Frankenstein" to "Frankley" during 1942, and in NYPG records for that year she is referred to both ways. When she later married Dr. Karl Gerstenberg her name became Frankley-Gerstenberg. Biographical directories of the American Psychiatric Association variously list her year of birth as 1889 and 1894.[41]

Born in Hamburg, Germany, she earned an M.D. at the University of Munich in 1920. Licensed to practice in Illinois, she was a psychiatrist with the Jewish Social Service Bureau in Chicago from 1924 to 1926. She returned to Germany to be a physician and psychiatrist in the Berlin School System from 1927 to 1933. Sometime between 1933 and 1936 she emigrated to America. She opened a private practice in 1939 after working for several years for the Jewish Board of Guardians in New York City. Her orientation was Freudian: a friend of Anna Freud's, she trained with Franz Alexander, her analyst.

In New York, Greta Frankley worked dedicatedly with Paul Tillich in Self-Help for Emigrés from Central Europe, a group that was founded in November 1936 to provide jobs for refugees and draw them into a community. Tillich was Self-Help's first chairperson, a position he held for fifteen years.[42]

*Ernst Schachtel* (1903–75) was another refugee, Freudian analyst. He taught at the William Alanson White Institute for twenty years and for the last fourteen years of his life in a postdoctoral psychology program at New York University.[43] Schachtel developed experimental approaches to Rorschach inkblot tests and published a book on the subject in 1966.[44] He and his wife, *Anna Hartoch Schachtel,* made a joint presentation to the NYPG in March 1943. His paper, "On Love, Knowledge and Perception," discussed the use of Rorschach tests for showing the connections between different perceptive types and different character structures, and between different perceptive types and the capacity for love and creative thought. Her paper, "Some Conditions of Love in Childhood," drew from Rorschach tests of nursery-school children to discuss the conditions under which they do or do not develop the capacity for love, particularly in wartime.

Schachtel, remembers Rollo May, spent several years in a Nazi concentration camp and was deeply affected by it.[45] Anna Schachtel made a remark during a NYPG meeting in March 1942 that implies an acute understanding of the threat to human society and culture caused by war. She said: "In this Psychology of Faith group, it is not what we learn that is important, but that in the middle of wartime we do not give up discussing these questions. This has a social as well as an educational value."

The human cost of war became tragically immediate to the group in March 1943 with the news that Nancy Roodenburg's husband had been killed in action two months earlier.[46] Seminar members highly valued Nancy Roodenburg, a stenographer, for her minutes of all NYPG meetings, which she mimeographed and distributed to everyone. Word that strafing enemy planes had killed Maj. William Roodenburg, in charge of an aviation ground force in North Africa, shocked and saddened everyone. He left not only a widow, but also a nineteen-month-old daughter.

Membership in the NYPG fluctuated somewhat as a result of comings and goings related to the war effort. *Ruth Benedict* (1887–1948), associate professor of anthropology at Columbia University, attended seven meetings of the group and delivered papers at two of them before she left for Washington, DC in 1943. Until 1945 Benedict worked for the Office of War Information in the field of overseas intelligence and foreign morale.[47] Because she was the only anthropologist in the group, Benedict's contribution was especially honored; her knowledge of other cultures made possible a more comprehensive, universal outlook.

*E. McClung Fleming* (1909–   ), who was born in India the son of Presbyterian missionaries,[48] was a history instructor at the College of the City of New York and a doctoral candidate in history at Columbia University when the NYPG organized. He attended group meetings regularly while teaching and working to complete his dissertation. In January 1944, Mac Fleming was inducted into the Army and left New York for officer candidate school at Camp Lee, Virginia. He was commissioned a second lieutenant, promoted to first lieutenant in December 1945, and discharged in 1947. As chief of the Field Services Branch, Information and Educational Division, he was responsible for the troop information program of the Middle Pacific Command.[49] In 1947 Fleming became professor of history and dean of Park College, Parkville, Missouri.

In the fall of 1944 *Carl Rogers* (1902–   ) moved to New York City to work with the United Service Organizations (USO) as director of counseling services. Formerly a professor of psychology at Ohio State University, he had agreed to spend a year training USO professional staff workers (about 3,000 of them) in counseling techniques that would enable them to handle more skillfully the problems of people who came to them.[50]

While he was in New York, the NYPG invited Rogers to join. He went to four meetings, and on March 3, 1945, he gave a paper at the group's final seminar. Although the psychologist made a vivid impression on some group members, the group made little or no impression on him. "I have no memory at all of meeting with that group and if you had not given me the dates on which I was present, I would have said I had never attended," Rogers wrote me. He continued:

> The psychoanalysts certainly resisted my client-centered approach to therapy, but whether they did at that meeting I have no recollection. . . . I did know a number of the people in the core group—Harry Bone, Grace Elliott, Harrison Elliott, Seward Hiltner, Rollo May—but I don't remember any particular association with them in this connection, although during those years I did know Harry Bone quite well and was much influenced by the Elliotts, especially Harrison, whose approach to group discussions stimulated me very much.[51]

Rogers based his presentation, in March 1945, on his pamphlet, "A Counseling Viewpoint for the USO Worker," which he distributed at the meeting. He began by reporting the situation caused by the war:

> It is commonplace knowledge that servicemen, their wives and relations, servicewomen, and industrial workers who have been transplanted into war production areas, are bringing many problems of personal adjustment to USO workers, chaplains, clergymen, college teachers and others who have not regarded the task of counseling as their primary responsibility. *These workers feel themselves doubtfully equipped to assist in the solution of personal problems* [italics added].[52]

Rogers then explained why his client-centered approach was especially useful for the person with little professional training or the person whose professional training is in some other field. Otis R. Rice, chairman of the Commission on Religion and Health of the Federal Council of Churches and a member of the NYPG, believed that Rogers' client-centered psychotherapy would prove rewarding to ministers and other religious workers; consequently, he arranged for the Commission on Religion and Health to reprint the pamphlet in May 1945 under the title "A Counseling Viewpoint." In the next decades Rogers' approach would deeply influence clinical training and pastoral counseling. Although it was not Freudian, his psychotherapeutic approach helped to spread knowledge of Freud's dynamic concepts, however partial and distorted.[53]

## The Kent Fellows

With the purpose of encouraging teaching and scholarship of distinction in the field of religion, Prof. Charles Foster Kent of Yale University and a number of his friends inaugurated, in 1923, a fellowship program for gifted young graduate students. The annual gatherings of Kent Fellows, which came to be called Week of Work, began with three days of meetings at Kent's home in Mount Carmel, Connecticut, before the opening of the academic year in September 1924. Stimulating discussions, mutual encouragement, and deepening friendships marked these days.

When the NYPG core group formed out of a Week of Work in 1941, eleven of its members were Kent Fellows. They were:

| | |
|---|---|
| Harry Bone | K '27 |
| Helen Nichol | K '27 |
| Otis Rice | K '27 |
| Elizabeth Rohrback | K '29 |
| Martha Jaeger Glickman | K '31 |
| Martha Biehle | K '35 |
| Seward Hiltner | K '35 |
| David Roberts | K '35 |
| E. McClung Fleming | K '38 |
| Daphne Hughes | K '42 |
| Rollo May | K '42 |

*Otis Rice* (1906–60), a Harvard graduate, was selected to receive a Kent Fellowship while he was a divinity student at the Episcopal Theological School in Cambridge, Massachusetts. Rice then did graduate work in England, France, and Germany. After being ordained in the Protestant Episcopal Church he served as an assistant minister and pastoral counselor at Trinity Church in Boston and St. Thomas Church in New York.[54]

From 1939 to 1958 Rice was religious director and chaplain of St. Luke's Hospital in New York and an instructor at General

Theological Seminary. His special fields of interest were pastoral psychology, religious education, and personal counseling. At the time of the NYPG meetings, Rice chaired the Commission on Religion and Health and was acting chaplain of Columbia.

*Dr. Harry Bone* (1899–1971), a clinical psychologist, made a lasting impression on NYPG members. As far as alignments in the group went, he was behind Fromm, not Tillich, May remembers, although his humanism May judged to be more profound than Fromm's.[55] Another member recalls that Bone was a remarkable thinker, putting together Freud, Jesus, and Marx long before others thought to do so.

Born in Topeka, Kansas, and raised in the First Presbyterian Church there, Bone did undergraduate work at Washburn University of Topeka. He served as general secretary for the YMCA in Vermont and Texas for several years before taking courses at Union Theological Seminary. From 1932 to 1935 he studied at the Sorbonne in Paris, where he earned his Ph.D. Certified by the William Alanson White Institute, he became a training and supervising psychoanalyst and for more than thirty-five years had a private practice in Manhattan.[56]

A conscientious NYPG participant, Bone missed only two meetings and made presentations at three. He expressed his thoughts about contemporary events in a Christmas letter he and his wife sent to NCRHE fellows in December 1941:

> The meaning of Christmas is deeper and clearer this year than ever before for us. First, because we believe confidently that the present world conflict is basically a healthy revolt against a social structure within which the brotherhood of man would have been forever impossible, and that it is therefore negative proof that humanity's deepest and most controlling need is for community of life—of all human life . . .[57]

In his message Bone recommended that fellows read, among other books, Fromm's *Escape from Freedom* and Tillich's *The Religious Situation*. He added, "Be on the lookout for Dr. Karen Horney's *Self-Analysis* (title uncertain) which will appear in a month or so." It is evident that the interests and concerns of the NYPG members who were Kent Fellows were carried to the

NCRHE through its newsletters, the annual Week of Work, and a network of professional and personal friendships.

*Helen Nichol* (1898–    ), who was single until her mid-seventies, when she married Richard Fernald, was elected a Kent Fellow the same year as Rice and Bone. She tells the story of how she once went to Dr. Bone saying, "Oh, Harry, I'd *love* to be psychoanalyzed." His reply:

> My dear girl, you have no more reason to be psychoanalyzed than a mosquito. No one who comes to me says, "I'd *love* to be psychoanalyzed." They come to me and say, "I am desperate. I am going to die. I wish I could die," and I say, "Come, let's work it out." Unless you come to me and say, "Harry, I'm dying," there's no point.[58]

Helen Nichol was born and raised in Canada and received both her B.A. (1920) and M.A. (1921) from McGill University. In her twenties she came under the influence of Henry Burton Sharman,[59] who enlisted her and many other students in the Student Christian Movement of Canada. Through Sharman, Nichol met his sister-in-law, Sophia Lyon Fahs. Fahs ran an experimental church school at Union Theological Seminary and encouraged Nichol to study there. She moved to New York and roomed at the International House with Kent Fellow Virginia Corwin, who was working on her Ph.D. thesis. After earning her B.D. in 1930, Nichol was fortunate during the Depression to get a teaching job at "Dobbs" (the Masters School in Dobbs Ferry, New York) with the help of Union president Henry Sloane Coffin, who served on the private school's board. She remained there for forty years with three leaves of absence.

The talkfests of the NYPG profoundly motivated Nichol. She learned that it is a person's responsibility to be imaginative, to be creative, to *act:* "If one doesn't act, one must take the consequences. Anyone who sits on the sidelines and doesn't get involved is not only a coward, but not a person. Well, I'd been sitting on the sidelines for decades."

So it was that Helen Nichol decided to leave for Rome to set up the British Club for Women in Uniform, thus dropping out of NYPG participation in 1944.

*Elizabeth Rohrbach* (1900–    ) had earned three M.A.s by the time of the NYPG meetings: in English literature (Columbia, 1924), in divinity (Union Theological Seminary, 1932), and in counseling (Columbia, 1938).[60] A teacher of English at St. Mary's School in Garden City, New York, she confided in her friend Helen Nichol. Rohrbach was distraught over her divorce; even though she felt it was right, it was terrible, an agony. Nichol suggested to Rohrbach that she see Harry Emerson Fosdick: "Fosdick's first words to her were, 'You have circular thinking. You cannot get a certain idea out of your head. It goes round and round. You cannot sleep at night.'" Fosdick described Rohrbach's situation so exactly that she thought he was a wizard. He then confided to her that *he* had had a nervous breakdown, which had taken him years to get over. Through what he called his confessional, "he took Betty through the ropes to God."[61]

*Martha Jaeger Glickman* (1894–1963) was married to Hyman Glickman (he attended eight meetings) in the early 1940s, but when they later divorced she dropped "Glickman" from her name. She worked for the YWCA in Cleveland after her graduation from Case Western Reserve University and after World War I served with a relief mission in Rumania. She earned a Ph.D. in psychology from Columbia and then taught at the College of William and Mary. To prepare for a career in psychotherapy, she worked with Dr. Otto Rank and NYPG member Frances Wickes. A Jungian analyst, Dr. Jaeger served as chairperson of the Friends' Conference on Religion and Psychology and as a member of the editorial board of *Inward Light*.

One of the five Program Committee members who scheduled and planned NYPG meetings, Glickman delivered one paper in May 1943. She discussed the relationship of social and economic factors to love in contemporary life, especially as seen through the eyes of a woman.

*Martha Biehle* (1906–77) was executive director of the NCRHE from 1938 to May 1943, when she resigned to become assistant to the dean of women at Swarthmore College.[62] During the period from 1942 to 1943 gifts to the NCRHE were so reduced that the Council could not both appoint new Fellows and employ another executive director to replace her. As a strategic step it chose to do

130

without an executive officer and instead administered its activities through Fellows' Committees. The Council moved its office from West 59th Street in New York to Swarthmore, where Fellows at the college and in the Philadelphia vicinity volunteered to help in their spare time. This was a makeshift arrangement until financial resources were reestablished.[63] Before her death Biehle compiled a history of the NCRHE, which includes a brief paragraph on the NYPG, one of the few references to the group in print.

The bright career of *David Roberts* (1911–55) was cut short with his early death. Born in Omaha the son of a minister, graduated from Occidental College in Los Angeles in 1931, he won the highest award of his graduating class at Union Theological Seminary in 1934: a Traveling Fellowship. Roberts studied for his Ph.D. at the University of Edinburgh from 1934 to 1936 and spent the summers studying at Oxford, Göttingen, and Marburg. In memoriam Albert Outler wrote:

> His student years at Union Theological Seminary and Edinburgh were a kind of Indian Summer for "Liberal Theology." The basic temper and shape of Dave's mind were established in the atmosphere dominated by William Adams Brown, Eugene Lyman and John Baillie.[64]

In view of this observation it is not surprising that Roberts was motivated to edit, with Henry Pitney Van Dusen, a collection of essays in honor of the liberal Christian thinker Eugene W. Lyman under the title *Liberal Theology*.[65]

In 1936 Roberts joined the faculty at Union as an instructor, advancing through the ranks to become Marcellus Hartley Professor of the Philosophy of Religion in 1950. During the years of the NYPG meetings he was also dean of students.

David Roberts demonstrated his considerable ability in the field of Religion and Health with the publication in 1950 of *Psychotherapy and a Christian View of Man*.[66] This book is an examination of the relations between "two complementary traditions of spiritual health." Providing common ground for a discussion between psychotherapy and Christian theology, it moves

131

toward a synthesis. Records of the NYPG indicated that initial groundwork for the study was laid in the two papers that Roberts gave at the meetings.[67]

*Daphne Hughes* (1910–73) might be considered the group's mystery member. The only person who, after joining, did not miss a single meeting, she then dropped out of contact.

*Rollo May* (1909–    ), pioneer in existential psychotherapy, had almost perfect attendance at the NYPG seminars in 1942, but the following year he went only occasionally, finally giving up the meetings entirely when a battle with tuberculosis forced him to enter a sanitarium. A graduate of Oberlin College (1930), May had taught for three years at the American College in Salonika, Greece, and during that time he had studied with psychoanalyst Alfred Adler in Vienna. After returning to the United States he had entered Union Theological Seminary, taken a leave, worked as a counselor at Michigan State University and then completed his divinity degree at Union in 1938. May became a Congregational minister and worked for two years in a parish in Verona, New Jersey, before concluding that he could be more helpful as a psychologist than as a pastor. He had then enrolled in Columbia University and was a doctoral candidate in clinical psychology at the time of the NYPG meetings.

Like Seward Hiltner, his close friend, May was a leader in demonstrating the practical applicability of depth psychological knowledge for pastors. During the war he wrote a pamphlet for military chaplains on "The Ministry of Counseling."[68] His first book, *The Art of Counseling* (1939), was intended as a guide with case studies and demonstrations. It reflects "on the whole the approach of liberal theology."[69] Appearing several years before the NYPG began meeting, it documents the fact that May had close prior association with men who were to become members. In the foreword he specifically thanks Bone, Tillich, Roberts, and Fleming. The introduction was written by Harry Bone.[70]

We know from May's reminiscences in *Paulus* that his intimate personal friendship with Paul Tillich had begun in Tillich's first course at Union in 1933. May's second book, *The Springs of Creative Living,* published in 1940, was based on a Tillichian concept—"the good news of sin"—and was dedicated to Tillich.[71]

132

May's doctoral dissertation, *The Meaning of Anxiety* (1950), was supervised by Tillich, whom May recalls as a relentless, though loving, taskmaster.[72] According to May, the Terry Lectures at Yale in 1950, published as *The Courage to Be* and described by Tillich as a decisive step "on my cognitive road,"[73] were a thoughtful response to May's thesis: courage being the answer to anxiety.

The interrelationships among the NYPG members as analyst and analysand, counselor and counselee, has been hinted at but is generally not a matter of public record. We do know, however, that Erich Fromm was one of the persons who guided May through his own psychoanalysis.[74]

## The Jungians

*Frances G. Wickes* (1875–1967), the senior group member, was approaching her seventies when the NYPG first organized; she lived to be ninety-one years old. A prominent Jungian analyst and a founder, in 1936, of the Analytical Psychology Club of New York, she had published two books on analytical psychology before the NYPG convened: *The Inner World of Childhood* (1927) and *The Inner World of Man* (1938). Like Violet de Laszlo, Wickes had worked with C.G. Jung personally. He introduced her first book, which is dedicated to the memory of her only child, a son named Eliphalet, who was drowned while acting as a counselor in a boys' camp, and which includes anecdotes from his life. Jung wrote: "True experience is never afraid of competent or incompetent objection. It has always the stronger position."[75]

A deeply feeling, intuitive person who started out as a teacher, Wickes pioneered in understanding emotionally disturbed children, not from the observer's point of view, but from the child's. Her work eventually expanded to include adults, especially "artists and creative people from many fields, who were drawn to her because of her open-mindedness and also because of her interest in the creative process, her love of art and her wide experience of many cultures which enabled her to accept the new and the different."[76]

At the second meeting of the NYPG, Frances Wickes presented a case study of a woman. Her talk was illustrated with ten vivid drawings that participants remembered long afterward. Later that year Wickes spoke about "The Eros Concept in Jungian Psychology." On both occasions the group called on her and the other Jungians—Kotschnig, Rohrbach, de Laszlo, Glickman, and Fleming—to explain Jung's use of terms and his ideas. Records of the discussions show that skeptical members often questioned if, in Bone's words, "terms used seemed to hinder rather than clarify interpretation of the correctly observed realities in clinical experience."[77] De Laszlo remembers that Jungians in the group did not have an easy time of it and felt generally isolated. "I think we felt we weren't speaking the same language. We were mostly introverts, slower to take initiative in speaking."[78]

## The Seminary Connection

Although Union Theological Seminary played no official role in hosting the NYPG, the ambience of the school was felt at the meetings. The group convened during the final few years of Henry Sloane Coffin's presidency, which was characterized by his liberal evangelicalism.[79] Of the group members, Grace Elliott, Rollo May, Helen Nichol, and Elizabeth Rohrbach were graduates of Union; David Roberts was both a graduate and a professor; Seward Hiltner and Harry Bone were lecturers; and Paul Tillich and Harrison Elliott were professors. The Elliotts' seminary apartment at 99 Claremont Avenue was the scene of many of the meetings.

*Harrison S. Elliott* (1882–1951) succeeded George Albert Coe at Union. From 1925 to 1950 he was professor of practical theology and head of the department of religious education and psychology. It was Elliott who was quoted in the first chapter as having written in 1927 that "the development of psychology probably has more bearing upon religion than has any other scientific advance." Greatly interested in mental hygiene, he helped introduce courses in mental hygiene into the Union Seminary curriculum. Harrison Elliott was known as an outstanding leader not only in religious education, but also in the field of group process and group discussion.[80] One student recalls:

Students were intrigued and stimulated by his genuine faith in the values which would come from group thinking and from individual student participation in the work of his classes. We came to realize that he meant what he said when he urged us to do our own thinking and to come to conclusions by a group process in which issues were fairly faced and every person shared in the quest for truth.[81]

Another student, Carl Rogers, was introduced to the world of psychology by Elliott and his wife. "Through them Rogers recognized for the first time that 'working with individual persons in a helping relationship could be a professional enterprise.' "[82]

Ordained to the ministry of the Methodist Church in 1944, Elliott had earned a B.A. from Ohio Wesleyan University (1905), a B.D. from Drew Theological Seminary (1911), an M.A. from Columbia (1922), and a Ph.D. from Yale (1940). Before teaching at Union he had worked for the Methodist Church in China and was secretary of the International Committee of the YMCA.

In 1927 President Henry Sloane Coffin officiated at the wedding of Harrison Elliott and Grace Loucks, a woman whom Coffin called "brilliant."[83] *Grace Loucks Elliott* (1891–1979) earned an M.A. from Columbia University and Union Seminary in 1924 and taught at the seminary summer school from 1936 to 1943. She received her Ph.D. from Columbia in 1936. Grace Elliott devoted much of her lifetime to the YWCA: as a student secretary (1917–26), as a member of the national board (1930–43), and as general secretary after 1943. She wrote several books and coauthored, with NYPG member Harry Bone, *Sex Life of Youth* (1929) and, with her husband, *Solving Personal Problems* (1936).

Group member *Thomas Bigham* (1911–    ) taught not at Union, but at Elwood Worcester's alma mater, General Theological Seminary. After earning his B.A. and M.S. from Columbia University, Bigham graduated from General Theological Seminary with his divinity degree in 1936. The following year he became a tutor in theology there, a position he held throughout the period of the NYPG meetings. Bigham was associated with General as instructor, associate professor, and professor through 1970, when he became a pastoral and psychiatric case worker in Massachusetts.

Interested particularly in theology and psychoanalytic theory, Tom Bigham presented a paper to the NYPG seminar in December 1943 in which he discussed Catholic moral theology and the transmoral conscience. From 1961 to 1978 he served on the Advisory Board of the *Journal of Religion and Health*. Among his articles is a tribute published in *Pastoral Psychology* to Dr. Gotthard Booth, who had acted as psychiatric consultant to General Theological Seminary for more than twenty years.[84]


## *"The Intellectuals Take Aim"*

Interviews with some NYPG members—Dr. de Laszlo, the Rev. Dr. Seward Hiltner, Dr. Rollo May, Helen Nichol Fernald, and Hannah Tillich—and correspondence with others reveals a consensus of opinion about the nature of the meetings. The NYPG functioned primarily as a forum for interdisciplinary dialogue: ideas of participants were essentially not changed, but exchanged. Having formulated their basic theological and psychological positions before the meetings, members gathered to listen and respond to one another. The seminar, in which diverse ideas and experiences were developed, deepened, and enriched, can be seen to reflect a cultural development of the times.

Around the period in which the NYPG met, there emerged in the United States a liberal intelligentsia, a phenomenon described by historian David Hollinger.[85] This intelligentsia—national, secular, ethnically diverse, and left of center—

> had become a prominent feature in American life by the end of the 1940s. Its most obvious leaders included Edmund Wilson, Lionel Trilling, and Dwight Macdonald, among men of letters; David Riesman and Daniel Bell among social scientists; and Reinhold Niebuhr and Sidney Hook among philosophical essayists. The discourse of this intelligentsia was largely institutionalized in the liberal arts divisions of several major universities and in such journals of opinion as the *New Republic,* the *Partisan Review, Commentary,* the *Nation,* and, more recently, the *New York Review of Books* and the *New York Times Book Review.* So influential was this intelligentsia during the 1940s, 1950s, and 1960s that most Americans who thought of

themselves as "intellectuals" were either members of it, or part of its audience.[86]

The liberal intelligentsia, writes Hollinger, was united by a cosmopolitan ideal, a desire to transcend the limitations of particularisms in order to achieve a more complete human experience.[87] This ideal "implicitly attributed to people the ability to confront, absorb, and profit from experience not only qualitatively different from, but *quantitatively greater* than that of any given provincial existence."[88] Liberal intellectuals maintained that sharing of human diversity offered a more authentic, reliable, and satisfying perspective than did narrow parochialism.

World War II had not a little to do with making the cosmopolitan ideal viable in the United States, particularly in New York City:

Although it would be an exaggeration to say that New York took the place of Paris as the cultural capital, the temporary ascendancy of Hitler in Europe suddenly transformed America, as Kazin put it in 1942, into "a repository of Western Culture" in a world overrun by its enemies. This impression was not simply a general one; it had the specific reinforcement of the new intellectual migration. . . . Values once associated with Europe, especially Paris, now had no physical, geographical, social foundation more solid than that provided by the United States. Suddenly, America did not seem so outrageously provincial.[89]

The character of the psychology group that met in New York in the early 1940s becomes clearer when viewed in this sociohistorical context. The NYPG self-consciously embodied the liberal, cosmopolitan ideal. It represented a broad cross section of human experience: male and female; American and European; old and young; Christian, Jew, and nonbeliever; teacher and student; Freudian and Jungian; single, married, and divorced; extravert and introvert; clergy, therapist, sociologist, anthropologist, philosopher, and historian. At the final meeting of the group's first year together (May 10, 1942), Martha Jaeger Glickman brought discussion to a close with a summary comment:

If each were to examine the reasons why he came into the group and spent so much time and effort, it would not be a question of

137

faith in certain values nor of whether he believed in God or not. It would rather be *to gather insights from all of these divergent points of view* to implement his faith in the very critical hour in which we are living [italics added].[90]

The one thing group members held surely in common was their liberal, intellectual style of thought. Indeed, if the secular liberal intelligentsia can be said to have had a *religious* counterpart in these years, most members of the NYPG belonged to it, and Tillich, Hiltner, Roberts, and May were among its nationally prominent leaders.

### The Impact of Psychoanalysis: Second Wave

World War II marked a turning point in the influence of Freud in America. According to John C. Burnham, historian of psychoanalysis in American culture, Freud's work came on Americans in two waves. The first wave coincided with the Progressive Movement before World War I, when "the followers of Freud clustered together in a few cities, reinforcing each other and attempting to convert others to the psychoanalytic viewpoint."[91] The second wave came with World War II, when psychiatry and psychoanalysis gained immense importance among physicians and the general public. This high tide of psychoanalytic influence lasted from the early 1940s to the late 1960s, when psychoanalysis came increasingly under attack in both medical and intellectual circles.

Wartime experience opened the door to dynamic, psychoanalytic thinking as physicians and service personnel had contact with psychiatric disabilities and treatment. Mental health statistics associated with the war were shocking: one out of eight applicants had been rejected for military service on the grounds of emotional instability; one half the admissions to military hospitals during the war were classified as psychiatric problems; 380,000 men were discharged from the military with psychiatric disabilities.[92] Burnham writes: "The great influx of psychoanalytic thinking came, presumably, in explaining to officers, physicians, public, and patients *why* the mental disability occurred and was to be taken seriously."[93] Although experience with shell shock in

World War I had led to the popularizing of mental hygiene, the scale and conspicuousness of psychiatry in World War II was more far-reaching.[94] Medical and public acceptance of Freud's teachings mushroomed.

By 1940 the center of world psychoanalysis had shifted to the United States with the influx of distinguished refugee analysts, who came to dominate American psychoanalysis. Although analysts were ultimately responsible for the propagation of psychoanalytic concepts, there were relatively few analysts; the core group never numbered more than several hundred.[95] Knowledge about the work of Freud and his successors was, then, disseminated by many others—psychiatrists, psychologists, clinical psychologists, and the new liberal intelligentsia. Through personal acquaintance and personal analysis, the contacts between liberal intellectuals and analysts were close: "To the liberal intelligentsia, the analysts represented scientists who were sensitive to the values of other intellectuals who shared the intellectuals' concern with preserving Western civilization."[96]

Just as the war gave impetus to the acceptance of Freud's ideas in the secular culture, so it affected religious life. Paul Tillich observed that the churches began to realize that something was wrong in their preaching and teaching when mental disturbances became a mass phenomenon hampering the war effort and when troubled Christians began seeking help not from ministers, but from psychoanalysts.[97] The experience of chaplains at the warfront increased the receptivity to depth psychology. Religion and Health leader Wayne Oates recalls: "Chaplains were coming back after having been through hell. They saw that the neat, flat consciousness psychologies they had learned before did not take into account the tragedies they had seen.[98]

In retrospect we see that an elite group of religious intellectuals and refugee analysts, the NYPG, played a pivotal role in introducing Freud into American Protestantism. Members of the NYPG helped to establish the Religion and Health Movement on the foundation of dynamic, psychoanalytic principles. At a time when the secular intelligentsia was bringing Freudian ideas before the public in the cause of mental health, the religious intelligentsia was relating these ideas to Christian theology in the cause of Religion and Health.

The articles and books of NYPG leaders had much to do with

the phenomenal growth of Religion and Health in the 1950s, 1960s, and 1970s. If Seward Hiltner served the CPE movement as "our Lenin," as has been said,[99] the NYPG may be seen to have played the same function for the movement that encompassed CPE: Religion and Health. Emmanuel had prepared the way; Boisen and Dunbar mapped it out; the NYPG legitimated it.

The NYPG provided an opportunity for a dialogue between Christianity and culture, theology and psychology, followers of Jesus, Freud, and Jung. Theologically liberal members were open-minded, willing to accept the truth from whatever quarter it might come. Knowledge of depth psychology convinced them that there are laws of mental health and that they can be discovered. When the group discussed the question of whether knowledge of the nature of humankind gives objectively valid insights into human nature, Harry Bone concluded that:

> Necessary structures for social health have operated all the time, even in their negation because in the individual negation produces neurosis. The laws of health are progressively discoverable, but it is hard to see how they were created by man, since they operate whether man is aware of them or not. In that sense man does not seem to have autonomy.[100]

God reveals Godself—is immanent—not only in the lawfulness of material nature, but also in the lawfulness of human nature. The findings of Freud and of those who followed him opened the door to new understanding of God's creation. By accommodating scientific, dynamic psychological findings, NYPG members were confident that their Christian faith would be enriched.

No one was more outspoken on the subject than Paul Tillich. One continuous theme threads through his work, early and late, on psychoanalysis: Freud's enormous contribution in revealing, or rather recovering, the realities of human existence. Tillich believed that the unconditioned character of religion becomes far more manifest "if it breaks out from within the secular, disrupting and transforming it."[101] In psychoanalysis the theologian of culture seems to have perceived the quality of holiness, the unconditioned breaking out from within the secular. Freud challenged the philosophy of consciousness in modern Protestantism by rediscovering the unconscious. Freud rediscovered the demonic structures that determine our consciousness, and he rediscovered confession and counseling, which had been lost in Protestantism.[102] Tillich claimed that analysts themselves did not need to know that theology had received these "tremendous gifts" from psychoanalysis, "but the theologians should know it."[103]

During the spring of 1945, just after the last meeting of the NYPG, David Roberts published an article about "Psychotherapy and the Christian Ministry."[104] His conclusion may be read as a summary statement of the thinking of Religion and Health liberals about God's immanence and human progress. Having discussed the transformation that is at the center of the therapeutic experience, Roberts writes:

> Therefore at the risk of displeasing both psychoanalysts and theologians, I shall conclude with the words of Gamaliel: "If this counsel and this work be of men, it will come to nought: But if it be of God, ye cannot overthrow it; lest haply ye be found even to fight against God."[105]

# CHAPTER 7

# The Religion and Health Movement

*And he called the twelve together and gave them power and authority over all demons and to cure diseases, and he sent them out to preach the kingdom of God and to heal.*

—LUKE 9:1–2

ELWOOD WORCESTER, Anton Boisen, Flanders Dunbar, the Blanton-Peale team, Seward Hiltner, and Paul Tillich were among the many who shaped the Religion and Health Movement in its early days. The scope of this work has necessarily been limited to beginnings. The Emmanuel Movement, the Council for Clinical Training, the Joint Committee on Religion and Health, and the Religio-Psychiatric Clinic represented *practical* efforts to bring together "sound religion and sound medicine," dynamic psychology and faith, in the cure of souls. The New York Psychology Group then worked to give a *theoretical* underpinning to the enterprise. Americans act first and theorize afterward, wrote Heije Faber, a Dutch scholar, in his study of *Pastoral Care and Clinical Training in America*. So it happened.[1]

Given the weighty body of facts and materials that have been assembled to document both practical and theoretical efforts to bring together religion and science in healing ministry, what conclusions may be drawn? First of all, evidence indicates that from the time Elwood Worcester founded the Emmanuel Clinic until the present day, there has been a significant movement in American Protestantism that may accurately be designated as the Religion and Health Movement. The evidence further indicates that the Religion and Health Movement represents Freud's impact on American Protestant ministry. The common denominator in all Religion and Health undertaking is the belief that dynamic psychological insights provide a tool that enables the minister to understand others (and himself or herself) with more clarity than ever before.

One may open the pages of *Pastoral Psychology* almost at random and find statements of this belief. An article from the February 1960 issue, "The Minister and Psychotherapy," by Harry Emerson Fosdick is one example. (Fosdick was the founding minister, in 1930, of New York's Riverside Church, which he served until 1946. He revealed in his autobiography, published in 1956, that during his adolescence he had spent time in a mental hospital.[2]) According to Fosdick, the good parish minister will be sought out for personal counseling. She or he cannot escape it, for it is in the air, an accepted means of seeking help: "The ques-

144

tion for him is not whether he will do it, but whether he will do it well or ill, with intelligent insight into the secrets of human behavior or with random, hit or miss attempts at improvised advice."[3]

When Fosdick recalled how he personally had mishandled some consultants in the early days—"before the insights of the new dynamic psychology were available"—he prayed for God's forgiveness. When he thought of the transformation of lives in the counseling room when the gospel was made applicable to a human need—"because one could understand what the real need was and why it was there"—he felt grateful beyond words. For Fosdick, the tragedy is that some ministers are mishandling personal counseling, doing more harm than good:

> The minister does not need to be a professional expert in the psychiatric field—that is impossible. But every minister can so acquaint himself with the basic principles of the new psychology that he will be at home in what *Pastoral Psychology* calls "the science of human behavior" in its specific application to the work of the minister.[4]

(To acquaint himself with the basic principles of the new psychology, Fosdick had turned in the early 1920s to Dr. Thomas W. Salmon, medical director of the National Committee for Mental Hygiene.) Fosdick ended his article on a note of liberal progressivism. He remarked that the tenth anniversary of *Pastoral Psychology* (1960) is a symbol of a new era, "of new possibilities in communicating the Gospel to needy persons."[5]

This concluding reference to the gospel is significant. From the beginning, the efforts of Religion and Health leaders were gospel-centered. Indeed, the facts suggest, although such an interpretation has never before been made, that *the Religion and Health Movement began as a movement in tension with and parallel to the Social Gospel.* With reference to the new sociological learning, proponents of the Social Gospel sought to carry on Jesus' social, prophetic ministry. With reference to the new depth psychological learning, proponents of Religion and Health sought to carry on Jesus' healing, priestly ministry. The Social Gospel, alone, was inadequate, Religion and Health leaders had learned. "Personal unbalance *never* leads to social stability."[6] And so, responding to felt human need, they sought to recover the unity of mind and body, to bring "wholeness."

To see the Religion and Health Movement as a movement in tension with and parallel to the Social Gospel is to see that its purpose was quite different from that of the Social Gospel; Religion and Health cannot be faulted, then, for not *being* the Social Gospel. Apart from the fact that Prof. Donald Meyer, in his study of *The Positive Thinkers,* makes the mistake of not disentangling mind-cure from Religion and Health, he makes the mistake of criticizing what he calls "religion as pop psychology" for its lack of a cultural or political critique. For Meyer, it seems that the trouble with Harry Emerson Fosdick's religious liberalism, for example, is that it was not the religious liberalism of Reinhold Niebuhr. Fosdick was not a "critic of comfortable people and comfortable religion,"[7] he was indifferent to economic and social reforms. In Meyer's assessment of the situation, Fosdick, author of *Adventurous Religion,* defined no adventures at all, "except on the definition that getting well was an adventure,"[8] and this failure was indicative of "the loss of Protestant creativity."

Meyer's thesis is that liberal religion was "helplessly unprepared for any kind of vital response to the rise of commercial mass culture."[9] He seeks to establish that the religious liberalism of the 1920s and 1930s was unadventurous and passive, and that part of its fatality was its failure to recognize this. To make such a judgment is to miss altogether the creativity, vitality, excitement, and sense of ground-breaking Religion and Health pioneers experienced as they grappled with the rise of Freudian depth psychology, a preeminent intellectual and cultural phenomenon of the twentieth century. The aims and objectives of Religion and Health were quite different from the aims and objectives of the Social Gospel. Taken together, the two movements of the American Protestant liberalism were complementary. In one important way the Religion and Health Movement was quite different from the Social Gospel: only in retrospect do we see its *coherence* as a movement. Unlike Social Gospelers, Religion and Health advocates acted spontaneously and independently with no real sense of common cause. They seem to have been unaware of the magnitude and significance of the movement that they led, oblivious of its essential unity: it had no identifying name. In the early

1930s advocates of clinical pastoral training quickly became self-conscious of their participation in a movement. They knew that they were trying to sell a radically new form of education and ministry to the seminaries and to the medical world at the same time.[10] But the clinical training movement constitutes only part of the greater Religion and Health Movement. Dynamic psychology made an impact not only on professional education for ministry, but also on pastoral care and counseling, pastoral psychology, pastoral theology, and the psychology of religion.[11]

Another conclusion to be drawn is that Religion and Health Movement leaders were innovators. They advanced the movement through its literature, through clinics and pastoral counseling centers, through Federal Council of Churches' agencies, through the seminaries, through institutes, commissions, and seminars—that is to say, everywhere in the early days except through denominational channels. This may partially explain why church historians have overlooked the significance of Religion and Health developments. Only in recent decades have denominations been slowly impressed by the movement and joined in promoting it.

When one observes the lives and work of Religion and Health leaders from a historical perspective, certain common characteristics become evident. These people were extraordinarily intelligent, highly educated, and deeply committed to Christian ministry. (All but Boisen had both B.D. and Ph.D. degrees; the one woman in the group had a B.D., a Ph.D., and an M.D. as well; Blanton and Peale joined together to form an M.D./B.D. team.) More than that, they were innovators; in seeking to build bridges between religion and science, they pioneered new paths, broke new ground, developed new channels of influence.

Sociological evidence confirms and amplifies these findings. A rich source of ideas for the historian is Samuel Klausner's study, begun in 1956, of the new alliance of ministers and psychiatrists, *Psychiatry and Religion.* It is based on the extensive Religion and Health ("Religio-Psychiatric") literature, and Blanton and Peale's Religio-Psychiatric Clinic is used as a case study. (Drs. Iago Galdston and Smiley Blanton helped to conceive and support the project.) Although the study is loaded with technical data, statistical tables, qualifying footnotes, and sociological terms, Klausner is

147

mindful of the uninitiated reader; he takes care to define and explain all sociological usage.

Ministers who choose nontraditional approaches to healing or counseling exhibit "variant behavior." Why? Why do some ministers elect the unorthodox path? Why do they introduce psychiatric elements into their work?

Klausner assumes that individuals are not prone to change unless the accustomed way produces some problem. What, then, are the conditions that provoke variant behavior? An examination of the literature (some 2,500 items) finds that "a feeling of incompetence in the face of their problems is the single most important reason given by ministers for seeking change."[12]

> What draws a minister or a psychiatrist to the periphery of his own group in search of help for healing? . . . Ministers tend to come to the movement from social positions where their traditional religious ethos is exposed to the impact of the ethos of science. . . . Ministering to a congregation of the higher socioeconomic strata or acquiring a higher education further increases exposure and the probability of recruitment. Under the influence of the scientific ethos, the minister is concerned to wreak change and is distressed if progress is imperceptible. He is encouraged to look to the instrumental techniques of science in general, and of psychiatry in particular, to effect that change.[13]

Sociological analysis further identifies three types of nonconformists, who differ in the degrees to which they depart from traditional counseling norms: ritualist, innovator, and rebel. Ritualist ministers "advocate traditional religious practices in the pastoral relationship, but these appear in the service of goals phrased in mental health language."[14] Innovating ministers "advocate the techniques of psychiatry to achieve the goals of religion."[15] Rebellious ministers "reformulate both the techniques and the goals of counseling in psychological terms."[16]

Innovation for ministers is the most common form of variant adaptation. Innovators support doctrinal positions while modifying some practices. Klausner points out that because applied science is essentially a method, stressing means, it offers religion a set of procedures and encourages ministerial innovation.[17]

Scholars will want to examine other findings in Klausner's report in studying the Religion and Health Movement—for example, statistics about the denominational affiliation of ministerial innovators. These particular conclusions are cited here because they support and augment understanding of Religion and Health leaders as innovators.

### *Religion and Health, a Product of Protestant Liberalism*

*1. Cultural accommodation.* Klausner's findings underscore still another conclusion to be drawn about the Religion and Health Movement: it is a product of American Protestant liberalism. The primary characteristic of the liberal impulse is the conscious, intended adaptation of religious ideas to modern culture. Evangelical liberal leaders of Religion and Health endeavored to reconcile Christian faith and scientific psychology. In so doing they worked to achieve a careful balance, a proper tension, between "Christ and culture," sacred and secular. The dual nature of their enterprise is expressed by the name of the movement itself: Religion *and* Health.

Research into the Religion and Health Movement reveals that some leaders deliberately downplayed or obscured the movement's roots in Freudian psychology. Not only would it have been impolitic to call attention to Freud's influence (psychoanalytic theories were controversial, misunderstood, and often distorted), but to do so would also have tipped the ever precarious balance between sacred and secular toward the secular. Religion and Health pioneers gave first allegiance to the gospel of Christ; they adapted the findings of Freud and his followers *in the service of ministry.* Grounded firmly in evangelical, liberal faith, they were not persons to flit from one passing theological or psychological fad to another in search of an elusive identity or security. Rather, with Christian purpose sure, they quickly identified and freely explored the significance for the Christian faith of the work of one of the most outstanding thinkers of the twentieth century. This they did discreetly, without fanfare.

If the movement is now in disarray, as some believe, it is partly because this delicate tension between sacred and secular has not been maintained: the sacred has yielded to the secular. Although *in* the world, Religion and Health has become too much *of* the world. To put the matter in sociological terms, nonconforming ministerial rebels (those who formulate both the techniques and the goals of counseling exclusively in psychological terms) have threatened the integrity of the movement. Unlike the innovators, they ignore or make incidental the Christian gospel.

Philip Rieff would applaud this "triumph of the therapeutic." He believes that in a time when people are no longer religious, "churchmen" should become "avowedly therapists, administering a therapeutic institution—under the justificatory mandate that Jesus himself was the first therapeutic."[18] But history teaches that a religious movement can be potent in a sustained and permanent way only by bringing to bear on contemporary life a distinctive testimony that is the vital possession of a community of believers.[19] The Religion and Health Movement is thus in a precarious position when it loses its grounding in Christian faith and community.

Criticism of religion's surrender to culture has come from the camps of psychiatry and psychology itself. Dr. Karl Menninger observes that what was once called "sin" is now called "symptom." He maintains that there *is* wrongdoing apart from disease, and he calls ministers back to their prophetic role in exposing human sinfulness and reconciling persons to God.[20] Paul Vitz characterizes contemporary psychology as religion and indicts Rollo May and Carl Rogers for leading "the cult of self-worship."[21]

Ernest Johnson observed in 1940 that "the rhythm of social existence tends for long periods to subordinate religion to the prevailing culture and then to bring religion into sharp encounter with the culture."[22] He wrote when "crisis," or "neoorthodox," theology was in its ascendancy—a time of confrontation between religion and culture. Today the pendulum swing is in the opposite direction as critics charge that the Religion and Health Movement has become captive of the prevailing culture, of our psychological society.

Social historian Christopher Lasch has been outspoken in describing his nightmare vision of a sick society run by a "psychiatric priesthood."[23] He has criticized psychiatry for rejecting

Freud's modest goals and becoming "a new religion, promising the traditional consolations of personal mastery, spiritual peace and 'meaning.' "[24] Lasch reminds readers that Freud felt that psychoanalysis "could do little more than substitute 'everyday unhappiness' for crippling neurosis."[25] In Freud's view, therapy could not satisfy the growing demand, in a world without religion, for meaning and faith. Even so, Americans have turned for spiritual relief to a new breed of doctors, and today the "psychiatric church still stands," despite factional "Protestant" and "Catholic" (the metaphor is stretched thin) dissensions. Lasch castigates psychiatry for falsifying its intellectual antecedents and arrogating to itself the work of humanizing the world.

The social historian does not hold Freud himself responsible for the new psychiatric church. No, it is the psychiatric establishment that is guilty of "sacrificing Freud." Lasch indicates that this has been possible because of the decline of religion and the decline of confidence in the clergy. He has grossly overestimated both. In fact, theological liberalism's accommodation of Freudian depth psychology largely accounts for the vitality of contemporary religion and the pastoral skill of today's clergy.

*2. God's immanence in human experience.* A second liberal belief we have examined is that God is immanent in human cultural development and revealed through it. In frequent reference to the crucial importance of the "Protestant principle," Tillich stressed the world-pervading character of God and refused to narrow the scope of God's revealing or redemptive activity. Tillich implied that he perceived God's action in Freud's contribution to theology: Freud rediscovered confession and counseling, which had been lost in Protestantism; Freud rediscovered the demonic structures that determine our consciousness; Freud challenged the philosophy of consciousness in modern Protestantism by rediscovering the unconscious.[26]

The concern of liberal Protestantism with God's action in human experience is a stream of thought that flows from Schleiermacher and was brought to America by Horace Bushnell. After World War I this experience-centered theology was opposed by neoorthodox conservatives, who charged that liberals glorified the immanence of God at the expense of God's transcendence.

Led by Karl Barth, they described God as "Wholly Other," and the Word of God as forever established, above everything human and created, representing a higher authority than experience. Liberals parried by pointing to the historically conditioned character of neoorthodoxy itself: Barth's theology was born in the pressure of a particular situation.

Liberal thought maintains that there can be no Christian theology apart from the insights of a historic community; in other words, there is no system of theology that is true, no matter what. Theology is worked out in the context of human experience. As Charles Clayton Morrison, editor of the liberal, ecumenical journal *The Christian Century,* wrote: "Experience is only our human response to something which comes to us from beyond experience, something objective, something *given,* something which comes to us *to be experienced by our participation in it.*[27]

Anton Boisen is an example of a liberal who relied on the authority of personal experience. Having perceived God's immanence in his own life (his psychotic episodes were occasions for integration, for healing), he pressed for the study of "living human documents" as legitimate ground for theological reflection. Although this empirical method became a touchstone for clinical pastoral education, the implications of Boisen's image of the human person as a living human document to be read and interpreted like a historical text were not fully explored until recently, when Charles V. Gerkin published a study revisioning pastoral counseling in a hermeneutical mode.[28]

Liberals maintain that the validity of theologies, doctrines, or religious movements is tested by their relevance to felt human need; thus the key to changing theologies, doctrines, or movements is the dominance of emergent needs. It has ever been the task of ministry to achieve a balance between the needs of the individual and the needs of the community, between the priestly and the prophetic. Historically, these shift in priority and emphasis.

Distressed when the prophetic emphasis of Social Gospelers became exclusive, Religion and Health leaders sought to restore the priestly, or pastoral, function of ministry. The needs of the individual were believed to have been eclipsed by the needs of the community. Critics of Religion and Health now charge that it focuses inordinately on the pastoral and neglects the prophetic. These competing claims of the Social Gospel and of Religion and Health in twentieth-century America can best be understood from a historical perspective:

> All religious movements acquire their vigor at the expense of valid emphases in other movements which their immediate concern has obscured. Their very strength is due to the existence of particular factors in the historical situation in which they emerge.[29]

We have been examining two of the three characteristics of the modernist impulse: belief in adaptionism and divine immanence. During the 1930s and 1940s these liberal convictions were beset by internal questioning, external attack, and the pressure of events.[30] It was a period of reassessment and reaffirmation, a period when the liberal movement was not routed or driven underground, but transformed in spirit.[31] Historian William Hutchinson finds that, in the face of the neoorthodox onslaught, liberals were nearly unanimous in refusing to renounce the immanence and accessibility of God. This was "far and away the most persistent note of liberal reaffirmation."[32] The sense of divine immanence supported cultural adaptionism; thus liberals also reaffirmed that the church is and must be in the world, that religion must inevitably be entangled in culture.

A striking example of a theologian who urged Protestantism to accommodate the new psychology, but who was then temporarily swayed by the neoorthodox critique, is Walter Marshall Horton (1895–1963). As a college freshman at Harvard in 1913–14 Horton had studied general psychology with Hugo Munsterberg, the German psychologist and philosopher whom William James was responsible for bringing to Harvard. Horton later said that reading William James' *Varieties of Religious Experience* was "one of the great religious experiences of my college years."[33] At Union Theological Seminary, Horton was deeply influenced by George Albert Coe. Soon after he began teaching at Oberlin College, in 1925, he offered theological students a course in applied psychology. This he kept up during more than thirty years of teaching there, gaining many new insights from the case studies of problem parishioners handed in by students.

153

In 1931 Horton published *A Psychological Approach to Theology,* dedicated to George Coe. Here Horton was sharply critical of Barth's leadership. He charged that Barth proposed to bring to naught the whole liberal movement as a punishment for its concessions to secular culture and the modern temper. But looking at modern theology's remarkable achievements, Horton was unwilling to admit that all had been a mistake:

> Can one regret that John Fiske and Henry Drummond espoused the doctrine of Evolution and made it the basis of their theism, just when most of their fellow Christians were denouncing it as atheistic? that, more recently, the influence of scientific Biblical criticism and the "new social conscience" permeated the thought of a whole generation of theologians? that the appeal to dogmatic authority has come to be generally replaced by the appeal to experience? One sees, to be sure, that many damaging concessions to secular thought have been made, which time has proven to have been unnecessary; but the type of theology which risks such concessions is at least *alive,* and intelligible to the man on the street.[34]

Then in 1934, the year that Sydney Ahlstrom calls the most remarkably productive year of the neoorthodox resurgence, Horton published *Realistic Theology,* a work that described a "personal change of mind."[35] The change was not radical. Although Hutchinson classifies this book in the corpus of early neoorthodox thought, he admits that Horton's position testifies to the continuities at least as much as to the reversals in American developments, and that Horton's position "could be called neoliberalism as easily as neo-orthodoxy."[36]

When, after twenty-five years, Walter Horton looked back on his call for a psychological approach to theology, he found that despite the fact that many of his views had changed, he still retained the strong conviction that the psychological approach will always be legitimate and necessary.[37] He was puzzled and troubled that for most of the time between 1931 and 1956 his lead had not been followed. Only recently had theologians (David Roberts, Paul Tillich, Albert Outler) substantially agreed with it and returned to it. Why?

Horton cited two causes: sociological and theological. First, economic depression and war had preoccupied the public mind.

Horton said that Franklin D. Roosevelt's declaration, "Private lives are repealed," was practically true. Second, neoorthodox theology transferred the emphasis from psychological experience to historical revelation. "God is met in His 'mighty acts' coming from above and beyond human experience."[38] Although the professor admitted that he sympathized with this shift to a considerable extent (a *purely* experience-centered approach obscures the supreme *source* of religious insight), nevertheless, there was no need to exclude the psychological approach. Like Tillich, Horton concluded that revelation must be received in experience.[39]

The contest between liberalism and neoorthodoxy was foreshadowed by Edward Scribner Ames in 1910, when he wrote *The Psychology of Religious Experience.* Ames insisted that psychology does not support a dualism of experience in which faith is regarded as the test of religion and knowledge is the sphere of science; in which religion as faith involves submission to authority (including a willingness to accept that which is intellectually inconsistent) and science as knowledge possesses absolute certainty and final truth. Having said this, Ames formulated a statement of the nature of religion and science, faith and knowledge, which religious liberals might endorse to this day: "Knowledge appears as instrumental, provisional, and practical; while faith becomes the attitude of confidence and expectation in reference to the further progress of experience."[40]

Yale philosopher of religion John E. Smith points out that modern thought has been dominated since the eighteenth century by an appeal to experience, but he clarifies that there are two competing philosophies of experience: the classic, empirical view of Locke and the British School, and John Dewey's rejection of the classical view. For Dewey, "Experience is a dynamic or temporal affair which is reciprocal and constituted by all the modes of intercourse between a conscious being and the environment, both physical and social."[41] Smith develops Dewey's ideas in *Experience and God,* saying that if religion is to challenge contemporary secularization, there must be a radical return to experience in the full range of encounter; that is, experience must be rescued from subjectivity:

> Experience may mislead us and it may be mistaken, but not because it is merely subjective ideas and feelings; experience

155

could not lead to real error if it were not an actual encounter with and participation in a real world that transcends human consciousness in every direction.[42]

If my reading of it is accurate, in this book Smith provides what could be shown to be a solid philosophical foundation for a movement that he and others have not yet recognized—the Religion and Health Movement.

*3. Progressivism.* The third characteristic of the modernist impulse we have examined is progressivism. Liberals did, finally, retreat from the progressive faith of the Social Gospel as they lost confidence that they could Christianize the social order, that they could advance the earthly kingdom, or realm, of God. Liberals came to see that they had counted too much on human progress. Their estimate of human nature had been too high. Writing in 1922, after "the Great War," Harry Emerson Fosdick pointed out in a study of *Christianity and Progress* that belief in inevitable or automatic progress had caused moderns to neglect the problem of sin. A superficial, ill-considered optimism, he said, had "largely lost sight of the terrific obstacles in human nature against which any real moral advance on earth must win its way."[43]

Neoorthodoxy's fundamental quarrel with modernism was with its optimistic interpretation of human nature. Rooted in the tradition of Reformed theology, the new orthodoxy emphasized human sinfulness. Its realism consisted in a "despairing anthropology" that was based on contemporary observations of human failure.[44] When, after a period of revisionism, liberals came to agree that they had erred in their estimate of human nature, the neoorthodox critique and current events (World War I and the Depression) were usually credited with having effected the change. An overlooked fact is that Freudian psychology was instrumental in persuading some liberal thinkers—most notably Paul Tillich—that liberal Protestant views of human nature were inadequate. Comments Tillich made on the subject in 1960 are worth quoting at length:

Present-day Protestantism has combined a basically Pelagian doctrine of man . . . with a serious emphasis on morals, individual as well as social. The most conspicuous symbolic expression of this attitude is the idea of a progressive actualization of the kingdom of God on earth by the "men of good will." . . . All these forms of open and hidden Pelagianism are undercut by contemporary psychology and the experience of everyone who does pastoral counseling. When a "pillar" of a suburban community, outstanding in moral and social activity, admits having suicidal tendencies, or if the mother of a happy family reveals, voluntarily and involuntarily, hatred against her children—then a Pelagian interpretation of these situations and any appeal to "free will" break down. The only thing the helper can do is to mobilize the healing powers, the forces of grace which are still working in the counselee and which may be strengthened by the way the counselor accepts him without moral demands. Such behavior in the pastoral situation follows the Augustinian-Reformation type of theology and is equally opposed to the Roman-legalistic and to the Protestant-moralistic attitudes. It is an astonishing fact that Protestant theology had to rediscover its own tradition about what man is, and about what healing powers are, through the impact of the psychology of the unconscious.[45]

The likeness between Freudian and Christian pessimism has been widely observed.[46] Neoorthodox theologian Reinhold Niebuhr noted that the realism of Freud was regarded by many as a welcome scientific (or secular) substitute for the presumably discredited traditional doctrine of sin.[47] Niebuhr, however, found the traditional Christian view of humankind superior to the Freudian one because Freud's system, a naturalistic one, did not do "full justice to the transcendent freedom of spirit of which the self is capable."[48]

Whatever the alleged defects in Freud's pessimistic view of human nature, the point is that *after Freud* the confident rationalism and buoyant optimism of Enlightenment faith were profoundly shaken. Intellectual and cultural historians have noted that Freud was a product of both the Enlightenment (which stressed the cult of reason and of society) and Romanticism (which emphasized the cult of the irrational and of the individual).[49] His metapsychology comprises a rational explanation of the irrational in human behavior. The situation is paradoxical, as Prof. Peter Gay explains:

Freud, the man who above all others is supposed to have destroyed the justification of Enlightenment rationalism, was the greatest child of the Enlightenment which our century has known. His fundamental assumption was that the search for truth must never stop, that only knowledge allows reason to function, and that only reason can make us free.[50]

Or, in the words of Prof. H. Stuart Hughes: "From one standpoint his discoveries seemed to throw into the discard the optimistic anticipations inherited from the Enlightenment. From another standpoint, they were a triumphant vindication of those same anticipations."[51]

This discussion may seem extraneous to our consideration of the progressivist belief of American Protestant liberalism, but it is, in fact, quite relevant. Liberal optimism about human progress did not vanish in the 1930s and 1940s; it was modified and redirected. Protestant liberals shared with Freud a profound faith in reason. By providing a scientific theory of human behavior that could be "studied with some objectivity, built upon, and within certain limits rendered teachable,"[52] Freud furnished ministry with a tool that made it possible to meet human need as never before. After Freud, the pastor was relieved of the necessity of relying on intuition and good intentions. By learning the "secrets" of human motivation, he or she could counsel more competently than in the past. He or she could also come to a deeper psychological self-understanding, a requisite in the practice of ministry.

Religion and Health pioneers universally felt the promise of a new era, or, as Fosdick said, "of new possibilities in communicating the gospel." There is an unmistakable note of progressive optimism in their writings, but it is different from that of the Social Gospel. It is not ebullient, but cautious, and it is not premised on the perfectability of the social order, but on the insights of scientific psychology. A statement in 1951 by Seward Hiltner, as he looked to the future of pastoral theology and psychology, may be taken as typical of the prevailing mood of Religion and Health leaders: "With superior psychological knowledge and tools, it would be strange indeed if we could not gain certain new and deeper appreciations of the faith through proper psychological study."[53]

158

However theological liberalism may be tempered by orthodox Christian realism or by Freudian psychological realism, it necessarily reflects its Enlightenment heritage. Human progress may not be ineluctable—reverses and failure abound—but progress there is.

## The Laws of Mental Health Progressively Discoverable

My purpose in this has been to demonstrate that the pivotal concern of Religion and Health leaders was the lawfulness of human behavior and motivation. The fact that laws of mental health seemed progressively discoverable answered a need— specifically, the need for confidence and competence in pastoral care and counseling without which ministry was threatened with becoming irrelevant in modern America.

Religion and Health leaders looked to scientific psychology for *laws* of human behavior because, like Freud, they believed that *knowledge,* or understanding, is a key to *mastery* of the irrational and hence a key to health. (Freud put it most succinctly when he said, "Where id was, ego shall be.") Unlike Freud, they were more interested in therapy than in theory. Americans characteristically promote applied science more than they do pure science. Scientific research is valued for its technological applicability. So it is with behavioral science.[54] Seward Hiltner wrote in *Religion and Health* in 1943:

> The essence of the mental hygiene point of view is less difficult to grasp than to state. It is that human behavior and conduct spring from real causes and that within limits these can and should be understood in the interests of the greater health of the individual and of society. It might be called the technology of human conduct.[55]

What is interesting is the felt need in America for such a technology. On the one hand, this may be, as Klausner suggests, because in America there is an overriding emphasis on effectiveness and accomplishment. The culture of industrial society "tends to be characterized by universalistic-performance norms."[56] On the other hand, he says, the felt need for human technology may have a deeper cause. It may be because Americans feel overwhelmed by a social order whose forces are out of control: knowledge of the laws of human behavior promises some measure of mastery.[57]

In locating a deeper cause Klausner is right. It is no accident that psychohistorians have focused more on Hitler than on any other figure. To *understand* the irrational, to make sense of it, gives hope for *control.* One day research into the Religion and Health Movement may uncover just how important a role was played by the determination of Religion and Health pioneers to control their own inner demons through self-insight. We know from their autobiographical writings, for example, that it was the experience of mental breakdown and confusion that led Boisen and Fosdick to their work in Religion and Health. What were the neuroses of scores of other leaders that influenced their professional interests and accomplishments?

Those who have investigated the history of the belief in progress[58] observe that human progress throughout the ages has been progress in knowledge of the laws of our physical environment, which has led to progress in mastery over it. What has proved problematic, however, is the use human beings frequently make of such mastery. Whereas technical progress is empirically observable, spiritual or moral progress is not. To put the matter in a different way, we have made enormous gains in understanding and controlling material nature, but few in understanding and controlling human nature.

With the fate of the earth and survival of the human species now at stake, peace activists frequently point out that spiritual progress is imperative. Advocates of nuclear disarmament frequently quote Albert Einstein's statement that "the unleashed power of the atom has changed everything save our modes of thinking, and we thus drift toward unparalleled catastrophe." Einstein wrote to Freud in 1932 to ask Freud to bring to bear his professional expertise, his "far-reaching knowledge of man's instinctive life," on the question, "Is there any way of delivering mankind from the menace of war?"[59] In a lengthy reply Freud reviewed his theory of the dual human instincts (erotic and aggressive) and explained that human aggressive impulses can never be gotten rid of, just diverted.

In concluding, Freud tells Einstein that he believes culture, or civilization, is in a *process* of organic evolution. The psychical modifications, attitudes, or characteristics that accompany this organic process are (a) strengthening of intellectual life and (b) restriction of instinctual impulse. Freud says he and Einstein are pacifists because they cannot help but be so—"We are obliged to be for organic reasons,"[60] in other words, because of the psychical attitude imposed on them by the process of civilization. Although Freud does not speak about "progress," his belief in "process" and cultural evolution implies forward motion, or progress. He ends his letter, "Whatever fosters the growth of civilization works at the same time against war."[61]

From the turn of the century, leaders of the Religion and Health Movement have believed that growth of civilization—progress—could come with the union of faith and science, religion and medicine. In an alienating, fractured, fragmented time, in a time when social theorists have seen a belief in progress at bay,[62] clergypersons and physicians have united to bring healing—understood as wholeness, integration, or "salvation."

The church has always aspired to heal, but with our modern knowledge of disease and our modern therapeutics there is more hope of implementing these aspirations. Margaret Mead put the matter well:

> The religious motive, the vision of a better world in which man could care for his neighbor more, has always come first. Our vision is not clearer or greater because it can now be implemented by science. But it is very much *surer.* The will to care for the leper is no greater than when Father Damian set sail, but today leprosy can be arrested and finally eradicated from a whole population. Spiritual health is the name we have given to our new goals for mankind which stress not so much the welfare of the body, as the welfare of the mind and spirit. The new understandings, the new methods of diagnosis and treatment of the ills of the mind . . . is the banner beneath which those of us who are scientists and those of us who work in specifically religious fields can forget our narrower professional allegiance,

and the limitation of our national identity, the specific loyalties to time and place.[63]

If Freud left ministry with a greater appreciation of the complexities of the human psyche, he also left ministers with greater resources to minister to the human condition.

# CHAPTER 8

# The Scientific Validity of Psychoanalysis and Religion and Health

> *The scientist is not even afraid of being wrong; he knows that the history of science is a history of erroneous but productive, pregnant statements from which new insights are born that overcome the relative wrongness of the older statement and lead to new insights.*

> —ERICH FROMM[1]

Rᴇʟɪɢɪᴏɴ ᴀɴᴅ Hᴇᴀʟᴛʜ leaders took for granted, or assumed, the *scientific* validity of dynamic psychology. Worcester, Boisen, Dunbar, Blanton, Hiltner, and Tillich all accepted Freud's description of the lawfulness of human behavior as a product of scientific method. Just as religious liberals before them believed that the truth of evolution by natural selection and the truth of Genesis were reconcilable, they perceived dynamic psychological truth and the truth of the gospel to be converging, not conflicting, truths. They were not troubled by a question that has become a common subject of study and debate in recent years: was Freud's work scientific?

Although particularly au courant, this has been an issue ever since Freud's visit to America in 1909. At that time he tried to demythologize psychoanalysis. In an interview printed in the *Boston Evening Transcript* he remarked: "The public has always had a certain weakness for everything that savors of mysteries and the mysterious, and these it probably suspects behind psychiatry, which, in reality has nothing, absolutely nothing mysterious about it.[2]

As a clinician, Freud believed that "those who study the same facts cannot possibly come to dissimilar conclusions"[3]; consequently, he did not ask anyone to take psychoanalysis on faith. After returning to Vienna he wrote to his new friend Dr. James Jackson Putnam (a man ten years older than himself), praising him for his high degree of open-mindedness and unprejudiced perceptiveness, qualities that he felt were to lay the foundation of their friendship.

> It is not at all important that you agree with me in every particular. My work demands from the reader only this: that he seek to undergo the experience on which it was based. Up to now I have not been disappointed in my hope that whoever does this will arrive at the same conclusions on all essential points. I neither demand nor expect that the reader accept everything I say without himself first gone down and explored the sources of my observations. . . . I assume that gradually you yourself will become convinced even of what may at the moment still appear inconceivable.[4]

The experience of the eminent Boston neurologist did, in fact, lead him to overcome his initial objections to psychoanalysis and to become a leading apologist in the United States until his death, in 1918.

About fifty years after Freud's visit to America the issue of the scientific status of his work was debated at a Symposium of the New York Institute of Philosophy. Engaged in the sometimes heated arguments and rebuttals were such distinguished psychoanalysts and philosophers as Heinz Hartmann, Lawrence Kubie, Abram Kardiner, Ernest Nagel, Morris Lazerowitze, and Sidney Hook.[5]

No consensus was reached, nor could it have been, for reasons described by Thomas Kuhn in a widely acclaimed study published several years later, *The Structure of Scientific Revolutions*. Kuhn, who was trained as a natural scientist, spent a year at the Center for Advanced Studies in the Behavioral Sciences. As a result of the experience he was struck by the disagreements among social scientists about the nature of scientific problems and methods:

> Both history and acquaintance made me doubt that practition-
> ers of the natural sciences possess firmer or more permanent
> answers to such questions than their colleagues in social sci-
> ence. Yet, somehow, the practice of astronomy, physics,
> chemistry, or biology normally fails to evoke the controversies
> over fundamentals that today often seem endemic among, say
> psychologists or sociologists.[6]

When Kuhn attempted to discover the source of the difference, he was led to recognize the role in scientific research of what he then called "paradigms," or "universally recognized scientific achievements that for a time provided model problems and solutions to a community of practitioners."[7]

Psychoanalytic theory has not emerged as a paradigm among behavioral scientists—nor is it conceivable that it will ever be universally recognized by them as a model for explaining human nature—and thus the "Freudian Revolution" cannot be considered a scientific revolution in the Kuhnian sense.

In recent years many have taken pleasure in debunking Freudian theory as unscientific. A review of representative critiques by journalists, historians, social scientists, and even psychoanalysts will suffice to give a picture of what has emerged as a prominent contemporary concern.

Psychoanalysis is not science, but a cult; not reality, but mythology; not methodology, but superstition. So charges Martin Gross in *The Psychological Society*.[8] Throughout the book, but particularly in the chapter "Psychoanalysis: Science or Delusion?" Gross insists that psychoanalysis is imaginative Victorian speculation, that Freud's attitude was really anti-science because Freud believed that his discoveries were self-evident, statistical studies of treatment outcomes being unnecessary. Freud, driven by ambition, was gullible, superstitious, and dogmatic. He first used his ploy (i.e., psychoanalysis as science) in a society "in which science is God and the distinctions between true science and *scientism* are cloudy to an uninstructed public and impressionable professionals."[9] Psychoanalysis answers all the criteria of a dogmatic faith, including a sense of infallibility and a claim to revealed truth about the reality of the human mind. "It might be viewed as a highly respectable mass delusion born from the typical human tendency to invent, then worship, what we do not yet know."[10]

For Gross, the danger that psychoanalysis now presents to this psychological society is that "true research" in psychiatry is blocked because the curious and the talented have been diverted into "the pursuit of Freudian ritual and dogma."[11] By "true research" he means biologically oriented research in which, for example, the genetic and biochemical bases of schizophrenia and manic-depressive disease are being explored. It is noteworthy that Gross's psychobiological bias is reminiscent of the "somatic style" that dominated American psychiatry before Freud.[12]

*The Psychological Society* is an example of what Yale University psychologist Willian Kessen calls the uniquely American "fright book," because it is biased and inflammatory. Nevertheless, Gross raises a troubling question, one that scholars are taking seriously: was Freud a scientist, as he maintained, or a humanist?

How one answers the question of the scientific status of psychoanalysis depends on how one defines "science." If one defines the essence of science, as Rollo May does, as the assumption that reality is lawful and therefore understandable,[13] Freud's contribution might well be called scientific. It was Freud's genius to develop "lawlike propositions" (Heinz Hartmann's term) about human behavior and motivation that transcend individual observations.

But even this is debated. Many argue today that psychoanalytic theory is unconfirmed because empirical observation either does not support or cannot be used to test Freud's theories. Of the numerous critics who have charged that psychoanalytic theory is unscientific because it is empirically unverifiable, one of the more recent is historian David Stannard. Although Stannard's ostensible subject in *Shrinking History* is the failure of psychohistory, the thrust of his work is an assault on psychoanalysis itself, on the grounds that it is therapeutically ineffective and theoretically disconfirmed on logical and empirical criteria.[14]

One merit of this "primer" is that it summarizes for the layperson the findings of recent research—beginning with that of Dr. Hans J. Eysenck, a name that appears frequently, as one might expect, in the Gross book as well. Stannard examines major experimental studies in an effort to discredit Freud's theories, including the existence of the unconscious and the defense mechanism of repression. In sum, Stannard hopes to demonstrate that

> the psychological facts allegedly discovered as a result of the employment of psychoanalytic theory are drastically few in number and even then are not beyond serious dispute; for the most part they are trivial; and further, no good evidence exists to establish the validity of psychoanalytically posited causality.[15]

In his last book, *The Greatness and Limitations of Freud's Thought,*[16] Erich Fromm deals with the charge that Freud's method was not scientific. In an opening chapter on the limitations of scientific knowledge he discusses the problem of scientific "truth" and Freud's scientific method. Fromm suggests that many people have a naive concept of the scientific method, for they think that problems that do not lend themselves to quantification and a statistical approach are of a nonscientific character, outside the field of scientific psychology.

But Fromm says that the principles of the scientific method—objectivity, observation, hypothesis formation, and revision by further study of the facts—are valid for all scientific endeavor even though they cannot be applied in the same way to all objects of scientific thought. The study of humankind is, obviously, different. The data obtained from a person are unlike the other scientific data. Because a person is in the constant process of change, and because every individual is unique, "even the possibility of generalizations and the formulation of laws is limited."[17] He concludes that Freud was a scientist "if we understand by the scientific method a method based on the belief in the potency of reason optimally free from subjective prejudices, detailed observation of facts, formation of hypotheses by the discovery of new facts, et cetera."[18]

That Freud used the scientific method does not necessarily mean that he was correct in his results. Fromm and Stannard share the opinion that Freud "often made constructions using scraps of evidence that led to conclusions which were nothing short of absurd."[19] Throughout his professional life Fromm took it as his task to distinguish what is essential and lasting from what is time-conditioned in Freud's theory.

Another scholar who has questioned the scientific nature of Freud's achievement is sociologist John Murray Cuddihy. In a remarkable, even audacious study, *The Ordeal of Civility,* Cuddihy claims that Freud's discovery was not science, but a social breakthrough. Freud, a Jew who happened to be a scientist, did not discover a secret of human nature, but rather told a secret of civil society. He was the first to mention the unmentionable—the sexual etiology of neurosis. In a brilliant word play reminiscent of the linguistic skill of his teacher, Peter Berger, Cuddihy writes: "Europe's social pariah, the 'Yid,' becomes in this way everybody's psychological pariah, the id."[20]

Cuddihy believes that because Freud's contribution derived from his social location as a Jew, Freud needed *goyim* to recognize the priority of his discovery. He needed to be reassured that it transcended ethnic interest. Freud himself denied this. In a conversation with Smiley Blanton in 1930, Freud commented that his Jewish background had helped him to stand "being criticized, being isolated, working alone," but that the suggestion that psychoanalysis was a product of a Jewish mind was nonsense. "As a scientific work, it is neither Jewish nor Catholic nor Gentile."[21]

Whereas Cuddihy praised Freud for telling the truth, a young psychoanalyst named Jeffery Moussaieff Masson stunned the psychoanalytic establishment in 1981 by excoriating Freud for suppressing truth. Masson succeeded Dr. Kurt Eissler as projects director of the Sigmund Freud Archives and in this trusted position had access to unpublished letters from Freud to his closest friend, Wilhelm Fliess. Using these letters as well as other evidence gathered in Freud's London home, Masson observed how between 1897 and 1903 Freud abandoned the seduction theory he had formulated in 1895, the theory that emotional disturbances in adults derive from actual childhood sexual trauma, the knowledge of which has been repressed. In studying the influences that led Freud away from his unpopular insights concerning the reality of child abuse, Masson concluded that "Freud gave up this theory, not for theoretical or clinical reasons, but because of a personal failure of courage."[22]

It is commonly known that Freud subsequently made a "breakthrough" in theorizing that the memories of his women patients of rape and seduction were really fantasies, products of the Oedipus complex, part of normal childhood sexuality. Masson sees this "breakthrough" as an assault on truth, an assault that calls into question the entire psychoanalytic enterprise.

> The time has come to cease hiding from what is, after all, one of the greatest issues of human history. For it is unforgiveable that those [psychoanalysts] entrusted with the lives of people who come to them in emotional pain, having suffered real wounds in childhood, should use their blind reliance on Freud's fearful abandonment of the seduction theory to continue the abuse their patients once suffered as children.[23]

Feminists were quick to take up Masson's cause. After his book was published, in 1984, *Ms.* magazine published an article on "The Hundred Year Cover-up: How Freud Betrayed Women."[24]

Although Cuddihy and Masson hold different opinions about

169

Freud's capacity for courage and truth-telling, they agree that his preeminent discovery was the sexual etiology of neurosis. Freud's theory of the unconscious is barely discussed, even though Freud believed this to be his essential contribution. Freud wrote in 1931 that *The Interpretation of Dreams,* which remained unaltered from 1900, "contains, even according to my present-day judgment, the most valuable of all the discoveries it has been my good fortune to make. Insight such as this falls to one's lot but once in a life-time."[25]

Erich Fromm, too, thought that Freud's greatest achievement was in being the first to make the unconscious the center of his system and painstakingly to investigate unconscious phenomena. Fromm wrote that neither Freud's theory of sex nor his meta-psychological speculations were radical, but that his theories of the central role of repression and the fundamental significance of the unconscious in our mental life were.

Many of the issues and questions raised by the authors considered here are carefully sorted out by philosopher of science Owen J. Flanagan Jr. in his *The Science of the Mind.* Addressing the vexing problem "Is Psychoanalysis Scientific?" he points out that psychoanalytic theory is really a large set of theories, or subtheories, that are bound together by the "general thesis that unconscious mental processes are essential causal forces": "Freud's overall theory is held together by the general theory of the unconscious in much the same way Newton's physics is held together by the theory of universal gravitation, and Darwin's biology is held together by the theory of natural selection."[26]

Like Fromm, Flangan makes it clear that some of the subtheories will fare well and some will fare badly on the scale of scientific acceptability. So it is that the discovery of one serious problem with any part of the theory—like Masson's discovery, for example—is not likely to bring down the entire theoretical edifice.

The most intellectually penetrating discussion to date of the scientific status of psychoanalysis is by another philosopher of science, who is also a clinical psychoanalyst, Marshall Edelson of the Yale University School of Medicine. *Hypothesis and Evidence in Psychoanalysis*[27] is a book for the cognoscenti, an abstract philosophical analysis of the challenge of falsification, logical positivism, and eliminative inductivism to psychoanalytic theory. Edelson skillfully defends psychoanalysis against the common claim that it is not genuinely scientific, but a branch of the humanities, a hermeneutic discipline comprising interpretative principles of human motivation. He concludes by challenging a new generation of psychoanalytic investigators to continue the task he has begun.

Reviewing the controversy about the scientific status of Freud's work, one might ask, "But what bearing does this have on the Religion and Health Movement? What if psychoanalysis is not science, but hermeneutics? Would establishing that make a difference?"

Surely not. Whatever philosophers of science, psychoanalysts, social scientists, historians, or journalists have to say about the question, in our psychological society the reality of the unconscious and of repression is now generally accepted by clergy and laypeople alike. Americans know themselves to be equipped with an unconscious, as Peter Berger says, as a sure fact of experience. In the face of objections that Freudian theory is empirically unverified, someone might well reply, "Psychoanalysis may be unscientific, but it is true."[28] Experience tells us so.

Speaking from the debunking point of view of the sociology of knowledge, Peter Berger cautions: "To say that psychoanalysis is verified in the experience of Americans is to say *no more* than that witchcraft is verified in the experience of people in the Middle Ages."[29]

It is noteworthy that Professor Berger chooses witchcraft as an example because the comparison is often made. In a recent book review about the life and times of Cotton Mather, Anatole Broyard commented: "As difficult as it is for us to understand this now, the people of Salem believed in the devil as much as we believe in the unconscious."[30]

There is a good reason why belief in witchcraft or the devil is compared with belief in the unconscious: the latter supplanted the former as an explanation for the irrational and incomprehensible in human behavior. So it was, for instance, that in searching for a reason for the horrifying and seemingly inexplicable People's Temple mass suicide at Jonestown, Guyana, in 1978, commentators did not speak in terms of witchcraft or the devil, but in

171

terms of depth psychology. The motives of Jim Jones and his followers were objects of psychoanalytic speculation.

Religion and Health leaders, who believe in human progress, would undoubtedly have difficulty with the relativizing viewpoint of the sociology of knowledge that does not view contemporary knowledge as necessarily advanced. For Religion and Health liberals, to say that psychoanalysis is verified in the experience of Americans *is* to say more than that witchcraft is verified in the experience of people in the Middle Ages. We have ceased to believe in witchcraft, and this represents progress toward objective knowledge of God's creation. As Dr. Richard Cabot wrote in 1938: "We are confident that nature contains no malignant or deceitful power which tries to trick us or to baffle us, when we put common sense or scientific method into our effort to understand. In this respect ours has become an age of faith." Today we are convinced that both material nature and human nature are intelligible. Continues Cabot, "We believe that if we put sensible questions to nature, we get either reasonable answers or none at all."[31]

From a different viewpoint than that of faith, the sociology of knowledge instructs us that "ideas do not succeed in history by virtue of their truth but of their relationship to specific social processes."[32] Or, as Ernest Johnson said when he reexamined the Social Gospel: "Ideas are neither created nor destroyed by other ideas; they are called forth by necessity and are relegated and superseded as they cease to be relevant to what people are concerned about."[33]

From this perspective one might conclude that it was no coincidence that the Religion and Health Movement took off after 1945. Sophisticated insight into human mental processes was a necessity called forth by the collective horror, revulsion, and dread Americans experienced when the dimensions of the Nazi holocaust and the atom bombing of Hiroshima were fully revealed and comprehended. Knowledge of the causal force of the unconscious and the mechanisms of repression, projection, and so on encouraged hope among the clergy, hope for understanding the irrational and for being a more effective influence in human behavior, individual and social. "Social peace can never be permanently achieved so long as individuals engage in civil war with

172

themselves," explained one Religion and Health leader in a popular book written in 1946.[34]

When they brought together faith and science, the gospel and depth psychology, Religion and Health pioneers shared with Freud a common faith in the integrative, healing power of truth. They believed, indeed, that "the Truth shall make you free [John 8:32]."

# *Appendix A*

# *A Conversation with Wayne Oates, Evangelical Liberal*

AS A STUDENT of the impact of Freud on American Protestant ministry, deeply puzzled by the dearth of scholarship on the subject, I was grateful when the Rev. Charles E. Hall Jr. called my attention to Wayne Oates' 1947 dissertation, "The Significance of the Work of Sigmund Freud for the Christian Faith." Learning that this Southern Baptist Theological Seminary thesis is available only through InterLibrary Loan, I promptly ordered it, read it, and was stunned: it is *brilliant*. Why was the work never published? The question haunted me. How could a work of such outstanding importance be sitting, a lone copy, on a library shelf in Louisville, Kentucky?

When I had an opportunity, through the ACPE, to visit Louisville in May 1979 and to meet Dr. Oates, I asked this leader in Religion and Health to tell me the story of his dissertation. The following is taken from our tape-recorded conversation.

As a student at Southern Baptist Seminary, Oates first met Anton Boisen in 1943. Dr. Gaines S. Dobbins, one of the "senior guard," a professor of the psychology of religion who had studied with George Albert Coe and John Dewey at Columbia, had invited Boisen to Louisville. Oates recalls that, at the time, Boisen made known his worries

175

about the Council for Clinical Training. It had become enamored of Freud and had apparently rejected Boisen's basic concern with theological problems of human existence: sin and salvation, redemption and despair.

The next year Oates took a unit of CPE with Ralph Bonacker. Bonacker had been psychoanalyzed and so "knew Freud from an existential point of view." This he communicated to Oates. During a period of Freudian propaganda, Bonacker taught a human, nonpropagandistic Freud. Bonacker suggested that Oates study with Boisen.

In the summer of 1945, at age twenty-eight, Wayne Oates traveled to Elgin State Hospital, near Chicago, where Boisen was chaplain. He found that the Council had taken Boisen's role of supervisor from him and given it to another man. This supervisor, like others in the Chicago area, was "heavily concentrated on Freud *as* interpreted by English and Pearson," "a simplistic" handling of Freud. Boisen, however, was a "primary source man." When Oates surveyed his roomful of books, Boisen indicated that "these over here are the trash and the hay. These over here are the finest of wheat." The latter, said Oates, were Freud, Adler, Jung, etc.

Oates remembers that he came "back to the shop here" and told Dobbins:

> You know nobody has really read Freud; that's what bothers me. I learned at Wake Forest that before you can critique a person you have to have read the primary sources. I learned at Duke, in church history with Ray Petrie, that you *dare* not quote a secondary source without getting *killed*.

Oates' dissertation, supervised by Dobbins, was an effort to find out what Freud himself, the primary source, said. "And I have always thanked God that I did that."

When Oates looked for copies of Freud, they were not easy to find. He finally went to the University of South Carolina, the University of North Carolina, and Columbia. Since that time he has raised money for primary source material and the Southern Baptist Seminary has two sets of Freud's complete works in its library. Oates' approach then, as now, is a classic approach, which insists on an analysis of the text.

Before I met Wayne Oates I wondered whether he had met resistance to his dissertation topic at the Southern Baptist Theological Seminary. In fact, I wondered whether the reason his dissertation was not published was that that would have offended conservative professors or denominational leaders. I could not have been further from the truth. My view of

Southern Baptists as narrowly conservative was wrong-headed. Oates corrected me:

> You'll find a strong evangelical liberal strain among Southern Baptists. It's been there since I have known them, which began about 1938, and to this very day is strong. If you went to our Christian Life Commission meeting, you'd find 300 to 500 persons there, 98 percent in the evangelical, liberal tradition. They are a zestful lot of people who are creative and curious and imaginative: kicking the slats out of this, kicking the slats out of that, and polemically related to establishmentarianism. This is not what gets in the popular press.

Thus seminary professors offered no resistance to Oates' dissertation. One New Testament professor did remark, however, "I didn't know Freud *had* any significance for the Christian faith," to which Oates replied: "Sir, that's why I'm writing the thesis, so that people who don't know what the significance of Freud is *will* know."

Why, then, was the highly commended work not published? Because a press editor advised against it. Pointing out that an author tends to be known by his first book, he asked Oates, "Do you want to be known as a Freudian?" The swift reply: "My God, no." The editor suggested that he publish the work in other forms, which he has subsequently done. The title of Oates' first published book signals the thrust of all his writing: *The Christian Pastor.* (The reader may remember that this was the title of a book by Social Gospel leader Washington Gladden, cited in chapter 1.)

Oates mentioned to me that David Roberts, a classic philosopher of religion (and a member of the New York Psychology Group), once told him that he had made a mistake in publishing *Psychotherapy and a Christian View of Man.* Because he was tagged as a "psychotherapy person," his career from then on was schematized by that interest.

Freud was important for Oates—"I was interested in the living human documents. He helped me find them"—but Oates did not want to be an apologist for Freud. He was not willing to be evangelical about Freud: "I'll be evangelical about one thing, and other things I'll put in place in relation to that. And that's the centrality of what God did for us in Jesus Christ. I'll be evangelical about that."

Oates knows that he could be evangelical about other things, like what he has seen the drug Elavil do for patients, but it would not last long, for something better would come along: "We were into Wilhelm Reich, into Harry Stack Sullivan, into Rogers, into Glasser, into Hobart Mowrer, into T. A. You see the hazard involved in the postulate you set forth. This is why I didn't go off on Freud. *I hold all that in focus because I know more history is on the way.*"

Oates observed that Freud had many constructive things to say about the religious life. He was a good pathologist of religion, and his theory of compulsive/obsessional neurosis is just as valid about religion today as when he wrote it. Oates has resisted memorizing from Freud's work, although many cannot believe that some quotations are from Freud, only because he would then be "using Freud as a Bible."

Concluding our interview Wayne Oates challenged:

> You look at Freud and see if my basic hypothesis is not right. That is, whoever is in the field of psychology/psychotherapy had better learn Freud because whether they agree with him or not, he is standing there in the door. You're going to have to climb over him, knock him down, push him aside, say something nasty about him, or shake hands with him and make friends—you've got to deal with him if you're in this field.

# Appendix B

# A Chronology: The Religion and Health Movement in Historical Context

1835    Amariah Brigham, New England psychiatrist, writes *Observations on the Influence of Religion on the Health and Physical Welfare.*

1849    Hartford clergyman Horace Bushnell publishes *Christian Nurture,* a primary inspiration of the religious education movement and of liberal theology.

1850    Ichabod S. Spencer, Presbyterian clergyman, publishes *A Pastor's Sketches,* unique in presenting actual case studies of personal religious problems encountered by an average pastor in the course of his ministry (vol. 2, 1853).

——    "Nathaniel Hawthorne described a psychoanalytic technique for the investigation and cure of a somatic condition associated with the feeling of guilt in a minister—*The Scarlet Letter.*"—Clarence Oberndorf, *A History of Psychoanalysis in America* (New York: Harper Torchbooks, 1953), p. 253.

1856    Sigmund Freud is born in Freiberg, Moravia, Austria.

1859    Charles Darwin publishes *The Origin of Species.*

1862    Phineas Parkhurst Quimby heals Mary Baker Eddy.

1870    "Oliver Wendell Holmes, M.D. in *Mechanism in Thought and Morals* called attention to the enormous influence of the unconscious on conscious thinking and illness."—Clarence Oberndorf

1874 Charles Hodge publishes an orthodox repudiation of natural selection, *What Is Darwinism?*

1875 First publication of Mary Baker Eddy's *Science and Health with Key to the Scriptures.*

1879 The Church of Christ (Scientist) is chartered in Boston.

1881 Dr. George Beard, a pioneer diagnostician of "neurasthenia," publishes *American Nervousness.*

1885–86 Freud goes to Paris to study with Charcot and returns to Vienna using the methods of hypnosis.

1887 G. Stanley Hall founds the *American Journal of Psychology,* the first psychological journal in America.

1889 William James is appointed professor of psychology at Harvard.

—— Elwood Worcester returns from the University of Leipzig with a Ph.D.

1892 Lyman Abbott's *The Evolution of Christianity* popularizes the "New Theology" (liberal theology).

—— The American Psychological Association is organized in G. Stanley Hall's study, and he serves as its first president.

1893 Freud and Josef Breuer publish their "Preliminary Communication Concerning the Psychic Mechanism of Hysterical Phenomena."

1896 William James points out the therapeutic potentiality of Freud's theories in appropriate cases (Lowell Lecture).

1897 Ralph Waldo Trine publishes *In Tune with the Infinite, or Fullness of Peace, Power, and Plenty.*

1899 The International Metaphysical League organizes and convenes its first convention to promote the New Thought Movement.

—— E.D. Starbuck writes *The Psychology of Religion,* the first important volume in this new discipline.

1900 Freud publishes *The Interpretation of Dreams.*

1901–02 William James delivers the Gifford Lectures at the University of Edinburgh, published later as *The Varieties of Religious Experience: A Study in Human Nature.*

1904 G. Stanley Hall publishes *Adolescence: Its Psychology, and Its Relations to Physiology, Anthropology, Sociology, Sex, Crime, Religion, and Education,* stressing Freud's findings about the importance of sexual trauma in the neuroses.

—— Pavlov begins his experiments on the conditioned reflex.

1906     The Rev. Drs. Elwood Worcester and Samuel McComb open a clinic at Emmanuel Episcopal Church in Boston for the psychotherapeutic treatment of functional nervous disorders.

1907     Walter Rauschenbusch publishes *Christianity and the Social Crisis,* classic of the Social Gospel movement.

1908     Delegates from thirty-three denominations in Philadelphia bring the Federal Council of Churches into existence, due largely to the efforts of social activists.

——     *Psychotherapy: A Course of Reading in Sound Psychology, Sound Medicine, and Sound Religion,* an elegantly printed and illustrated magazine devoted to medical psychotherapy and the Emmanuel Movement, appears.

——     Clifford Beers makes a plea for the humane treatment of the mentally ill in telling about his two years as a mental patient in *A Mind That Found Itself.*

1909     Freud gives five lectures at Clark University, Worcester, Massachusetts, at the invitation of President G. Stanley Hall. He is accompanied on his only trip to America by Carl Jung and Sando Ferenczi.

——     Ray Stannard Baker publishes *New Ideas in Healing.* Worcester, McComb, and Coriat publish *Religion and Medicine.*

——     The National Committee for Mental Hygiene is organized by Clifford Beers, Dr. Adolf Meyer, and William James.

1910     William James dies.

——     James J. Putnam presents a paper on "Personal Experience with Freud's Psychoanalytic Method" before the American Neurological Association in Washington, DC, securing for Freud's views a serious public hearing.

——     The "Psychology of Religion" begins to appear as a separate subject in colleges and universities.

1911     The American Psychoanalytic Association is founded by J.J. Putnam, who serves as its first president.

1913     Carl Jung separates from Freud and develops the school he calls "Analytic Psychology."

1914     Communication between American analysts and Austria is interrupted by World War I.

1915     Henry Preserved Smith, professor of biblical history at Amherst College, publishes a paper, "Luther's Early Development in the Light of Psychoanalysis" in the *American Journal of Psychology.*

1917     The quarterly "Mental Hygiene" begins publication.

1918     James Jackson Putnam dies.

1919　Adolph Stern is the first American psychoanalyst to visit Vienna for didactic analysis.

1920　Anton Boisen suffers an acute psychotic breakdown and is admitted to Boston Psychopathic Hospital.

1922　Frenchman Emile Coué tours America with his formula, "Day by day, in every way, I am getting better and better."

1923　William S. Keller, M.D., founds the Bexley Hall Plan in Ohio, the first clinical pastoral education program. Theological students are put to work in social agencies under social casework supervision.

——　G. Gresham Machen's *Christianity and Liberalism* (a fundamentalist attack) appears.

1925　Anton Boisen begins working with theological students at Worcester State Hospital, Worcester, Massachusetts.

——　John Watson writes *Behaviorism*.

——　Friction develops between American and European analysts over the question of training laypersons as analysts.

——　The Scopes trial takes place in Dayton, Tennessee.

1927　A Joint Committee on Religion and Health of the Federal Council of Churches and the New York Academy of Medicine is organized.

——　Dr. Harry Emerson Fosdick addresses the Eighteenth Annual Meeting of the National Committee for Mental Hygiene on the subject "A Clergyman's View of Mental Hygiene."

——　Harrison Elliott publishes *The Bearing of Psychology upon Religion*.

——　Freud attacks religion in *The Future of an Illusion*.

1930　The Council for the Clinical Training of Theological Students, founded by Anton Boisen, Richard Cabot, and Philip Guiles, is incorporated in Boston. Dr. H. Flanders Dunbar is appointed director.

——　The First International Congress for Mental Hygiene in Washington, DC brings many European psychoanalysts as participants.

1931　Andover and Newton Theological Schools merge and appoint A. Philip Guiles to its faculty. This is the first theological school to employ a professor in the clinical field on a full-time basis.

——　Walter Marshall Horton, professor at Oberlin College, calls for an "adequate general theory of spiritual diagnosis" in *A Psychological Approach to Theology*.

1932　Flanders Dunbar moves the Council for Clinical Training to

New York City after a rupture with Philip Guiles. Guiles develops clinical training in Boston—the rival camps grow until their merger in 1967.

—— Beginning about this time political persecution in Central Europe compels a large migration of psychoanalysts, especially to America.

1933 Paul Tillich moves to New York and begins teaching at Union Theological Seminary. Rollo May is one of his first students.

1937 The Religio-Psychiatric Clinic is founded by the Rev. Norman Vincent Peale and Dr. Smiley Blanton as a free service of the Marble Collegiate Church.

—— The Commission of Religion and Health of the Federal Council of Churches of Christ in America is organized. Seward Hiltner is appointed executive secretary several months later.

1938 The American Psychiatric Association schedules a seminar on Religion and Psychiatry at its annual convention. More than 1,000 persons appear at a room meant to accommodate fifty.

1939 Sigmund Freud dies in London.

1940 Elwood Worcester dies.

1941 The New York Psychology Group organizes. Membership includes Fromm, Hiltner, May, and Tillich.

1943 Hiltner publishes a comprehensive study of *Religion and Health.*

1944 The First National Conference on Clinical Training meets in juxtaposition with the American Association of Theological Schools in Pittsburgh.

—— The Institute of Pastoral Care incorporates in Boston with Rollin Fairbanks as the first executive director.

1945 Columbia University offers an interdisciplinary Religion and Health Seminar as the New York Psychology Group disbands.

1947 The Council for Clinical Training launches the *Journal of Clinical Pastoral Work* at roughly the same time as the Institute of Pastoral Care launches *Journal of Pastoral Care.* Competition between the New York and Boston centers motivates these publishing ventures.

—— Rabbi Joshua Liebman calls one of the first interdisciplinary conferences on Religion and Psychiatry at Temple Israel in Boston.

—— Wayne E. Oates completes his Th.D. dissertation at Southern Baptist Theological Seminary, "The Significance of the Work of Sigmund Freud for the Christian Faith." Although unpublished, it informs Oates' later books.

—— Charles F. Kemp writes *Physicians of the Soul, A History of Pastoral Counseling*

1948 The Association of Mental Hospital Chaplains is organized.

1949 The House of Bishops of the Protestant Episcopal Church makes it mandatory that all candidates for the ministry undergo a psychological examination and "urged the examiners to use, whenever possible, psychological and psychodiagnostic tests as part of their examinations."

—— The Lutheran Advisory Council on Pastoral Care organizes to promote and oversee clinical training in Lutheran seminaries. (In 1967 it becomes part of the ACPE.)

—— Dr. Flanders Dunbar publishes *Mind and Body.*

1950 *Pastoral Psychology* begins as an influential monthly publication with Hiltner as consultant.

—— The National Council of Churches of Christ in the United States of America is formed.

—— David Roberts' book *Psychotherapy and a Christian View of Man* is published.

—— Anna Freud, at the invitation of Clark University, visits America, presenting papers in several cities.

1951 The American Foundation of Religion and Psychiatry is organized in New York, the successor to the Blanton-Peale Clinic.

1953 The Menninger Foundation sets up the Edward F. Gallahue Seminars on Religion and Psychiatry.

—— The *Journal of the American Psychoanalytic Association* begins publication.

—— Pope Pius XII addresses the Fifth International Congress of Psychotherapy and Clinical Psychology.

1954 The Institute of Religion is set up at the Texas Medical Center of Houston, bringing together five Protestant seminaries of Texas in a graduate program of pastoral care and counseling.

—— H. Richard Niebuhr, Daniel Day Williams, and James M. Gustafson begin a study of theological education sponsored by the American Association of Theological Schools and the Carnegie Corporation. In 1957 they published *The Advancement of Theological Education,* affirming the new emphasis on psychology and pastoral counseling as a significant new development.

—— The Rev. George Christian Anderson founds the Academy of Religion and Mental Health, an educational venture.

1956 The Cathedral of St. John the Divine in New York City celebrates the centenary of Freud's birth.

—— Granger E. Westberg is appointed associate professor of religion and health in the School of Medicine and Federated Theological Faculty, the University of Chicago.

—— Samuel Klausner begins his sociological study to examine the relationship between the ideas espoused and the social positions of ministers and psychiatrists in the Religio-Psychiatric Movement.

1957 The Southern Baptist Association for Clinical Pastoral Education forms. Within a decade it is a national, pan-Protestant group numbering one third of all the clinical pastoral educators in the nation. (In 1967 it becomes part of the ACPE.)

1958 The National Institute of Mental Health, a department of the U.S. Public Health Service, grants $426,000 to Harvard Divinity School, Yeshiva University of New York, and Loyola University of Chicago to establish courses to integrate the teaching of mental health principles with the functions and needs of the clergy.

—— A graduate program in psychiatry and religion is established at Union Theological Seminary.

—— Psychoanalyst Erik Erikson publishes *Young Man Luther.*

1959 Dr. Flanders Dunbar dies.

—— The Menninger Foundation announces one-year "Fellowships in Psychiatric Theory for Clergymen and Theological Scholars."

1962 Sociologist Samuel Klausner estimates that, between 1900 and 1962, perhaps 2,500 items were published in the religio-psychiatric field.

1964 The American Association of Pastoral Counselors is organized by pastoral counseling specialists. It is opposed by persons fearing that by giving up preaching and conducting worship, clergy would become indistinguishable from psychotherapists or social workers.

1965 Anton Boisen dies on October 1; Paul Tillich, on October 22. *Pastoral Psychology* publishes a memorial issue for Tillich in February 1968; for Boisen in September 1968.

1966 Dr. Smiley Blanton dies.

1967 The Association for Clinical Pastoral Education is incorporated, culminating efforts to bring together four groups. Charles E. Hall Jr. is named executive director.

1970 Edward E. Thornton publishes *Professional Education for Ministry, A History of Clinical Pastoral Education.*

1972 *Pastoral Psychology* ceases publication.

—— The Institutes of Religion and Health is formed by the merger of the American Foundation of Religion and Psychiatry (1951) and the Academy of Religion and Mental Health (1954).

1973 Dr. Karl Menninger writes a "long letter" to the clergy entitled *Whatever Became of Sin?*

1975 The National Institute of Mental Health designates a $566,000 grant to the Institutes of Religion and Health for the establishment of ten pastoral counseling centers across the country.

—— The Golden Anniversary of the founding of clinical pastoral education is celebrated in Minneapolis.

1978 The *Journal of Religion and Health* is taken over by Human Sciences Press.

1980 Erich Fromm dies in Switzerland. *Greatness and Limitations in Freud's Thought* is published posthumously.

—— Seward Hiltner receives the first Distinguished Service Award of the Association of Clinical Pastoral Education.

1983 The 350th anniversary of publication of Galileo's theory that the earth revolves around the sun, a theory that disputed the church's view of the earth as center of the universe and that he was forced to recant under threat of torture. Pope John Paul II observed that through the experience the church was led "to a more proper attitude." "It is only through humble and assiduous study that she learns to dissociate the essentials of faith from the scientific systems of a given age." *New York Times,* May 10, 1983.

1984 Seward Hiltner dies.

—— Norman Vincent Peale publishes his autobiography, *The True Joy of Positive Living.*

1985 The parents of Kenneth Nally, who committed suicide in 1979 at the age of 24, lose a clergy malpractice suit filed against pastors at Grace Community Church in Sun Valley, California. The Nallys alleged that the pastors had provided incompetent counseling and failed to send their son to a psychiatrist. Church attorneys argued that referrals had been made. In rejecting a bid for a new trial, the judge ruled that Nally was an adult who had the right to choose his counselors.

# Notes

**PREFACE**

1. James Luther Adams and Seward Hiltner, eds., *Pastoral Care in the Liberal Churches* (Nashville: Abingdon Press, 1970), p. 241.

2. O. Hobart Mowrer, *The Crisis in Psychiatry and Religion* (New York: Van Nostrand Reinhold Co., 1961).

3. Thomas Oden, "Recovering Lost Identity," *Journal of Pastoral Care* 34:1 (March 1980): 14.

4. Sidney Hook, ed., *Psychoanalysis, Scientific Method and Philosophy, A Symposium* (New York: New York University Press, 1959), p. xi.

5. This is the conclusion of E. Brooks Holifield in "Ethical Assumptions of Clinical Pastoral Education," *Theology Today* 36:1 (April 1979): 30–44; reprinted in *Journal of Pastoral Care* 34:1 (March 1980): 39–53.

6. For an evaluation of Paul's intention in this text and of the prevalent misreading of it, see Krister Stendahl, "The Apostle Paul and the Introspective Conscience of the West," in *The Writings of St. Paul*, ed. Wayne A. Meeks (New York: W.W. Norton & Co., 1972), pp. 422–34.

7. For pioneering studies of the cure of souls in America see Charles F. Kemp, *Physicians of the Soul, A History of Pastoral Counseling* (New York: Macmillan, 1947), and Carl J. Scherzer, *The Church and Healing* (Philadelphia: Westminster Press, 1950). For a survey of *cura animarum* or *Seelsorge,* see John T. McNeill's classic, *A History of the Cure of Souls* (1951; reprint, New York: Harper & Row, 1977). For a collection of readings, see William A. Clebsch and Charles R. Jaekle, eds., *Pastoral Care in Historical Perspective, An Essay with Exhibits* (Englewood Cliffs, NJ: Prentice-Hall, 1964; reprinted New York: Jason Aronson, 1975).

187

8. E. Brooks Holifield, *A History of Pastoral Care in America, From Salvation to Self-realization* (Nashville: Abingdon Press, 1983).

9. Samuel K. Klausner, *Psychiatry and Religion, A Sociological Study of the New Alliance of Ministers and Psychiatrists* (Glencoe, IL: Free Press of Glencoe, 1964), p. 19. An article about "The Religio-Psychiatric Movement" by Klausner appears in the *International Encyclopedia of the Social Sciences* 12:632–38.

10. There have been few references to the New York Psychology Group in print. Paul Tillich's participation in the seminar is mentioned by Wilhelm and Marion Pauck only in a footnote of their biography, *Paul Tillich, His Life and Thought,* vol 1, Life (New York: Harper & Row, 1976) p. 320. David Moss briefly discussed the group in "An Interview with Seward Hiltner," *Pilgrimage* 6:2 (Summer 1978): 93.

11. Henri Ellenberger, *The Discovery of the Unconscious: The History and Evolution of Dynamic Psychiatry* (New York: Basic Books, 1970), pp. 289–91.

12. Albert Outler, *Psychotherapy and the Christian Message* (New York: Harper & Bros., 1954), pp. 10–11.

13. Edward E. Thornton, *Professional Education for Ministry, A History of Clinical Pastoral Education* (Nashville: Abingdon Press, 1970), p. 92.

14. Peter Berger, "Toward a Sociological Understanding of Psychoanalysis," in *Facing Up to Modernity: Excursions in Society, Politics, and Religion* (New York: Basic Books, 1977), pp. 29–30.

15. For an annotated bibliography of bibliographies, see G. Allison Stokes, "Bibliographies of Psychology/Religion Studies," *Religious Studies Review* 4:4 (October 1978): 273–79. For a concise bibliographical essay on the Religion and Health Movement, see "Dynamic Psychology and Religion," in the *American Quarterly* article, "Religion and America" by Edwin S. Gaustad, Darline Miller, and G. Allison Stokes 31:3 (Bibliography Issue 1979): 258–65.

**CHAPTER 1**  The Freudian Revolution and American Protestant Liberalism

1. Erik Erikson, *Young Man Luther* (New York: W.W. Norton & Co., 1962), p. 21.

2. Harrison Elliott, *The Bearing of Psychology Upon Religion* (New York: Associated Press, 1927), p. 7.

3. John Seeley, *The Americanization of the Unconscious* (New York: International Science Press, 1967), p. 16.

4. Sigmund Freud, *Introductory Lectures on Psychoanalysis,* in *The Standard Edition of the Complete Psychological Works of Sigmund*

*Freud*, vol. 16, trans. and ed. James Strachey (London: Hogarth Press, 1963), p. 285.

5. Helen Walker Puner, *Freud, His Life and His Mind* (1947; reprint, New York: Charter Books, 1978), p. 244.

6. Heinrich Meng and Ernst L. Freud, eds., *Psychoanalysis and Faith, The Letters of Sigmund Freud and Oskar Pfister* (New York: Basic Books, 1963), p. 17.

7. Ibid., p. 126.

8. See Bruce Mazlish's epilogue to Andrew Dickson White's, *A History of the Warfare of Science with Theology in Christendom* (1896; reprint, New York: The Free Press, 1965), p. 507.

9. Krister Stendahl, "Responsible Scientific Investigation and Application," in *The Nature of a Human Society,* ed. H. Ober Hess (Philadelphia: Fortress Press, 1976), p. 159.

10. Ruth Marcus, "Psychoanalysis Through Jesus, The Gospel According to Ruth," *The Yale Daily News Magazine,* October 5, 1978, p. 16.

11. Ruth Stapleton, *The Gift of Inner Healing* (Waco, TX: Word Books, 1977), pp. 62–63.

12. When Carl Wernerstrom inquired into *Pastoral Care in the Liberal Churches* (edited by James Luther Adams and Seward Hiltner [Nashville: Abingdon Press, 1970]), his focus was Unitarian-Universalism.

13. Lloyd J. Averill premises his study of *American Theology in the Liberal Tradition* (Philadelphia: Westminster Press, 1967) on the idea that Darwinism, biological and social, is central; thus every one of the twelve characteristics listed in his profile of liberalism has an evolutionary reference.

14. Seward Hiltner, "The Contribution of Liberals to Pastoral Care," in *Pastoral Care in the Liberal Churches,* op. cit., p. 239.

15. Peter Berger, *The Heretical Imperative: Contemporary Possibilities of Religious Affirmation* (New York: Doubleday, Anchor Books, 1979), pp. xii–xiii.

16. See Mary Ely Lyman, "The Liberal Spirit in the New Testament," in *Liberal Theology,* ed. David E. Roberts and Henry Pitney Van Dusen (New York: Charles Scribner's Sons, 1942), pp. 76–91.

17. William R. Hutchinson, ed., *American Protestant Thought: The Liberal Era* (New York: Harper & Row, 1968), pp. 1–3.

18. William R. Hutchinson, *The Modernist Impulse in American Protestantism* (Cambridge, MA: Harvard University Press, 1976), p. 2.

19. Kenneth Cauthen, *The Impact of American Religious Liberalism* (New York: Harper & Row, 1962), p. 29.

20. Ibid., p. 30.

21. Hutchinson, *The Modernist Impulse,* op. cit., p. 63.

22. Meng and Freud, *Psychoanalysis and Faith,* op. cit., p. 63.

23. Ibid., p. 104.

24. Ibid., p. 127.

25. Nathan G. Hale Jr., ed., *James Jackson Putnam and Psychoanalysis: Letters Between Putnam and Sigmund Freud, Ernest Jones, William James, Sandor Ferenczi, and Morton Prince, 1877–1917* (Cambridge, MA: Harvard University Press, 1971), pp. 196–97.

26. Ibid., p. 62.

27. Paul Maves, *The Church and Mental Health* (New York: Charles Scribner's Sons, 1953), p. 267.

28. This appears as chapter 10 in *Theology of Culture* (New York: Oxford University Press, 1969), p. 124.

29. Joshua Loth Liebman, *Peace of Mind* (1946; reprint, New York: Simon & Schuster, 1973), p. 14.

30. Erikson, *Young Man Luther,* op. cit., p. 252.

31. These appear respectively in *Gandhi's Truth, On the Origins of Militant Nonviolence* (New York: W.W. Norton & Co., 1969), pp. 229–54; and in *Insight and Responsibility, Lectures on the Ethical Implications of Psychoanalytic Insight* (New York: W.W. Norton & Co., 1964), pp. 217–43.

32. See Nathan G. Hale Jr., *Freud and the Americans, the Beginnings of Psychoanalysis in the United States, 1876–1971* (New York: Oxford University Press, 1971); Donald Meyer, *The Positive Thinkers: A Study of the American Quest for Health, Wealth and Personal Power from Mary Baker Eddy to Norman Vincent Peale* (New York: Doubleday, 1965); and Gail Thain Parker, *Mind Cure in New England, From the Civil War to World War I* (Hanover, NH: University Press of New England, 1973).

33. See Seward Hiltner, "History," ch. 3 in *Preface to Pastoral Theology* (Nashville: Abingdon Press, 1958), pp. 40–51.

34. Washington Gladden, *The Christian Pastor and the Working Church* (New York: Charles Scribner's Sons, 1898), p. vii.

35. Ibid., p. 9.

36. Ibid., p. 14.

37. Hutchinson, *The Modernist Impulse,* op. cit., pp. 4–5.

38. Gladden, *The Christian Pastor,* op. cit., p. 195.

39. Raymond Cunningham, "From Preachers of the Word to Physicians of the Soul: The Protestant Pastor in Nineteenth Century America," *Journal of Religious History* 3:4 (1964–65): 332ff.

40. E. Brooks Holifield convincingly describes the late nineteenth-century turn to the interpersonal in his article "Ethical Assumptions of

Clinical Pastoral Education," *Theology Today* 36:1 (April 1979): 30–44. Holifield's argument that clinical pastoral education is a product of the Progressive Movement, that its original impetus was primarily an ethical, reforming impulse, is unconvincing and contrary to the thesis of this study.

41. Cunningham, "From Preachers of the Word," op. cit., pp. 342–43.
42. Gladden, *The Christian Pastor,* op. cit., pp. 185–86.

**CHAPTER 2**   Elwood Worcester and the Emmanuel Movement

1. Elwood Worcester, Samuel McComb, and Isador A. Coriat, *Religion and Medicine, The Moral Control of Nervous Disorders* (New York: Moffat, Yard & Co., 1908), p. 13.
2. Elwood Worcester, *Life's Adventure, The Story of a Varied Career* (New York: Charles Scribner's Sons, 1932), p. 76.
3. Henry B. Washburn, "Elwood Worcester," *Dictionary of American Biography,* vol. 22, suppl. 2 (New York: Charles Scribner's Sons, n.d.), p. 735. See also "Elwood Worcester," *New York Times,* Obituary, July 20, 1940, p. 15.
4. Worcester, *Life's Adventure,* op. cit., p. 75. Copyright 1932 Charles Scribner's Sons; copyright renewed. Reprinted with the permission of Charles Scribner's Sons.
5. Ibid., p. 76.
6. Ibid., p. 78.
7. Ibid., pp. 80–81.
8. Ibid., p. 91.
9. Ibid., p. 87.
10. Ibid., p. 92.
11. Ibid., pp. 92–93.
12. Washburn, "Elwood Worcester," op. cit., p. 736.
13. Raymond Cunningham, "Ministry of Healing: The Origins of the Psychotherapeutic Role of the American Churches," Ph.D. diss., The Johns Hopkins University, 1965, p. 122.
14. Worcester, *Life's Adventure,* op. cit., p. 357.
15. Worcester, et al., *Religion and Medicine,* op. cit., p. 372.
16. Ibid.
17. Ray Stannard Baker, *New Ideals in Healing* (New York: Frederick A. Stokes Co., 1909), pp. 6–7.
18. Worcester et al., *Religion and Medicine,* op. cit., p. 380.
19. Ibid., p. 8.
20. Ibid., p. 10.
21. Ibid., p. 6.
22. Ibid., p. 12.

23. Ibid., p. 7. See Raymond J. Cunningham, "The Impact of Christian Science on the American Churches, 1890–1910," *American Historical Review* 72:3 (April 1967): 885–905.

24. Worcester et al., *Religion and Medicine,* op. cit., p. 379.

25. Gail Thain Parker, *Mind Cure in New England, From the Civil War to World War I* (Hanover, NH: University Press of New England, 1973), esp. pp. 152, 175. Nathan G. Hale Jr., *Freud and the Americans, the Beginnings of Psychoanalysis in the United States, 1876–1971* (New York: Oxford University Press, 1971), ch. 9. See also Sydney E. Ahlstrom, "Mary Baker Eddy," in *Notable American Women,* vol. 1 (Cambridge, MA: Harvard University Press, Belknap Press, 1980), pp. 551–61, esp. the conclusion.

26. John Semonche, *Ray Stannard Baker, A Quest for Democracy in Modern America, 1870–1918* (Chapel Hill, NC: University of North Carolina Press, 1969), p. 215. See Semonche's discussion on pp. 215–20. See also Robert C. Bannister Jr., *Ray Stannard Baker, The Mind and Thought of a Progressive* (New Haven, CT: Yale University Press, 1966), pp. 137–39.

27. Quoted in ibid., p. 217.

28. Ibid., pp. 216–17.

29. Raymond J. Cunningham, "The Emmanuel Movement: A Variety of American Religious Experience," *American Quarterly* 14 (Spring 1962): 56.

30. Worcester, *Life's Adventure,* op. cit., pp. 355–56.

31. Ibid.

32. Washburn, "Elwood Worcester," op. cit., p. 736. In addition to articles previously mentioned, see John Gardner Greene, "The Emmanuel Movement 1906–1929," *New England Quarterly* 3:3 (September 1934): 494–532.

33. Cunningham, "The Emmanuel Movement," op. cit., p. 57.

34. Worcester et al., *Religion and Medicine,* op. cit., p. 13.

35. Ibid., p. 385.

36. Ibid., pp. 373–74.

37. Historian Barbara Sicherman writes that Coriat's participation in the Emmanuel Movement is perhaps the most puzzling phase of his career. For her conjecture about the significance to him of his position as chief medical consultant to a movement of Christian healing, see "Isador H. Coriat: The Making of an American Psychoanalyst," in *Psychoanalysis, Psychotherapy and the New England Medical Scene,* ed. George E. Gifford Jr. (New York: Science History Publications/USA, 1978).

38. Worcester et al., *Religion and Medicine,* op. cit., p. 9.

39. Ibid., p. 13.

40. Worcester, *Life's Adventure*, op. cit., p. 355. This is taken from Worcester's Letter of Resignation submitted to the Wardens and Vestry of Emmanuel Church, January 22, 1929.

41. Worcester et al., *Religion and Medicine*, op. cit., p. 2.

42. Ibid., p. 5.

43. Hale, *Freud and the Americans*, op. cit., pp. 231–32; Cunningham, "Ministry of Healing," op. cit., p. 152.

44. W.B. Parker, ed., *Psychotherapy*, vol. 1 (New York: Center Publishing Co., 1908–09), pp. ii–v. For a discussion of Fallow's role in *Psychotherapy*, Cunningham, "Ministry of Healing," pp. 151–52; of the Hartford Theological Seminary course given by Dr. Simpson and the Rev. Dr. McComb, pp. 157–58.

45. Worcester et al., *Religion and Medicine*, op. cit., p. 386.

46. Worcester, *Life's Adventure*, op. cit., pp. 349–50.

47. Worcester et al., *Religion and Medicine*, op. cit., p. 4.

48. See Cunningham, "Ministry of Healing," op. cit., pp. 1–44.

49. David Edwin Harrell Jr., *All Things Are Possible: The Healing and Charismatic Revivals in Modern America* (Bloomington, IN: Indiana University Press, 1975).

50. Parker, *Psychotherapy*, op. cit., p. 1.

51. Worcester et al., *Religion and Medicine*, op. cit., p. 374.

52. Ibid.

53. Ibid., p. 368.

54. John C. Burnham, "Psychiatry, Psychology and the Progressive Movement," *American Quarterly* 12 (1960): 457.

55. Sigmund Freud, *An Autobiographical Study,* in *The Standard Edition of the Complete Psychological Works of Sigmund Freud*, vol. 20, trans. and ed. James Strachey (London: Hogarth Press, 1959), pp. 51–52.

56. Nathan G. Hale Jr., ed., *James Jackson Putnam and Psychoanalysis: Letters Between Putnam and Sigmund Freud, Ernest Jones, William James, Sandor Ferenczi, and Morton Prince, 1877–1917* (Cambridge, MA: Harvard University Press, 1971), p. 188.

57. Worcester, *Life's Adventure*, op. cit., p. 356.

58. "The Ministry of Mental Healing," in *The Christian Ministry and the Social Order*, ed. Charles MacFarland (New Haven, CT: Yale University Press, 1909), p. 268.

59. Ibid., p. 256.

60. Hale, *James Jackson Putnam*, op. cit., p. 17.

61. James Jackson Putnam, "The Service to Nervous Invalids of the Physician and of the Minister," *Harvard Theological Review* 2 (1909): 241.

62. Ibid., p. 244.

63. Ibid., p. 249.

64. Charles Reynolds Brown, *Faith and Health* (New York: Thomas Y. Crowell Co., 1910).

65. Ibid., p. 50.

66. Ibid.

67. Ibid., p. 152.

68. Ibid., p. 157. See also Hale, *Freud and the Americans,* op. cit., pp. 225–29.

69. Putnam, "The Service to Nervous Invalids," op. cit., p. 242.

70. Ibid., p. 237.

71. Elwood Worcester and Samuel McComb, *Body, Mind and Spirit* (Boston: Marshall Jones Co., 1931). See the introduction written by Worcester, p. vii.

72. Freud, *An Autobiographical Study,* op. cit., p. 27.

73. Ibid., p. 30.

74. Ibid., p. 31.

75. Worcester and McComb, *Body, Mind and Spirit,* op. cit., p. x.

76. Worcester, *Life's Adventure,* op. cit., p. 339.

77. Worcester and McComb, *Body, Mind and Spirit,* op. cit., p. xi.

78. Letter from Freud to Pfister, February 9, 1909. Heinrich Meng and Ernest L. Freud, eds., *Psychoanalysis and Faith* (New York: Basic Books, 1963), p. 17. In 1927 an American physician wrote Freud telling him of a personal religious experience that had enabled him to retain his faith. When Freud replied that God had not done so much for him, the American responded that prayers were being offered that Freud might be granted faith to believe. "I am still awaiting the outcome of this intercession," Freud commented dryly in 1928. Sigmund Freud, "A Religious Experience," in *The Standard Edition of the Complete Psychological Works of Sigmund Freud,* vol. 21, op. cit., p. 170.

**CHAPTER 3** Anton Boisen and the Council for the Clinical Training of Theological Students

1. Anton Boisen, *Out of the Depths* (New York: Harper & Row, 1960), p. 109. Copyright © 1960 by Anton T. Boisen. Used by permission of Harper & Row, Publishers, Inc.

2. Anton Boisen, *The Exploration of the Inner World, A Study of Mental Disorder and Religious Experience* (Willett, Clark & Co., 1936; reprint, Philadelphia: University of Pennsylvania Press, 1971), p. 1.

3. Anton Boisen, "The Period of Beginnings," *Journal of Pastoral Care* 5:1 (Spring 1951): 15.

4. Boisen, *Inner World,* op. cit., p. 5. Copyright 1936 by Willett, Clark

and Company. Reprinted by permission of Harper & Row, Publishers, Inc.

5. Ibid.

6. Boisen, *Out of the Depths,* op. cit., p. 103.

7. Not until the publication of his autobiography *Out of the Depths,* when he was eighty-four years old, did Boisen reveal the story of his love for Alice and the part it played in his illness. His first book, *The Exploration of the Inner World,* published just after her death from cancer, in December 1935, is dedicated simply "To the Memory of A.L.B." For insightful comments about their relationship and Alice's "curing authority," see Henri J.M. Nouwen, "Anton T. Boisen and Theology Through Living Human Documents," *Pastoral Psychology* 19:185 (September 1968): 55–57.

8. Boisen, *Inner World,* op. cit., p. 4.

9. Boisen, *Out of the Depths,* op. cit., p. 109.

10. Ibid. On November 20, 1921, Boisen would write a letter to Elwood Worcester, complaining: "Just last Christmas I was denied permission to visit a friend on the ground that I still believed that in the experience through which I had passed there might be the working out of a divine plan. And yet, as I understand it, some such faith has always been fundamental in the Christian philosophy of life. I think there can be little question that such men as Saul of Tarsus and George Fox would fare badly before a present-day psychiatric staff." Ibid., p. 139.

11. Letter to Fred Eastman, December 11, 1920. *Out of the Depths,* op. cit., p. 107. The Rev. Fred Eastman told clinical pastoral educators at their twenty-fifth anniversary celebration in 1950: "With the increasing complexities of modern life—the stress on nerves and hearts due to wars and depressions and the general depersonalizing of individual life—human beings in great numbers have broken under the strain. They have need of ministers specially trained in understanding the psychological factors that wreck mind and nerves and characters." *Journal of Pastoral Care* 5:1:3.

12. Boisen, *Inner World,* op. cit., p. 6.

13. Boisen wrote that he found his conversations with Worcester very helpful. They maintained communication until Worcester's death. *Out of the Depths,* op. cit., p. 138.

14. Ibid., p. 39.

15. Nouwen, "Anton T. Boisen," op. cit., p. 54. See also Peter Homans' discussion of "The Psychology of Religion and the Thought of Freud," in *Theology After Freud* (New York: Bobbs-Merrill, 1970), pp. 94–107, esp. 97–98.

16. Nouwen, "Anton T. Boisen," op. cit., pp. 54–55.

17. Boisen, *Out of the Depths,* op. cit., p. 60.

18. Nouwen, "Anton T. Boisen," op. cit., p. 55.

19. Boisen, *Out of the Depths,* op. cit., p. 97.

20. Ibid., p. 134.

21. Anton T. Boisen, "Pioneer of Pastoral Psychology [George Albert Coe]," *Pastoral Psychology* 3:27 (October 1952): 65.

22. Ibid., p. 66.

23. Paul Pruyser, *Dynamic Psychology of Religion* (New York: Harper & Row, 1976), p. 9. Portions of this book were first given as the Lyman Beecher Lectures at Yale Divinity School in 1968.

24. E. Brooks Holifield, "Ethical Assumption of Clinical Pastoral Education," *Theology Today* 36:1 (April 1979): 39. Reprinted in *Journal of Pastoral Care* 34:1 (March 1980): 48.

25. Peter Homans writes that the reasons for the "quick and thoroughly undramatic decline" of the psychology of religion are more interesting and important than the work of the movement itself. He sees the cause to be the beginnings of both psychoanalysis and theological existentialism. *Theology After Freud,* op. cit., p. 99. Because pastoral psychology derives from Freudian psychology, as I seek to demonstrate in this study, it is no surprise that Homans also associates the decline of the psychology of religion with the appearance of pastoral psychology (p. 107).

26. Ibid., pp. 98–99.

27. Boisen, *Out of the Depths,* op. cit., pp. 67–68.

28. Ibid., p. 74.

29. Sydney Ahlstrom, *A Religious History of the American People* (New Haven, CT: Yale University Press, 1972), p. 897.

30. Boisen, *Out of the Depths,* op. cit., p. 75.

31. Ahlstrom, *A Religious History,* op. cit., p. 898.

32. Boisen's close friend Fred Eastman, who became Professor of Biography and Drama at Chicago Theological Seminary, remarked that the collapse of IWM precipitated the nervous breakdown. "Father of the Clinical Pastoral Movement," *Journal of Pastoral Care* 5:1 (Spring 1951): 4.

33. Nouwen, "Anton T. Boisen," op. cit., p. 51.

34. Boisen wrote to Elwood Worcester two months after he left Westboro: "In view of this experience of mine I have sometimes dared to wonder if in the old Hebrew prophets there may not have been some sort of madness in which the consciousness of national danger was the determining factor." *Inner World,* op. cit., p. 121. For other statements about Hebrew prophecy, messianic consciousness, and national danger, see pp. 75 and 138.

35. Ahlstrom, *A Religious History,* op. cit., p. 899.

36. Nouwen, "Anton T. Boisen," op. cit., pp. 58–60. Henri Nouwen discusses Boisen's use of the medical model of differential diagnosis for supervision in his unpublished manuscript "Pastoral Supervision in Historical Perspective," October 1965.

37. This agency took over the IWM survey findings. Boisen writes that he had been connected with the Institute before his illness and was encouraged by them to present his plan. *Out of the Depths,* op. cit., p. 148.

38. Ibid., p. 149.

39. This letter is quoted by Dr. Robert C. Powell in a footnote in his unpublished dissertation, "Healing and Wholeness: Helen Flanders Dunbar and an Extra-Medical Origin of the American Psychosomatic Movement," Duke University, 1974, p. 147.

40. Boisen, *Out of the Depths,* op. cit., p. 167.

41. Ibid., p. 176.

42. Ibid.

43. Quoted by Dr. Robert C. Powell in a dissertation footnote. "Healing and Wholeness," op. cit., p. 147.

44. Boisen, "The Period of Beginnings," op. cit., p. 13.

45. Boisen is called "Pappy" to this day in clinical pastoral education circles. Presidents of the ACPE hand down his cane as a venerable symbol of the office.

46. Dr. Richard C. Cabot, "A Plea for a Clinical Year in the Course of Theological Study," ch. 1 in *Adventures of the Borderline of Ethics* (New York: Harper & Bros., 1926), p. 7.

47. Ibid., p. 16.

48. Anton T. Boisen, "The Challenge to Our Seminaries," *Journal of Pastorl Care* 5:1 (Spring 1951): 8. Reprinted from *Christian Work,* January 23, 1926.

49. Ibid., p. 9.

50. Ibid.

51. Ibid., p. 10.

52. Ibid., p. 11.

53. Although the ACPE celebrates the coming of students to Worcester in 1925 as the founding of clinical pastoral education, the first clinical training of theological students was in Cincinnati, Ohio, in the summer of 1923. Students of Bexley Hall, an Episcopal seminary, lived and worked with Dr. William S. Keller. This program, called the Bexley Hall Plan, became the Graduate School of Applied Religion, and from 1938 until 1944 Joseph F. Fletcher was Dean. See Edward E. Thornton, *Professional Education for Ministry: A History of Clinical Pastoral Education* (Nashville: Abingdon Press, 1970), pp. 41–46.

54. Eastman, "Father of the Clinical Pastoral Movement," op. cit., p. 4.

55. Ibid.

56. Charles F. Hall Jr., "Some Contributions of Anton T. Boisen (1876–1965) to Understanding Psychiatry and Religion," *Pastoral Psychology* 19:185 (September 1968): 45.

57. September 1978 interview with Rosamond Grant Fisher, personal secretary to Dr. Dunbar, 1925–43.

58. Hall, "Some Contributions," op. cit., p. 46. Perhaps it was necessary for both the Emmanuel and the Clinical Pastoral Education Movements to have begun in Boston considering Freud's comment, "I understand that all important intellectual movements in America have originated in Boston." Letter to Dr. Putnam, June 16, 1910. Nathan G. Hale Jr., *James Jackson Putnam and Psychoanalysis: Letters Between Putnam and Sigmund Freud, Ernest Jones, William James, Sandor Ferenczi, and Morton Prince, 1877–1917* (Cambridge, MA: Harvard University Press, 1971), p. 101.

59. Thornton, *Professional Education,* op. cit., p. 76. Used by permission of Abingdon Press.

60. Ibid., p. 79.

61. Ibid.

62. Eastman, "Father of the Clinical Pastoral Movement," op. cit., p. 6.

63. Thornton, *Professional Education,* op. cit., p. 54.

64. Boisen, *Inner World,* op. cit., pp. 238–49.

65. Thornton, *Professional Education,* op. cit., pp. 51–52.

66. Boisen, *Inner World,* op. cit., p. 246.

67. Ibid., p. 248.

68. Thornton, *Professional Education,* op. cit., p. 32.

69. Keller was the founder of the Bexley Hall Plan described in note 53.

70. Thornton, *Professional Education,* op. cit., p. 72.

71. Holifield, "Ethical Assumption," op. cit., p. 36.

72. Ibid., p. 44.

73. Hiltner writes: "I am less convinced than Holifield that [Cabot's] general philosophy and view of morality (which the article summarizes very well) had much influence upon the New England group." "Symposium: Clinical Pastoral Education," *Theology Today* 36:1 (April 1979): 51. *Theology Today* published Holifield's paper, "Ethical Assumption of Clinical Pastoral Education," which was commissioned by the Historical Committee of the ACPE for its May 1978 meeting in Lexington, Ken-

tucky. The Symposium, with responses by Hiltner, Rollin J. Fairbanks, and Joseph Fletcher, appeared in the same issue.

74. Boisen, *Out of the Depths,* op. cit., pp. 190–91.

75. *Lift Up Your Hearts* (Boston: Pilgrim Press, 1926).

76. Boisen wrote Frederick Kuether, Director of the Council, "It has been my policy to let the student work out his own problems except in so far as he comes to me for help." *Out of the Depths,* op. cit., p. 186.

77. Nouwen, "Anton T. Boisen," op. cit., p. 61.

78. Boisen, *Out of the Depths,* op. cit., p. 190.

79. For an elaboration of this point, see Appendix A, "A Conversation with Wayne Oates, Evangelical Liberal."

80. Boisen, *Out of the Depths,* op. cit., p. 186.

81. Ibid., p. 130.

82. Boisen, *Inner World,* op. cit., p. 103.

83. Ibid., p. 152.

84. Ibid.

85. Ernest Becker, *Revolution in Psychiatry, The New Understanding of Man* (New York: The Free Press, 1964).

86. Ibid., p. 81.

87. Even before he met Alice, Boisen associated his near psychotic episode of Easter 1898 with sexual conflict. Of his decision to study forestry he wrote, "I was also aware of the danger within, and fearful of my ability to win out in what was for me a temptation-laden situation. Since in French literature I was constantly confronted with the unassimilated sex problem, a change of occupation seemed called for." *Out of the Depths,* op. cit., p. 50.

88. E. Brooks Holifield, *A History of Pastoral Care in America, From Salvation to Self-realization* (Nashville: Abingdon Press, 1983, p. 246.

89. Becker, *Revolution in Psychiatry,* op. cit., p. 81.

90. Boisen, *Out of the Depths,* op. cit., pp. 138–39.

91. Pruyser, *A Dynamic Psychology,* op. cit., p. 292.

92. Holifield, *A History,* op. cit., p. 42.

93. Letter to Dr. Putnam, May 14, 1911, in Hale, *James Jackson Putnam,* op. cit., p. 121.

94. O. Hobart Mowrer, *The Crisis in Psychiatry and Religion* (New York: Van Nostrand Reinhold Co., 1961).

95. Ibid., p. 165. Copyright © 1961 by Litton Educational Publishing, Inc. Used by permission of Van Nostrand Reinhold Company.

96. Ibid., p. 159.

97. Ibid., p. 175.

98. Ibid., p. 70.

99. Ibid., p. 60.

100. Ibid., p. 65.

101. Ibid., p. 64.

102. Ibid., p. 66.

103. Ibid., p. 72.

104. Ibid., p. 165. Mowrer blames Calvinism for making humans helpless to effect their salvation. The Protestant Reformation, in certain respects deviant and incomplete, must go on, he says.

105. Ibid., pp. 81–102.

106. Ibid., p. 99.

107. Ibid., pp. 170–71.

108. Ibid., p. 165. Philip Rieff has made it quite plain that, "being analytical rather than remissive, the Freudian doctrine was never to be put in systematic service to either interdiction or release, under pain of ceasing to be analytic. . . . Americans, in particular, have managed to use the Freudian doctrine in ways more remissive than he intended." Mowrer makes no effort to draw clear distinctions between those who read Freud's intentions accurately and those who did not. Philip Rieff, *The Triumph of the Therapeutic, Uses of Faith After Freud* (New York: Harper & Row, Harper Torchbook, 1966), p. 238.

109. See Appendix A, "A Conversation with Wayne Oates."

110. Anton Boisen, "In Defense of Mr. Bryan, A Personal Confession by a Liberal Clergyman," *American Review* 3 (1925): 323–28.

111. Boisen, *Out of the Depths,* op. cit., p. 152.

112. Hugh Hammett, "The Historical Context of the Origins of CPE," *Journal of Pastoral Care* 2:2 (June 1975): 76.

113. Boisen, "In Defense of Mr. Bryan," op. cit., pp. 323–24.

114. Ibid., p. 324.

115. Ibid.

116. Ibid., p. 238.

117. Boisen, "The Period of Beginnings," op cit., p. 15.

118. Boisen, *Inner World,* op. cit., pp. 181–215.

119. Ibid., p. 200.

120. Boisen made an extensive survey of liberal literature (journals and books), which he found deficient in the empirical method, in his article "Cooperative Inquiry in Religion,"*Religious Education,* September–October 1945. This was reprinted in the *Journal of Pastoral Care* 5:1 (Spring 1951): 17–26.

121. Boisen, *Out of the Depths,* op. cit., pp. 209–10.

122. Boisen, "The Challenge to Our Seminaries," op. cit., p. 11.

123. Ibid.

124. Thornton, *Professional Education,* op. cit., p. 35. Thornton sug-

gests three reasons for the failure of Emmanuel: (1) its leaders did not train other ministers, (2) Worcester did not grow with the movement, and (3) doctor-clergy relationships broke down. The inadequacy of outdated psychotherapeutic methods is not mentioned.

125. Hammett, "The Historical Context," op. cit., p. 82.

126. Thornton, *Professional Education,* op. cit., p. 37.

127. Association for Clinical Pastoral Education, Inc., *ACPE News* 9:9 (September 1976): 5.


**CHAPTER 4** Flanders Dunbar and the Joint Committee on Religion and Medicine

1. Flanders Dunbar, "Medicine, Religion, and the Infirmities of Mankind," *Mental Hygiene* 18 (January 1934): 24.

2. Robert Charles Powell's unpublished Ph.D. dissertation, "Healing and Wholeness: Helen Flanders Dunbar (1902–59) and an Extra-Medical Origin of the American Psychosomatic Movement," Duke University, 1974, covers in detail Dunbar's life and thought until 1939. Another source of information about Dunbar is Edward E. Thornton's *Professional Education for Ministry, A History of Clinical Pastoral Education* (Nashville: Abingdon Press, 1970). See also my article "Helen Flanders Dunbar," in *Notable American Women, The Modern Period, A Biographical Dictionary* (Cambridge, MA: Harvard University Press, Belknap Press, 1980), pp. 210–12.

3. Powell, "Healing and Wholeness," op. cit., p. 91.

4. Anton Boisen, *Out of the Depths, An Autobiographical Study of Mental Disorder and Religious Experience* (New York: Harper & Row, 1960), p. 154. Copyright © 1960 by Anton T. Boisen. Used by permission of Harper & Row, Publishers, Inc.

5. George Soule Jr. (unsigned), "In Memoriam," *Psychosomatic Medicine,* October 1959, p. 350.

6. Powell, "Healing and Wholeness," op. cit., p. 95.; Thornton, *Professional Education,* op. cit., p. 77.

7. Boisen, *Out of the Depths,* op. cit., p. 160.

8. Ibid.

9. Powell, "Healing and Wholeness," op. cit., p. 100.

10. Interview with Rosamond Grant Fisher, September 1978.

11. Powell, "Healing and Wholeness," op. cit., p. 102, footnote #1.

12. Personal letter to the author from Dr. Helene Deutsch on September 14, 1978.

13. Personal letter to Dr. Robert Powell from Dr. Helene Deutsch, September 17, 1969, courtesy of Dr. Powell, Arlington Heights, IL.

14. Felix Deutsch, "The Riddle of the Mind-Body Correlations," in *On the Mysterious Leap from the Mind to the Body,* ed. Felix Deutsch (New York: International Universities Press, 1959), p. 8.

15. A personal interview with Rosamond Grant Fisher established that Dunbar moved to Zurich. That Grant accompanied Dunbar to Europe was information they kept secret because Grant's parents would not have approved of the trip.

16. Powell, "Healing and Wholeness," op. cit., pp. 102, 104.

17. Thornton, *Professional Education,* op. cit., p. 77.

18. Powell, "Healing and Wholeness," op. cit., p. 201.

19. Ibid., p. 195.

20. Ibid., p. 201.

21. Boisen, *Out of the Depths,* op. cit., p. 164.

22. Ibid., p. 165.

23. Ibid., p. 169.

24. Powell, "Healing and Wholeness," op. cit., p. 210.

25. Boisen, *Out of the Depths,* op. cit., p. 170.

26. Powell, "Healing and Wholeness," op. cit., pp. 210, 212.

27. Boisen, *Out of the Depths,* op. cit., p. 169.

28. Ibid., p. 171.

29. Ibid., p. 170.

30. Soule, "In Memoriam," op. cit., p. 352.

31. Taken from the Association for Clinical Pastoral Education's Historical Archives (File A, Drawer 1), now deposited in the Yale Divinity School Library.

32. "Anson Phelps Stokes," *Dictionary of American Biography,* vol. 9 (New York: Charles Scribner's Sons, n.d.), pp. 66–67; "Olivia Egleston Phelps Stokes," ibid., p. 68; "Rose Harriet Pastor Stokes," ibid., pp. 68–69; "Isaac Newton Phelps Stokes," *Who Was Who in America,* vol. 2, 1943–50 (Chicago: A. Marquis Co., 1950), p. 513. Despite the many points at which my life and the life of the Stokes family touch, there is no family relationship.

33. "John Sherman Hoyt," *The National Cyclopaedia of American Biography,* vol. 53, p. 19.

34. Robert Powell first called attention to Ethel Hoyt's role in the CPE Fiftieth Anniversary issue of *Journal of Pastoral Care* 29:2 (June 1975): 99–105. See "Mrs. Ethel Phelps Stokes Hoyt and the Joint Committee on Religion and Medicine: A Brief Sketch."

35. In Ethel Phelps Stokes Hoyt, *Spirit* (New York: E.P. Dutton, 1921).

36. ACPE Archives, op. cit.

37. Ibid.

38. Ibid.

39. "Frederick Peterson," *The National Cyclopaedia of American Biography,* vol. 47, op. cit., pp. 30–32.

40. Nathan G. Hale Jr. *Freud and the Americans, The Beginnings of Psychoanalysis in the United States, 1876–1917* (New York: Oxford University Press, 1971), p. 231.

41. Ibid., p. 451.

42. Raymond Cunningham, "Ministry of Healing: The Origins of the Psychotherapeutic Role of the American Churches, Ph.D. diss., The Johns Hopkins University, 1965, p. 232.

43. Ibid., p. 233.

44. ACPE Archives, op. cit.

45. Ibid.

46. Ibid.

47. Ibid.

48. Elwood Worcester, *Life's Adventure, The Story of a Varied Career* (New York: Charles Scribner's Sons, 1932), p. 345. Copyright 1932 Charles Scribner's Sons; copyright renewed. Reprinted with the permission of Charles Scribner's Sons.

49. "Frederick Peterson," op. cit., p. 31.

50. Powell, "Healing and Wholeness," op. cit., p. 116.

51. Cunningham, "Ministry of Healing," op. cit., p. 235.

52. ACPE Archives, op. cit.

53. Powell, "Healing and Wholeness," op. cit., p. 107.

54. Ibid., p. 108.

55. Ibid., p. 109.

56. "Kate Everit Macy Ladd," *The National Cyclopaedia of American Biography,* vol. 32, op. cit., p. 48.

57. Quotation from Dr. Dunbar's daughter, Marcia Dunbar-Soule, Stokes, "Helen Flanders Dunbar," op. cit., p. 211.

58. Quotation from Irma Waterhouse Hewlett, who began psychoanalysis with Dunbar in 1934 and was a research secretary for the American Psychosomatic Society founded by Dunbar. From interview notes by Dr. Robert Powell, April 18, 1973.

59. Flanders Dunbar, *Emotion and Bodily Changes: A Survey of the Literature on Psychosomatic Interrelationships* (New York: Columbia University Press, 1935), p. xi.

60. Flanders Dunbar, "What Happens at Lourdes? Psychic Forces in Health and Disease," *The Forum Magazine* 91 (April 1934): 231.

61. For more information about Wolfe, see Gladys Meyer Wolfe, "America's First Orgonomist," *Journal of Orgonomy* 4:19–30.

62. Powell, "Healing and Wholeness," op. cit., pp. 237–38.

63. Thornton, *Professional Education,* op. cit., p. 92.

64. "In Memoriam," *American Journal of Psychiatry,* volume 117 (1960), p. 189.

65. *Time,* October 6, 1947.

66. *New York Times,* October 26, 1947, VII, p. 38.

CHAPTER 5   Norman Vincent Peale, Smiley Blanton, and the
Religio-Psychiatric Clinic

1. Norman Vincent Peale, *The Power of Positive Thinking* (Englewood Cliffs, N.J.: Prentice-Hall, 1956), p. 186.

2. Smiley Blanton, "Where Do You Take Your Troubles?" *The American Magazine* 147 (March 1949): 137.

3. Arthur Gordon, *Norman Vincent Peale, Minister to Millions* (Englewood Cliffs, NJ: Prentice-Hall, 1958), p. 155.

4. Norman Vincent Peale, op. cit., p. 177.

5. Gordon, *Norman Vincent Peale,* op. cit., p. 178. See also Peale's own account of this meeting and the partnership in *The True Joy of Positive Living, An Autobiography* (New York: William Morrow & Co., 1984), pp. 228–30.

6. Smiley Blanton, "A Pioneering Partnership: The American Foundation of Religion and Psychiatry." Paper prepared for the first International Congress of Social Psychiatry, London, 1964, p. 1.

7. Gordon, *Norman Vincent Peale,* op. cit., p. 5.

8. "Blow the Trumpets! An Appreciation of 50 Years of the Ministry of Dr. and Mrs. Norman Vincent Peale," *Creative Help for Daily Living,* Foundation for Christian Living, 33:5 (June 1982): 23.

9. Gordon, *Norman Vincent Peale,* op. cit., p. 138.

10. "Norman Vincent Peale," *Current Biography 1946,* p. 472.

11. Gordon, *Norman Vincent Peale,* op. cit., p. 161.

12. Margaret Gray Blanton, "Biographical Notes and Comments," in Smiley Blanton, *Diary of My Analysis with Sigmund Freud* (New York: Hawthorn Books, 1971), p. 123. Copyright © 1971 by Margaret Gray Blanton. A Hawthorn Book. Reprinted by permission of E.P. Dutton, Inc.

13. Ibid., p. 128.

14. Margaret Gray Blanton, Preface, in S. Blanton, *Diary,* op. cit., p. 27.

15. Explanatory footnote in S. Blanton, *Diary,* op. cit., p. 49.

16. Ibid., p. 129.

17. Ibid., p. 131.

18. Smiley Blanton and Norman Vincent Peale, *Faith Is the Answer* (Nashville: Abingdon-Cokesbury Press, 1940), p. 17.

19. Ibid., p. 209.

20. Smiley Blanton, *Love or Perish* (New York: Simon & Schuster, 1956), pp. 4–5.

21. Donald Meyer, *The Positive Thinkers, Religion as Pop Psychology from Mary Baker Eddy to Oral Roberts* (New York: Pantheon Books, 1980), p. 277.

22. Ibid., p. 273.

23. Ibid., p. 277.

24. Blanton and Peale, *Faith Is the Answer,* op. cit., p. 25.

25. Ibid., p. 209. Blanton quotes from Hebrews 11:1.

26. S. Blanton, *Diary,* op. cit., p. 97.

27. Ibid., p. 84.

28. Ibid., p. 86.

29. Blanton and Peale, *Faith Is the Answer,* op. cit., p. 12.

30. Margaret Gray Blanton, *Bernadette of Lourdes* (New York: Longmans, Green, 1939), p. 242. This biography was republished in 1962 by Prentice-Hall under the title *The Miracle of Lourdes.*

31. S. Blanton, *Diary,* op. cit., p. 122.

32. Ibid., p. 128.

33. S. Blanton, "A Pioneering Partnership," op. cit., p. 2.

34. "Dr. Norman Vincent Peale Still an Apostle of Cheer," *New York Times,* January 2, 1978, p. 38.

35. Samuel K. Klausner, "How the Clinic Came to Be," in *Psychiatry and Religion, A Sociological Study of the New Alliance of Ministers and Psychiatrists* (Glencoe, IL: Free Press of Glencoe, 1964), p. 199.

36. S. Blanton, *Diary,* op. cit., p. 104.

37. Norman Vincent Peale, *A Guide to Confident Living* (New York: Prentice-Hall, 1948).

38. S. Blanton, *Diary,* op. cit., p. 104.

39. "Clinic of the Soul," *Newsweek,* March 15, 1948, p. 74.

40. "Are You Looking for God?" *The American Magazine,* October 1947, p. 138.

41. "Where Do You Take Your Troubles?" *The American Magazine,* March 1949, p. 138.

42. S. Blanton, "A Pioneering Partnership," op. cit., p. 3.

43. Ibid.

44. Peale, *The Power of Positive Thinking,* op. cit., p. 187.

45. Meyer, *The Positive Thinkers,* op. cit., p. 274.

46. Ibid., p. 269.

47. S. Blanton, *Diary,* op. cit., p. 109.

48. Meyer, *The Positive Thinkers,* op. cit., p. 287.

49. Peale, *The Power of Positive Thinking,* op. cit., p. 172.

50. Ibid., p. 268.

51. S. Blanton, *Love or Perish,* op. cit., pp. 9–10.

52. "Are You Looking for God?" op. cit., p. 21.

CHAPTER 6:   Seward Hiltner, Paul Tillich, and the New York
Psychology Group

1. Paul Tillich, "Heal the Sick; Cast Out Demons," p. 7.

2. Seward Hiltner, "Pastoral Theology and Psychology," in Arnold S.
Nash, ed., *Protestant Thought in the Twentieth Century, Whence and
Whither?* (New York: Macmillan Co., 1951), p. 198.

3. Hannah Tillich, *From Time to Time* (New York: Stein and Day,
1973). Rollo May, *Paulus: Reminiscences of a Friendship* (New York:
Harper & Row, 1973).

4. Wilhelm and Marion Pauck, *Paul Tillich: His Life and Thought,*
Vol. 1, *Life* (New York: Harper & Row, 1976), p. 320.

5. Seward Hiltner, "Tillich the Person: A Review Article," *Theology
Today* 30 (January 1974): 383.

6. David M. Moss III, "The Early Pastoral Psychology Movement: An
Interview with Seward Hiltner," *Pilgrimage* 6:2 (Summer 1978): 93.

7. Records of the National Council for Religion in Higher Education
facilitated my study of the role of the Council and the eighteen Kent
Fellows who joined the NYPG.

8. Interview with the Rev. Dr. Seward Hiltner at a meeting of the
Association for Clinical Pastoral Education Historical Committee in
Lexington, Kentucky, on May 12, 1978. I first learned of the NYPG at
this meeting when Dr. Robert C. Powell conducted a videotape interview
of Dr. Hiltner for the ACPE Archives.

9. Interview with Rollo May in Holderness, New Hampshire, on July
30, 1979. I am grateful to Dr. May for his generous hospitality—for
memories he shared, questions he raised, suggestions he made.

10. Kenneth C. Haugk and Barry A. Hong, "Pastoral Care and Counseling: A Survey of Recommended Readings," *Journal of Religion and
Health* 14:1 (January 1975): 58–62. (Eighty-nine schools responded to the
inquiry.)

11. National Council on Religion in Higher Education, *Report of the
Sixteenth Week of Work,* August 27–September 3, 1941.

12. "Memo Re: Plans for the Group, 1942–43, discussed at the first
meeting, October 2, 1942," signed by Martha H. Biehle, Secretary. Taken
from the NCRHE records.

13. For Seward Hiltner's self-assessment of his life's work and its
reception, see "A Descriptive Appraisal, 1935–1980," *Theology Today*
37:2 (July 1980): 210–20.

14. In 1945 Hiltner edited a volume on *Clinical Pastoral Training* that was published by the Commission on Religion and Health of the Federal Council of Churches.

15. Hiltner, "Tillich the Person," op. cit., p. 384.

16. Paul Tillich, "The Relationship of Religion and Health: Historical Considerations and Theoretical Questions," *The Review of Religion* 10:4 (May 1946): 348–84.

17. For a partial list see "Bibliography of Seward Hiltner," *Pastoral Psychology,* January 1968, pp. 6–22. Hiltner was pastoral consultant to *Pastoral Psychology* magazine from 1950 to 1969.

18. Seward Hiltner, "Freud for the Pastor," *Pastoral Psychology,* January 1955, pp. 41–57.

19. Ibid., p. 46.

20. Rollo May interview, op. cit.

21. *New York Times,* Obituary, October 23, 1965, p. 31, col. 1. See also *Current Biography* (New York: H.W. Wilson Co., 1954), pp. 608–10.

22. Earl A. Loomis Jr., "The Psychiatric Legacy of Paul Tillich," in *The Intellectual Legacy of Paul Tillich,* ed. James R. Lyons (Detroit: Wayne State University Press, 1969), p. 82.

23. Recollections of Robert C. Johnson, Professor of Theology, Yale Divinity School, January 1980. See also Wilhelm Pauck's eulogy, "The Sources of Paul Tillich's Richness," *Union Seminary Quarterly Review,* 21:1 (November 1965): 8.

24. Interview with Hannah Tillich, July 18, 1979. She graciously received me as a guest during a two-day stay with her in Montauk, Long Island, New York.

25. "Author's Introduction," *The Protestant Era* (abridged), trans. James Luther Adams (Chicago: University of Chicago Press, 1948), p. vi.

26. *New York Times,* Obituary, March 19, 1980, p. B11. See also *Current Biography* (New York: H.W. Wilson Co., 1967), pp. 129–31.

27. Erich Fromm, *Escape from Freedom* (New York: Holt, Rinehart and Winston, 1941), p. viii.

28. Rollo May interview, op. cit., 7/30/79. For biographical information about Fromm, see the *New York Times,* Obituary, op. cit., and *Current Biography,* 1967, op. cit.

29. Interview with Helen Nichol Fernald in York, Maine, on May 15, 1979.

30. Rollo May interview, op. cit.

31. "Gotthard Booth, M.D., The Man of the Month," *Pastoral Psychology,* June 1962, p. 65. (For additional biographical information see the *New York Times,* Obituary, November 17, 1975, p. 34.)

32. Ibid., p. 66.

33. For information write the Gotthard Booth Society for Holistic Health, P.O. Box 736, Waterloo, Ontario, Canada.

34. "Elined Prys Kotschnig," *Who's Who of American Women,* vol. 7 (1972–73), p. 494.

35. Walter Kotschnig and Elined Prys, eds., *The University in a Changing World, A Symposium* (London: Oxford University Press, 1932).

36. Laura Fermi, *Illustrious Immigrants, the Intellectual Migration from Europe 1930–1941,* 2d ed. (Chicago: University of Chicago Press, 1971), p. 71. See also Stephen Duggan and Betty Drury, *The Rescue of Science and Learning* (New York: Viking Press, 1952), p. 185.

37. Personal letter from Elined Kotschnig in Washington, DC on May 23, 1979. Kotschnig died 6/23/85 (*New York Times* obit. 6/25/85).

38. Personal letter from Teresina Havens in Shutesbury, Massachusetts on May 7, 1979. She is married to Dr. Joseph Havens, a clinical psychologist who edited *Psychology and Religion: A Contemporary Dialogue* (New York: Van Nostrand, 1968). She and I discussed historical efforts to integrate psychology and religion at a New England regional meeting of the American Academy of Religion in Hartford, Connecticut, in April 1977.

39. All biographical information is taken from interviews with Dr. de Laszlo at the Stanhope Hotel in New York City on June 13 and July 4, 1979.

40. Violet de Laszlo, ed., *Psyche and Symbol, A Selection from the Writings of C.G. Jung,* (New York: Doubleday, Anchor Books, 1958) and Violet de Laszlo, ed., *The Basic Writings of C.G. Jung* (New York: Modern Library, 1959).

41. "Greta Frankley Gerstenberg," *Biographical Dictionary of the American Psychiatric Association,* 1958, 1963, 1973.

42. Telephone interview on March 18, 1985, with Theodore Farris, Tillich's son-in-law, who remembers Greta Frankley as an intimate friend of the family whom they often consulted.

43. *New York Times,* Obituary, November 30, 1975, p. 73.

44. Ernst Schachtel, *Experimental Foundations of Rorschach's Test* (New York: Basic Books, 1966).

45. Rollo May interview, op. cit., 7/30/79.

46. *New York Times,* Obituary, March 4, 1943.

47. Donald Fleming, "Ruth Fulton Benedict," in *Notable American Women, 1607–1950, A Biographical Dictionary,* vol. 1, ed. Edward T. James (Cambridge, MA: Harvard University Press, Belknap Press), p. 130. See also *New York Times,* Obituary, September 18, 1948, p. 17.

48. Daniel Johnson Fleming became a Professor of Missions at Union Theological Seminary in 1918, where he taught for thirty-four years. Author of numerous books on missions, Fleming served as consultant on India with the State Department during World War II.

49. "Dr. Edward McClung Fleming Is Named Academic Dean," *Park College Record,* Parkville, Missouri, June 1947.

50. Howard Kirschenbaum, *On Becoming Carl Rogers* (New York: Delacorte Press, 1979), pp. 149–52.

51. Personal letter from Dr. Carl Rogers in La Jolla, California, on April 23, 1979.

52. *A Counseling Viewpoint* (New York: Commission on Religion and Health, Federal Council of the Churches of Christ in America, May 1945), p. 3.

53. John C. Burnham, "The Influence of Psychoanalysis Upon American Culture," in *American Psychoanalysis: Origins and Development,* ed. Jacques M. Quen and Eric T. Carlson (New York: Brunner/Mazel Pub., 1978), p. 63.

54. *New York Times,* Obituary, July 9, 1960, p. 19.

55. Rollo May interview, op. cit.

56. *New York Times,* Obituary, May 1, 1971, p. 36.

57. National Council on Religion in Higher Education files.

58. Helen Nichol Fernald interview, op. cit., 5/15/79.

59. Henry Burton Sharman (1865–1953) earned his Ph.D. at the University of Chicago in New Testament. His thesis, "The Teachings of Jesus About the Future," was published in 1909. Other works include *Records of the Life of Jesus* (1917, 1937) and *Jesus as Teacher* (1935).

60. *Directory of Fellows, 1978,* Society for Values in Higher Education, New Haven, Connecticut, p. 86.

61. Helen Nichol Fernald interview, op. cit.

62. Martha H. Biehle, ed., *Fifty Years: 1923–1973, A Brief History of The National Council on Religion in Higher Education and the Society for Religion in Higher Education* (New Haven, CT: Society for Values in Higher Education, 1974), p. 5.

63. Letter from Martha Biehle to Dr. Cyril Richardson, May 17, 1943, National Council on Religion in Higher Education files.

64. Albert Outler, "David E. Roberts—In Memoriam," *Journal of Pastoral Care* 9:2 (Summer 1955): 65–66.

65. David E. Roberts and Henry Pitney Van Dusen, eds., *Liberal Theology* (New York: Charles Scribner's Sons, 1942).

66. David E. Roberts, *Psychotherapy and a Christian View of Man* (New York: Charles Scribner's Sons, 1950).

67. January 14, 1944, and January 12, 1945.

68. The pamphlet was published in 1943 by the Army and Navy Department of the Young Men's Christian Association and the Commission on Religion and Health of the Federal Council of the Churches of Christ in America.

69. Herbert Spiegelberg, "The American Scene: Beginnings," in *Phenomenology in Psychology and Psychiatry* (Evanston, IL: Northwestern University Press, 1972), p. 159. This chapter includes sections on both Rollo May and Carl Rogers.

70. Bone says, "The present book is one of the few but growing number of those which are exploring an area of fundamental importance, the interrelation of Christianity and mental hygiene." In Rollo May, *The Art of Counseling* (1937; Nashville: Abingdon Press, 1967), p. 17.

71. This book, subtitled "A Study of Human Nature and God," was published by the Abingdon-Cokesbury Press.

72. Rollo May, *Paulus, Reminiscences of a Friendship* (New York: Harper & Row, 1973), pp. 112–13. May's eulogy, "Paul Tillich: In Memoriam," appeared earlier in *Pastoral Psychology* 19:181 (February 1968): 7–10.

73. Paul Tillich, *My Search for Absolutes* (New York: Simon & Schuster, 1967), p. 44.

74. Rollo May, *Current Biography 1973*, op. cit., p. 283.

75. Frances G. Wickes, *The Inner World of Childhood, A Study in Analytical Psychology* (New York: D. Appleton & Co., 1930), p. xiv.

76. M. Esther Harding, "Obituary Notice, Frances G. Wickes," *Journal of Analytical Psychology,* The Society of Analytical Psychology, London, 13 (1968): 68. See also the tributes in *Frances G. Wickes, A Memorial Meeting, October 25, 1967, New York* published by the Analytical Psychology Club of New York.

77. Record of the December 3, 1942, NYPG meeting.

78. Dr. Violet de Laszlo interview, op. cit. Using Jung's typology, de Laszlo called the Freudians on the whole "extraverted," while the Jungians were "intuitive/introverted types," who were not inclined to band together.

79. Henry Sloane Coffin, *A Half Century of Union Theological Seminary, 1896–1946, An Informal History* (New York: Charles Scribner's Sons, 1954), p. 119.

80. Elliott's books included *The Why and How of Group Discussion* (1923), *The Process of Group Thinking* (1928), and *Group Discussion in Religious Education* (1946).

81. Coffin, *A Half Century,* op. cit., p. 156.

82. Kirschenbaum, *On Becoming Carl Rogers,* op. cit., p. 46.

83. Coffin, *A Half Century,* op. cit., p. 157.

84. See note #22.

85. "Ethnic Diversity, Cosmopolitanism and the Emergence of the American Liberal Intelligentsia," *American Quarterly* 27:2 (May 1975): 133–51.

86. Ibid., p. 134.

87. Ibid., p. 135.

88. Ibid., p. 50.

89. Ibid., pp. 146–47.

90. Records of the meetings of the New York Psychology Group.

91. "The Influence of Psychoanalysis Upon American Culture," op. cit., p. 53.

92. Leo M. Croghan, "Psychoanalysis and the Community Mental Health Movement," *Journal of Religion and Health,* 14:1 (January 1975), p. 29.

93. Burnham, "The Influence of Psychoanalysis," op. cit., p. 58.

94. Ibid., p. 57.

95. Ibid., p. 56.

96. Ibid., p. 55.

97. Paul Tillich, "The Impact of Pastoral Psychology on Theological Thought," in *The Ministry and Mental Health,* ed. Hans Hofmann (New York: Association Press, 1960), pp. 15–16. Reprinted from *Pastoral Psychology,* February 1960.

98. Personal interview with Wayne Oates in Louisville, Kentucky, on May 12, 1979. For the Rev. Dr. Oates' observation about the significance of Freud for Christian faith, see Appendix A.

99. Porter French, "Innocents Abroad: Clinical Training in the Early Days," *Journal of Pastoral Care* 29:1 (March 1975) 9.

100. May 20, 1942.

101. Paul Tillich, *On the Boundary, An Autobiographical Sketch* (New York: Charles Scribner's Sons, 1966), p. 72.

102. Paul Tillich, "The Theological Significance of Existentialism and Psychoanalysis," in *Theory of Culture,* ed. Robert C. Kimball (New York: Oxford University Press, 1959), pp. 123–25.

103. Ibid., p. 126.

104. David E. Roberts, "Psychotherapy and the Christian Ministry," *Religion in Life* 14:2: 184–94.

105. Ibid., p. 194.

CHAPTER 7   The Religion and Health Movement

1. Heije Faber, *Pastoral Care and Clinical Training in America* (Arnhem: Van Loghum Slaterus, 1961). To use the words of F. Ernest Johnson, "Life moves faster than thought, for purpose is prior to thinking."

*The Social Gospel Re-examined* (New York: Harper & Bros., 1940), p. 24.

2. Harry Emerson Fosdick, *The Living of These Days* (New York: Harper & Bros., 1956).

3. Ibid., p. 13.

4. Ibid.

5. Ibid.

6. Joshua Loth Liebman, *Peace of Mind* (New York: Simon & Schuster, 1946), p. 6.

7. Donald Meyer, *The Positive Thinkers, Religion as Pop Psychology from Mary Baker Eddy to Oral Roberts* (New York: Pantheon Books, 1980), p. 218.

8. Ibid., p. 219.

9. Ibid., p. 228.

10. Edward E. Thornton, *Professional Education for Ministry, A History of Clinical Pastoral Education* (Nashville: Abingdon Press, 1970), p. 75.

11. For a more detailed discussion see Seward Hiltner, "Pastoral Theology and Psychology," in *Protestant Thought in the Twentieth Century,* ed. Arnold Nash (New York: Macmillan, 1951), pp. 181–99.

12. Samuel K. Klausner, *Psychiatry and Religion, A Sociological Study of the New Alliance of Ministers and Psychiatrists* (Glencoe, IL: Free Press of Glencoe, 1964), p. 25.

13. Ibid., p. 258.

14. Ibid., p. 113.

15. Ibid., p. 114.

16. Ibid.

17. Ibid., p. 118.

18. Philip Rieff, *The Triumph of the Therapeutic, Uses of Faith After Freud* (New York: Harper & Row, 1966), p. 251.

19. Johnson, *Social Gospel Re-examined,* op. cit., p. 6.

20. Karl Menninger, *Whatever Became of Sin?* (New York: Hawthorn Books, 1973).

21. Paul C. Vitz, *Psychology as Religion, The Cult of Self-worship* (Grand Rapids, MI: William B. Eerdmans Publishing Co., 1977).

22. Johnson, *Social Gospel Re-examined,* op. cit., p. 12.

23. See "Sacrificing Freud," *New York Times Magazine,* February 22, 1976, pp. 11, 70–72; *Haven in a Heartless World: The Family Besieged* (New York: Basic Books, 1977); and *The Culture of Narcissism: American Life in an Age of Diminishing Expectations* (New York: W.W. Norton, 1978).

24. Lasch, "Sacrificing Freud," op. cit., p. 11.

25. Ibid., p. 70.

26. Paul Tillich, "The Theological Significance of Existentialism and Psychoanalysis," in *Theology of Culture,* ed. Robert C. Kimball (New York: Oxford University Press, 1959), pp. 112–126.

27. Quoted in Johnson, *Social Gospel Re-examined,* op. cit., p. 25.

28. See Gerkin's thoughtful and skilled study, *The Living Human Document, Revisioning Pastoral Counseling in a Hermeneutical Mode* (Nashville: Abingdon Press, 1984).

29. Johnson, *Social Gospel Re-examined,* op. cit., p. 22.

30. William R. Hutchinson, *The Modernist Impulse in American Protestantism* (Cambridge, MA: Harvard University Press, 1976), p. 289.

31. Ibid., p. 299.

32. Ibid., p. 308.

33. Walter Marshall Horton, "A Psychological Approach to Theology—After 25 Years," in *Healing: Human and Divine,* ed. Simon Doniger (New York: Association Press, 1957), p. 101.

34. Walter Marshall Horton, *A Psychological Approach to Theology* (New York: Harper & Bros., 1931), pp. 37–38.

35. Sydney Ahlstrom, *A Religious History of the American People* (New Haven, CT: Yale University Press, 1972), p. 943.

36. Hutchinson, *The Modernist Impulse,* op. cit., p. 291.

37. Horton, "A Psychological Approach to Theology—After 25 Years," op. cit.

38. Ibid., p. 104.

39. Ibid.

40. Edward Scribner Ames, *The Psychology of Religious Experience* (Boston: Houghton Mifflin, 1910), p. 413.

41. John E. Smith, *Reason and God, Encounters of Philosophy with Religion* (New Haven, CT: Yale University Press, 1961), p. 97.

42. John E. Smith, *Experience and God* (New York: Oxford University Press, 1968), p. 36.

43. Harry Emerson Fosdick, *Christianity and Progress* (New York: Fleming H. Revell Co., 1922), p. 169.

44. Ibid., p. 295.

45. Paul Tillich, "The Impact of Pastoral Psychology on Theological Thought," in *The Ministry and Mental Health,* ed. Hans Hofmann, (New York: Association Press, 1960), p. 14.

46. For a fascinating analysis of the congruence of structure between the Puritan procedure for the preparation of the heart for salvation and the technique of psychoanalysis, see Howard M. Feinstein, "The Prepared Heart: A Comparative Study of Puritan Theology and Psychoanalysis," *American Quarterly* 22 (Summer 1970): 166–76.

47. Reinhold Niebuhr, "Human Creativity and Self-Concern in Freud's Thought," in *Freud and the Twentieth Century,* ed. Benjamin Nelson (1957; reprint, Gloucester, MA: Peter Smith, 1974), p. 272.

48. Ibid., p. 269.

49. Henri F. Ellenberger, *The Discovery of the Unconscious, The History and Evolution of Dynamic Psychiatry* (New York: Basic Books, 1970), p. 245. See esp. ch. 4, "The Background of Dynamic Psychiatry."

50. Quoted in H. Stuart Hughes, *Consciousness and Society, The Reorientation of European Social Thought, 1890–1930* (New York: Vintage Books, 1958), p. 152.

51. Ibid.

52. Rollo May, "The Origins and Significance of the Existential Movement in Psychology," in *Existence,* ed. Rollo May, Ernest Angel, and Henri F. Ellenberger (New York: Simon & Schuster, 1958), p. 33.

53. Hiltner, "Pastoral Theology and Psychology," op. cit., p. 198.

54. Rollo May discusses this phenomenon—with reference to Tillich's distinction between "technical" and "ecstatic" reason—in describing the origin of the existential psychotherapy movement. The crucial significance of this movement, he says, is its protest against the tendency to identify psychotherapy with technical reason. "It is based on the assumption that it is possible to have a science of man which does not fragmentize man and destroy his humanity at the same moment as it studies him." *Existence,* op. cit., pp. 34–36. During his professional life May's allegiance was transferred from a religious movement that unites science and theology to a secular movement that "unites science and ontology."

55. Seward Hiltner, *Religion and Health* (New York: Macmillan, 1943), p. 19.

56. Klausner, *Religion and Psychiatry,* op. cit., pp. 37–38.

57. Peter Berger has pointed out the fit between the psychological model of the unconscious and a social situation of such complexity that the individual can no longer perceive society in its totality. "The interpretation of one's own being in terms of the largely submerged Freudian iceberg is thus subjectively verified by one's ongoing experience of a society with these characteristics." "Toward a Sociological Understanding of Psychoanalysis," in *Facing Up to Modernity: Excursions in Society, Politics, and Religion* (New York: Basic Books, 1977), p. 33. Berger's considerations are, as he says, distressingly abbreviated. One wishes he had expanded his observation of psychoanalysis as a technique of rational control.

58. See John Baillie, *The Belief in Progress* (New York: Charles Scribner's Sons, 1951); Fosdick, *Christianity and Progress,* op. cit., and

Robert Nisbet, *History of the Idea of Progress* (New York: Basic Books, 1980).

59. "Why War?" Einstein and Freud, 1933, found in James Strachey, ed., *The Standard Edition of the Complete Psychological Works of Sigmund Freud,* vol. 22 (London: Hogarth Press, 1964), p. 199.

60. Ibid., p. 214.

61. Ibid., p. 215.

62. Robert Nisbet imagines that "when the identity of our century is finally fixed by historians, not faith but abandonment of faith in the idea of progress will be one of the major attributes." Nevertheless, he believes that a major religious renaissance is forming in the world. "If so, it seems highly probable that the fusion of science and religion achieved by Teilhard de Chardin, one based upon the inexorable progress of human knowledge into the very distant future—and with this progress, the progress also of man's spirit and his estate on earth—will hold a very prominent place in it." *History of the Idea of Progress* (New York: Basic Books, 1980), pp. 316–17.

63. Margaret Mead, *Twentieth Century Faith, Hope, and Survival* (New York: Harper & Row, 1972), pp. 1–2.

**CHAPTER 8.**   The Scientific Validity of Psychoanalysis and Religion and Health

1. Erich Fromm, *The Greatness and Limitations of Freud's Thought* (New York: Harper & Row, 1980), p. 11.

2. Nathan G. Hale Jr., *Freud and the Americans, the Beginnings of Psychoanalysis in the United States, 1876–1917* (New York: Oxford University Press, 1971), p. 226.

3. Freud to Putnam, March 10, 1910, in *James Jackson Putnam and Psychoanalysis,* ed. Nathan G. Hale Jr. (Cambridge, MA: Harvard University Press, 1971), p. 6.

4. Freud to Putnam, December 5, 1909, in ibid., p. 90.

5. Sidney Hook, ed., *Psychoanalysis, Scientific Method and Philosophy, A Symposium* (New York: New York University Press, 1959).

6. Thomas S. Kuhn, *The Structure of Scientific Revolutions,* 2d ed. (Chicago: University of Chicago Press, 1970), p. viii.

7. Ibid.

8. Martin L. Gross, *The Psychological Society: The Impact—and the Failure—of Psychiatry, Psychotherapy, Psychoanalysis and the Psychological Revolution* (New York: Random House, 1978).

9. Ibid., p. 202.

10. Ibid., p. 229.

11. Ibid., p. 231.

12. For a discussion of the somatic style (1870–1910) and Freud's revolutionary break with it, Hale's *Freud and the Americans,* op. cit., is invaluable.

13. Rollo May, "The Origins and Significance of the Existential Movement in Psychology" in *Existence: A New Dimension in Psychiatry and Psychology,* ed. Rollo May, Ernest Angel, and Henri 4F. Ellenberger (New York: Simon & Schuster, 1958), p. 9.

14. David Stannard, *Shrinking History, On Freud and the Failure of Psychohistory* (New York: Oxford University Press, 1980).

15. Ibid., p. 149.

16. Erich Fromm, *The Greatness and Limitations in Freud's Thoughts* (New York: Harper & Row, 1980).

17. Ibid., p. 14.

18. Ibid., p. 15.

19. Stannard, *Shrinking History,* op. cit. p. 152.

20. Subtitled *Freud, Marx, Levi-Strauss, and the Jewish Struggle with Modernity* (New York: Dell Publishing Co., 1974), pp. 96–97.

21. Smiley Blanton, *Diary of My Analysis with Sigmund Freud* (New York: Hawthorn Books, 1971), p. 43. Copyright © 1971 by Margaret Gray Blanton. A Hawthorn Book. Reprinted by permission of E.P. Dutton, Inc.

22. Jeffrey Moussaieff Masson, *The Assault on Truth, Freud's Suppression of the Seduction Theory* (New York: Farrar, Straus & Giroux, 1984), p. 189.

23. Ibid., pp. 191–92.

24. Carol Tavris, *The Hundred Year Cover-up: How Freud Betrayed Women," Ms.* magazine, March 1984, pp. 78–80.

25. *The Standard Edition of the Complete Psychological Works of Sigmund Freud,* vol. 4, trans. and ed. James Strachey (London: Hogarth Press, 1953), p. xxxii.

26. Owen J. Flanagan Jr., *The Science of the Mind* (Cambridge, MA: MIT Press, 1984), p. 75.

27. Marshall Edelson, *Hypothesis and Evidence in Psychoanalysis* (Chicago: University of Chicago Press, 1984).

28. Sidney Hook, "Science and Mythology in Psychoanalysis," in *Psychoanalysis, Scientific Method and Philosophy* (New York: New York University Press, 1959), p. 213.

29. From a personal letter from Peter Berger to the author, August 25, 1980.

30. Anatole Broyard, "Entertaining God," *New York Times,* March 17, 1984, p. 15.

31. Richard Cabot, Preface to *Honesty* (New York: Macmillan, 1938), p. iv.

32. Berger, "Toward a Sociological Understanding of Psychoanalysis," op. cit., p. 27.

33. Johnson, *Social Gospel Re-examined,* op. cit., p. 23.

34. Joshua Loth Liebman, *Peace of Mind* (1946; reprint, New York: Simon & Schuster, 1973), p. xi.

# Bibliography

**BOOKS**

Adams, James Luther, and Seward Hiltner, eds. *Pastoral Care in the Liberal Churches.* Nashville: Abingdon Press, 1970.

Ahlstrom, Sydney E. *A Religious History of the American People.* New Haven, CT: Yale University Press, 1972.

Ames, Edward Scribner. *The Psychology of Religious Experience.* Boston: Houghton Mifflin, 1910.

Analytical Psychology Club of New York. *Frances G. Wickes, A Memorial Meeting, October 25, 1967, New York.* New York: Analytical Psychology Club of New York, 1968.

Averill, Lloyd J. *American Theology in the Liberal Tradition.* Philadelphia: Westminster Press, 1967.

Baillie, John. *The Belief in Progress.* New York: Charles Scribner's Sons, 1951.

Baker, Ray Stannard. *New Ideals in Healing.* New York: Frederick A. Stokes Co., 1909.

Bannister, Robert C., Jr. *Ray Stannard Baker, The Mind and Thought of a Progressive.* New Haven, CT: Yale University Press, 1966.

Becker, Ernest. *Revolution in Psychiatry, the New Understanding of Man.* New York: The Free Press, 1964.

Berger, Peter L. *The Heretical Imperative, Contemporary Possibilities of Religious Affirmation.* New York: Doubleday, Anchor Book, 1979.

Biehle, Martha H., ed. *Fifty Years: 1923–1973, A Brief History of the National Council on Religion in Higher Education and the Society for Religion in Higher Education.* New Haven, CT: Society for Values in Higher Education, 1974.

219

Blanton, Margaret Gray. *Bernadette of Lourdes.* New York: Longmans, Green, 1939.

Blanton, Smiley. *Diary of My Analysis with Sigmund Freud.* New York: Hawthorn Books, 1971.

———. *The Healing Power of Poetry.* New York: Thomas Y. Crowell Co., 1960. Foreword by Norman Vincent Peale.

———. *Love or Perish.* New York: Simon & Schuster, 1956.

Blanton, Smiley, and Norman Vincent Peale. *Faith Is the Answer.* Nashville: Abingdon-Cokesbury Press, 1940.

Boisen, Anton T. *The Exploration of the Inner World, A Study of Mental Disorder and Religious Experience.* 1936. Reprint. Philadelphia: University of Pennsylvania Press, 1971.

———. *Out of the Depths, An Autobiographical Study of Mental Disorder and Religious Experience.* New York: Harper & Bros., 1960.

Brown, Charles Reynolds. *Faith and Health.* New York: Thomas Y. Crowell Co., 1910.

Cabot, Richard. *Honesty.* New York: Macmillan, 1938.

Cauthen, Kenneth. *The Impact of American Religious Liberalism.* New York: Harper & Row, 1962.

Clebsch, William A., and Charles R. Jaekle, eds. *Pastoral Care in Historical Perspective, An Essay with Exhibits.* 1964. Reprint. New York: Jason Aronson, 1975.

Coffin, Henry Sloane. *A Half Century of Union Theological Seminary, 1896–1945.* New York: Charles Scribner's Sons, 1954.

Cuddihy, John Murray. *The Ordeal of Civility: Freud, Marx, Levi-Strauss and the Jewish Struggle with Modernity.* New York: Dell Publishing Co., 1974.

de Laszlo, Violet S., ed. *The Basic Writings of C.G. Jung.* New York: Modern Library, 1959.

———, ed. *Psyche & Symbol, A Selection from the Writings of C.G. Jung.* New York: Doubleday, Anchor Book, 1958.

Deutsch, Felix, ed. *On the Mysterious Leap from the Mind to the Body.* New York: International Universities Press, 1959.

Doniger, Simon, ed. *Healing: Human and Divine, Man's Search for Health and Wholeness Through Science, Faith, and Prayer.* New York: Association Press, 1957.

———, ed. *Religion and Human Behavior.* New York: Association Press, 1954.

Dunbar, (Helen) Flanders. *Emotion and Bodily Changes: A Survey of the Literature on Psychosomatic Interrelationships.* New York: Columbia University Press, 1935.

———. *Mind and Body: Psychosomatic Medicine.* New York: Random House, 1947.

220

————. *Psychosomatic Diagnosis.* New York: Hoeber, 1943; revised, 1956.

————. *Symbolism in Mediaeval Thought and Its Consumation in the Divine Comedy.* New Haven, CT: Yale University Press, 1929.

————. *Your Child's Mind and Body: A Practical Guide for Parents.* New York: Random House, 1949.

————. *Your Pre-Teenager's Mind and Body.* New York: Random House, 1962.

————. *Your Teenager's Mind and Body.* New York: Random House, 1962.

Edelson, Marshall. *Hypothesis and Evidence in Psychoanalysis.* Chicago: University of Chicago Press, 1984.

Ellenberger, Henri F. *The Discovery of the Unconscious: The History and Evolution of Dynamic Psychiatry.* New York: Basic Books, 1970.

Elliott, Harrison. *The Bearing of Psychology upon Religion.* New York: Association Press, 1927.

Erikson, Erik H. *Gandhi's Truth, On the Origins of Militant Nonviolence.* New York: W.W. Norton & Co., 1969.

————. *Insight and Responsibility, Lectures on the Ethical Implications of Psychoanalytic Insight.* New York: W.W. Norton & Co., 1964.

————. *Young Man Luther, A Study in Psychoanalysis and History.* New York: W.W. Norton & Co., 1958.

Faber, Heije. *Pastoral Care and Clinical Training in America.* Arnhem: Van Loghum Slaterus, 1961.

Fermi, Laura. *Illustrious Immigrants, The Intellectual Migration from Europe 1930–1941.* 2d ed. Chicago: University of Chicago Press, 1971.

Flanagan, Owen J., Jr. *The Science of the Mind.* Cambridge, MA: MIT Press, 1984.

Fosdick, Harry Emerson. *Christianity and Progress.* New York: Fleming H. Revell Co., 1922.

————. *The Living of These Days.* New York: Harper & Bros., 1956.

Freud, Sigmund. *An Autobiographical Study,* in *The Standard Edition of the Complete Psychological Works of Sigmund Freud.* Vol. 20. Edited by James Strachey. London: Hogarth Press, 1959.

————. *The Interpretation of Dreams,* in the *Standard Edition.* Vol. 4. Edited by James Strachey. London: Hogarth Press, 1953.

————. *Introductory Lectures on Psychoanalysis,* in *The Standard Edition.* Vol. 16. Edited by James Strachey. London: Hogarth Press, 1963.

Fromm, Erich. *Escape from Freedom.* New York: Holt, Rinehart and Winston, 1941.

221

————. *The Greatness and Limitations in Freud's Thoughts*. New York: Harper & Row, 1980.

Gerkin, Charles V. *The Living Human Document, Re-Visioning Pastoral Counseling in a Hermeneutical Mode*. Nashville: Abingdon Press, 1984.

Gladden, Washington. *The Christian Pastor and the Working Church*. New York: Charles Scribner's Sons, 1898.

Gordon, Arthur. *Norman Vincent Peale, Minister to Millions*. Englewood Cliffs, NJ: Prentice-Hall, 1958.

Gross, Martin L. *The Psychological Society: The Impact—and the Failure—of Psychiatry, Psychotherapy, Psychoanalysis, and the Psychological Revolution*. New York: Random House, 1978.

Gurin, Gerald, Joseph Veroff, and Sheila Feld. *Americans View Their Mental Health*. New York: Basic Books, 1960.

Hale, Nathan G., Jr. *Freud and the Americans, the Beginnings of Psychoanalysis in the United States, 1876–1917*. New York: Oxford University Press, 1971.

————, ed. *James Jackson Putnam and Psychoanalysis: Letters Between Putnam and Sigmund Freud, Ernest Jones, Williams James, Sandor Ferenczi and Morton Prince, 1877–1917*. Cambridge, MA: Harvard University Press, 1971.

Harrell, David Edwin, Jr. *All Things Are Possible, the Healing and Charismatic Revivals in Modern America*. Bloomington, IN: Indiana University Press, 1975.

Havens, Joseph, ed. *Psychology and Religion: A Contemporary Dialogue*. Princeton, NJ: D. Van Nostrand Co., 1968.

Hiltner, Seward, ed. *Clinical Pastoral Training*. Commission on Religion and Health, Federal Council of the Churches of Christ in America, 1945.

————. *Preface to Pastoral Theology*. Nashville: Abingdon Press, 1958.

Hoffman, Hans, ed. *The Ministry and Mental Health*. New York: Association Press, 1960.

Holifield, E. Brooks. *A History of Pastoral Care in America: From Salvation to Self-Realization*. Nashville: Abingdon Press, 1983.

Homans, Peter. *Theology After Freud*. New York: Bobbs-Merrill Co., 1970.

Hook, Sidney, ed. *Psychoanalysis, Scientific Method and Philosophy, A Symposium*. New York: New York University Press, 1959.

Horton, Walter Marshall. *A Psychological Approach to Theology*. New York: Harper & Bros., 1931.

Hoyt, Ethel Phelps Stokes. *Spirit*. New York: E.P. Dutton & Co., 1921.

Hughes, H. Stuart. *Consciousness and Society, The Reorientation of*

*European Social Thought, 1890–1930*. New York: Vintage Books, 1958.

Hutchinson, William R., ed. *American Protestant Thought: The Liberal Era*. New York: Harper & Row, 1968.

———. *The Modernist Impulse in American Protestantism*. Cambridge, MA: Harvard University Press, 1976.

Johnson, F. Ernest. *The Social Gospel Re-examined*. New York: Harper & Bros., 1940.

Kegley, Charles W., ed. *The Theology of Paul Tillich*. New York: The Pilgrim Press, 1982.

Kemp, Charles F. *Physicians of the Soul, A History of Pastoral Counseling*. New York: Macmillan, 1947.

Kirschenbaum, Howard. *On Becoming Carl Rogers*. New York: Delacorte Press, 1979.

Klausner, Samuel K. *Psychiatry and Religion, A Sociological Study of the New Alliance of Ministers and Psychiatrists*. Glencoe, IL: Free Press of Glencoe, 1964.

Kotschnig, Walter, and Elined Prys, eds. *The University in a Changing World, A Symposium*. London: Oxford University Press, 1932.

Kuhn, Thomas S. *The Structure of Scientific Revolutions*. Chicago: University of Chicago Press, 1970.

Lasch, Christopher. *The Culture of Narcissism: American Life in an Era of Diminishing Expectation*. New York: W.W. Norton & Co., 1978.

———. *Haven in a Heartless World: The Family Besieged*. New York: Basic Books, 1977.

Liebman, Joshua Loth. *Peace of Mind*. 1946. Reprint. New York: Simon & Schuster, 1973.

McNeill, John T. *A History of the Cure of Souls*. 1951. Reprint. New York: Harper & Row, 1977.

Masson, Jeffrey Moussaieff. *The Assault on Truth, Freud's Suppression of the Seduction Theory*. New York: Farrar, Straus & Giroux, 1984.

Maves, Paul B., ed. *The Church and Mental Health*. New York: Charles Scribner's Sons, 1953.

May, Rollo, *The Art of Counseling*. 1939. Reprint. Nashville: Abingdon Press, 1967.

———.*The Ministry of Counseling*. Army and Navy Department: 1943.

———. *Paulus, Reminiscences of a Friendship*. New York: Harper & Row, 1973.

———. *The Springs of Creative Living, A Study of Human Nature and God*. Nashville: Abingdon-Cokesbury Press, 1940.

Mead, Margaret. *Twentieth Century Faith, Hope and Survival*. New York: Harper & Row, 1972.

223

Meng, Heinrich, and Ernst L. Freud, eds. *Psychoanalysis and Faith, the Letters of Sigmund Freud and Oskar Pfister.* New York: Basic Books, 1963.

Menninger, Karl. *Whatever Became of Sin?* New York: Hawthorn Books, 1973.

Meyer, Donald. *The Positive Thinkers, A Study of the American Quest for Health, Wealth and Personal Power from Mary Baker Eddy to Norman Vincent Peale.* New York: Doubleday, 1965.

————. *The Positive Thinkers, Religion as Pop Psychology from Mary Baker Eddy to Oral Roberts.* Reissue with a new preface and conclusion. New York: Pantheon Books, 1980.

Mowrer, O. Hobart. *The Crisis in Psychiatry and Religion.* New York: Van Nostrand Reinhold Co., 1961.

National Council on Religion in Higher Education. *Report of the Sixteenth Week of Work, August 27–September 3, 1941.*

Niebuhr, H. Richard, Daniel Day Williams, and James M. Gustafson. *The Advancement of Theological Education.* New York: Harper & Bros., 1957.

Nisbet, Robert. *History of the Idea of Progress.* New York: Basic Books, 1980.

Obendendorf, Clarence. *A History of Psychoanalysis in America.* 1953. Reprint. New York: Harper Torchbooks, 1964.

Outler, Albert. *Psychotherapy and the Christian Message.* New York: Harper & Bros., 1954.

Parker, Gail Thain. *Mind Cure in New England, From the Civil War to World War I.* Hanover, NH: University Press of New England, 1973.

Parker, W.B., ed. *Psychotherapy, A Course of Reading in Sound Psychology, Sound Medicine, and Sound Religion.* Vols. 1 and 2. New York: Center Publishing Co., 1908–09.

Pauck, Wilhelm, and Marion Pauck. *Paul Tillich, His Life and Thought.* Vol. 1. *Life.* New York: Harper & Row, 1976.

Peale, Norman Vincent. *A Guide to Confident Living.* (New York: Prentice-Hall, 1948.

————. *The Power of Positive Thinking.* Englewood Cliffs, NJ: Prentice-Hall, 1952.

————. *The True Joy of Positive Living, An Autobiography.* New York: William Morrow & Co., 1984.

The President's Commission on Mental Health. *Report to the President.* Vol. 1. Washington, DC: U.S. Government Printing Office, 1978.

Pruyser, Paul W. *A Dynamic Psychology of Religion.* 1968. Reprint. New York: Harper & Row, 1976.

Puner, Helen Walker. *Freud, His Life and His Mind.* 1947. Reprint. New York: Charter Books, 1978.

Rieff, Philip. *The Triumph of the Therapeutic, Uses of Faith After Freud.* New York: Harper & Row, 1966.

Roberts, David E. *Psychotherapy and a Christian View of Man.* New York: Charles Scribner's Sons, 1950.

Roberts, David E., and Henry Pitney Van Dusen, eds. *Liberal Theology.* New York: Charles Scribner's Sons, 1942.

Robeson, Harriet. *Emmanuel Church in the City of Boston, 1860–1960. The First One Hundred Years.* Published by the Vestry, 1960.

Rogers, Carl R. *A Counseling Viewpoint.* New York: Commission on Religion and Health, Federal Council of the Churches of Christ in America, May 1975.

Schachtel, Ernst. *Experimental Foundations of Rorschach's Test.* New York: Basic Books, 1966.

Schneider, Herbert Wallace. *Religion in 20th Century America.* Rev. ed. New York: Atheneum, 1964; Cambridge, MA: Harvard University Press, 1952.

Schurzer, Carl J. *The Church and Healing.* Philadelphia: Westminster Press, 1950.

Seeley, John. *The Americanization of the Unconscious.* New York: International Science Press, 1967.

Semonche, John E. *Ray Stannard Baker, A Quest for Democracy in Modern America, 1870–1918.* Chapel Hill, NC: University of North Carolina Press, 1969.

(Sharman, Henry Burton.) *This One Thing, A Tribute of Henry Burton Sharman.* Toronto: Student Christian Movement of Canada, 1959.

Smith, John E. *Experience and God.* New York: Oxford University Press, 1968.

———. *Reason and God, Encounters of Philosophy with Religion.* New Haven, CT: Yale University Press, 1961.

Society for Values in Higher Education. *Directory of Fellows, 1978.* New Haven, CT: Society for Values in Higher Education, 1978.

Stannard, David. *Shrinking History, On Freud and the Failure of Psychohistory.* New York: Oxford University Press, 1980.

Stapleton, Ruth Carter. *The Gift of Inner Healing.* Waco, TX: Word Books, 1977.

Thornton, Edward E. *Professional Education for Ministry, A History of Clinical Pastoral Education.* Nashville: Abingdon Press, 1970.

Tillich, Hannah. *From Time to Time.* New York: Stein and Day, 1973.

Tillich, Paul. *The Courage to Be.* New Haven, CT: Yale University Press, 1952.

———. *My Search for Absolutes.* New York: Simon & Schuster, 1967.

———. *On the Boundary, An Autobiographical Sketch.* New York: Charles Scribner's Sons, 1966.

————. *The Protestant Era,* abridged. Trans. by James Luther Adams. Chicago: University of Chicago Press, 1948.

————. *The Religious Situation.* Trans. by H. Richard Niebuhr. New York: Henry Holt and Co., 1932.

————. *Systematic Theology.* Vol. 2. Chicago: University of Chicago Press, 1957.

————. *Theology of Culture.* Edited by Robert C. Kimball. New York: Oxford University Press, 1959.

Vitz, Paul C. *Psychology as Religion, The Cult of Self-worship.* Grand Rapids, MI: William B. Eerdmans Publishing Co., 1977.

White, Andrew Dickson. *A History of the Warfare of Science with Theology in Christendom,* abridged. Notes, preface, and epilogue by Bruce Mazlish. New York: The Free Press, 1965.

Wickes, Frances G. *The Inner World of Childhood, A Study in Analytical Psychology.* Introduced by Carl G. Jung. New York: D. Appleton & Co., 1930.

Worcester, Elwood. *Life's Adventure, the Story of a Varied Career.* New York: Charles Scribner's Sons, 1932.

Worcester, Elwood, and Samuel McComb. *Body, Mind and Spirit.* Boston: Marshall Jones Co., 1931.

Worcester, Elwood, Samuel McComb, and Isador H. Coriat. *Religion and Medicine, The Moral Control of Nervous Disorders.* New York: Moffat, Yard & Co., 1908.

### ARTICLES

Ahlstrom, Sydney E. "Mary Baker Eddy." In *Notable American Women, 1607–1950, A Biographical Dictionary.* Edited by Edward T. James. Cambridge: Harvard University Press, 1971, pp. 551–61.

Alexander, Franz. "In Memoriam: Flanders Dunbar, 1902–1959." *American Journal of Psychiatry* 117 (1960): 189–90.

Association for Clinical Pastoral Education, Inc. *ACPE News* 9:9 (September 1976): 5.

Berger, Peter. "Toward a Sociological Understanding of Psychoanalysis." In *Facing Up to Modernity: Excursions in Society, Politics, and Religion.* New York: Basic Books, 1977, pp. 23–42.

Bigham, Thomas J., Jr. "Gotthard Booth, M.D., The Man of the Month." *Pastoral Psychology,* June 1962, pp. 6, 65–66.

Blanton, Smiley. "A Pioneering Partnership: The American Foundation of Religion and Psychiatry." Paper prepared for the first International Congress of Social Psychiatry, London, 1964.

————. "Where Do You Take Your Troubles?" *The American Magazine* 147 (March 1949): 30 to end.

Boisen, Anton T. "The Challenge to Our Seminaries." *Journal of Pastoral Care* 5:1 (Spring 1951): 8–12.

———. "Cooperative Inquiry in Religion." *Journal of Pastoral Care* 5:1 (Spring 1951): 8–12.

———. "In Defense of Mr Bryan, A Personal Confession by a Liberal Clergyman." *American Review* 3 (1925): 323–28.

———. "The Period of Beginnings." *Journal of Pastoral Care* 5:1 (Spring 1951): 13–16.

———. "Pioneer of Pastoral Psychology [George Albert Coe]." *Pastoral Psychology* 3:27 (October 1952): 8, 64–66.

Broyard, Anatole. "Entertaining God." *New York Times,* March 17, 1984, p. 15.

Burnham, John C. "The Influence of Psychoanalysis upon American Culture." In *American Psychoanalysis: Origins and Development.* Edited by Jacques M. Quen and Eric T. Carlson. New York: Brunner/Mazel, Pub., 1978, pp. 52–72.

———. "Psychiatry, Psychology and the Progressive Movement." *American Quarterly* 12 (1960): 457–65.

Cabot, Richard C. "A Plea for a Clinical Year in the Course of Theological Study." Ch. 1 in *Adventures on the Borderlands of Ethics.* New York: Harper & Row, 1926, pp. 1–22.

Clebsch, William A. "American Religion and the Cure of Souls." In *Religion and America.* Edited by William G. McLoughlin and Robert N. Bellah. Boston: Beacon Press, 1968, pp. 249–65.

Croghan, Leo M. "Psychoanalysis and the Community Mental Health Movement." *Journal of Religion and Health* 14:1 (January 1975): 28–39.

Cunningham, Raymond J. "The Emmanuel Movement: A Variety of American Religious Experience." *American Quarterly* 14 (Spring 1962): 48–63.

———. "From Preachers of the Word to Physicians of the Soul: The Protestant Pastor in Nineteenth Century America." *Journal of Religious History* 3:4 (1964–65): 327–46.

———. "The Impact of Christian Science on the American Churches, 1880–1910." *American Historical Review* 72:3 (April 1967): 885–905.

*Current Biography* (New York: H.W. Wilson Co.):

"Erich Fromm." 1967, pp. 129–31.

"Norman Vincent Peale." 1946, pp. 472–73.

"Carl Rogers." 1962, pp. 357–59.

"Anson Phelps Stokes, Jr." 1962, pp. 406–08.

"Paul Tillich." 1954, pp. 608–10.

Cutten, George B. "The Ministry of Mental Healing." In *The Christian*

*Ministry and the Social Order.* Edited by Charles MacFarland. New Haven, CT: Yale University Press, 1909.

*Dictionary of American Biography* (New York: Charles Scribner's Sons):

"Anson Phelps Stokes." Vol. 9, pp. 66–67.

"Olivia Egleston Phelps Stokes." Vol. 9, p. 68.

"Rose Harriet Pastor Stokes." Vol. 9, pp. 68–69.

Dunbar, (Helen) Flanders. "Medicine, Religion, and the Infirmities of Mankind." *Mental Hygiene* 18 (January 1934): 16–25.

————. "What Happens at Lourdes? Psychic Forces in Health and Disease." *The Forum Magazine* 91 (April 1934): 226–31.

Eastman, Fred. "Father of the Clinical Pastoral Movement." *Journal of Pastoral Care* 5:1 (Spring 1951): 3–7.

Feinstein, Howard M. "The Prepared Heart: A Comparative Study of Puritan Theology and Psychoanalysis." *American Quarterly* 22 (Summer 1970): 166–76.

Fleming, Donald. "Ruth Fulton Benedict." In *Notable American Women, 1607–1950, A Biographical Dictionary.* Vol. 1. Edited by Edward T. James. Cambridge, MA: Harvard University Press, Belknap Press, 1971, pp. 128–31.

Fosdick, Harry Emerson. "The Minister and Psychotherapy" in *Pastoral Psychology,* vol. ii (February 1960), pp. 11–13.

"Frances G. Wickes—Obituary Notice." *Journal of Analytical Psychology,* The Society of Analytical Psychology, London. vol. 13 (1968), pp. 67–69.

French, Porter. "Innocents Abroad: Clinical Training in the Early Days." *Journal of Pastoral Care* 29:1 (March 1975): 7–10.

Freud, Sigmund. "A Religious Experience" in *The Standard Edition of the Complete Psychological Works of Sigmund Freud.* Vol. 21. Edited by James Strachey. London: Hogarth Press, 1961, pp. 167–72.

————. "Why War?" Einstein and Freud, 1933. Correspondence in *The Standard Edition.* Vol. 22. Edited by James Strachey. London: Hogarth Press, 1964, pp. 197–215.

Gaustad, Edwin S., Darlene Miller, and G. Allison Stokes. "Religion in America." *American Quarterly* 31:3 (Bibliography Issue 1979): 250–83.

"Gerstenberg, Greta Frankley." *Biographical Directory of the American Psychiatric Association,* 1973.

Greene, John Gardner. "The Emmanuel Movement 1906–1929." *New England Quarterly* 7:3 (September 1934): 494–532.

Hall, Charles E., Jr. "Some Contributions of Anton T. Boisen (1876–

1965) to Understanding Psychiatry and Religion." *Pastoral Psychology* 19:185 (September 1968): 40–48.

Hammett, Hugh B. "The Historical Context of the Origins of CPE." *Journal of Pastoral Care* 29:2 (June 1975): 76–85.

Haugk, Kenneth C., and Barry H. Hong, "Pastoral Care and Counseling: A Survey of Recommended Readings." *Journal of Religion and Health* 14:1 (January 1975): 58–62.

Hiltner, Seward. "The American Association of Pastoral Counselors: A Critique." *Pastoral Psychology* 15:143 (April 1964): 8–16.

———. "Bibliography of Seward Hiltner." *Pastoral Psychology,* January 1968, pp. 6–122.

———. "A Descriptive Appraisal, 1935–1980." *Theology Today* 37:2 (July 1980): 210–20.

———. "Freud for the Pastor." *Pastoral Psychology,* January 1955, pp. 41–57.

———. "Pastoral Theology and Psychology." In *Protestant Thought in the Twentieth Century.* Edited by Arnold Nash. New York: MacMillan, 1951, pp. 181–89.

———. "Tillich the Person: A Review Article." *Theology Today* 30 (January 1974): 382–88.

———. "Toward an Ethical Conscience." *Journal of Religion* 20:1 (January 1945): 1.

Holifield, E. Brooks. "Ethical Assumptions of Clinical Pastoral Education." *Theology Today* 36:1 (April 1979): 30–44; reprinted in *Journal of Pastoral Care* 34:1 (March 1980): 39–53.

Hollinger, David A. "Ethical Diversity, Cosmopolitanism and the Emergence of the American Liberal Intelligentsia" in *American Quarterly,* 27:2 (May 1975) 133–151.

Institutes of Religion and Health. *Institutes Reporter* 3:1 (February 1975): 1, 4; 5:5 (December 1977): 4.

Klausner, Samuel Z. "The Religio-Psychiatric Movement." *International Encyclopedia of Social Science* 12:632–38.

"Kotschnig, Elined Prys." *Who's Who of American Women.* Vol. 7, 1972–73, p. 494.

Lasch, Christopher. "Sacrificing Freud." *New York Times Magazine,* February 22, 1976, pp. 11, 70–72.

Loomis, Earl A. "The Psychiatric Legacy of Paul Tillich." In *The Intellectual Legacy of Paul Tillich.* Edited by James R. Lyons. Detroit: Wayne State University Press, 1969, pp. 81–89.

Marcus, Ruth. "Psychoanalysis Through Jesus, The Gospel According to Ruth." *The Yale Daily News Magazine,* October 5, 1978, p. 16.

May, Rollo. "The Origins and Significance of the Existential Movement in Psychology." In *Existence: A New Dimension in Psychiatry and Psychology*. Edited by Rollo May, Ernest Angel, and Henri F. Ellenberger. New York: Simon & Schuster, 1958, pp. 3–36.

———. "Paul Tillich: In Memoriam." *Pastoral Psychology* 19:181 (February 1981): 7–10.

Moss, David M. "The Early Pastoral Psychology Movement: An Interview with Seward Hiltner." *Pilgrimage* 6:2 (Summer 1978): 83–101.

*The National Cyclopaedia of American Biography*. New York: James T. White & Co.:

"John Sherman Hoyt." Vol. 53, p. 19.

"Kate Macy Ladd." Vol. 32, pp. 48–49.

"Adolf Meyer." Vol. 38, pp. 45–46.

"Frederick Peterson." Vol. 47, pp. 30–32.

"Anson Phelps Stokes." Vol. 24, pp. 109–10.

*New York Times* obituaries:

"Ruth Benedict." September 18, 1948, p. 17.

"Harry Bone." May 1, 1971, p. 36.

"Gotthard Booth." November 17, 1975, p. 34.

"Harrison Elliott." June 28, 1951, p. 25.

"Erich Fromm." March 19, 1980, p. B11.

"Martha Jaeger." December 3, 1963, p. 43.

"Otis Rice." July 9, 1960, p. 19.

"David E. Roberts." January 5, 1955.

"Major William H. Roodenberg." March 4, 1943.

"Ernest Schachtel." November 30, 1975, p. 73.

"Paul Tillich." October 23, 1965, p. 31.

"Elwood Worcester." July 20, 1940, p. 15.

Niebuhr, Reinhold. "Human Creativity and Self-concern in Freud's Thought." In *Freud and the Twentieth Century*. Edited by Benjamin Nelson. 1957. Reprint. Gloucester, MA: Peter Smith, 1974, pp. 259–76.

Nouwen, Henri J.M. "Anton T. Boisen and Theology Through Living Human Documents." *Pastoral Psychology* 19:185 (September 1968): 49–63.

Oden, Thomas C. "Recovering Lost Identity." *Journal of Pastoral Care* 34:1 (March 1980): 4–19.

Outler, Albert. "David E. Roberts—In Memoriam." *Journal of Pastoral Care* 9:2 (Summer 1955): 65–67.

*Park College Record*. "Dr. Edward McClung Fleming Is Named Academic Dean" (Parkville, Missouri), June 1947.

Pauck, Wilhelm. "The Sources of Paul Tillich's Richness." *Union Seminary Quarterly Review* 21:1 (November 1965): 3–9.

Peale, Norman Vincent, and Smiley Blanton. "Are You Looking for God?" *The American Magazine* 144 (October 1947): 21ff.

Powell, Robert C. "Mrs. Ethel Phelps Stokes Hoyt and the Joint Committee on Religion and Medicine: A Brief Sketch." *Journal of Pastoral Care* 29:2 (June 1975): 99–105.

Putnam, James Jackson. "The Service of Nervous Invalids of the Physician and of the Minister." *Harvard Theological Review* 2 (1909): 235–50.

Roberts, David E. "Psychotherapy and the Christian Ministry." *Religion in Life* 14:2 (Spring 1945): 184–94.

Sicherman, Barbara. "Isador H. Coriat: The Making of an American Psychoanalyst." In *Psychoanalysis, Psychotherapy and the New England Medical Scene, 1894–1944*. Edited by George E. Gifford. New York: Science History Publications/USA, 1978.

Slaughter, Frank. "Emotions and Disease." *New York Times,* October 26, 1947, Sec. VII, p. 38.

Soule, George Henry, Jr. "In Memoriam" (an unsigned memorial of Flanders Dunbar). *Psychosomatic Medicine* 21 (1959): 349–52.

Spiegelberg, Herbert. "The American Scene: Beginnings." In *Phenomenology in Psychology and Psychiatry.* Evanston, IL: Northwestern University Press, 1972, pp. 143–68.

Stendahl, Krister. "The Apostle Paul and the Introspective Conscience of the West." In *The Writings of St. Paul.* Edited by Wayne A. Meeks. New York: W.W. Norton & Co., 1972, pp. 422–34.

———. "Responsible Scientific Investigation and Application." In *The Nature of a Humane Society.* Edited by H. Ober Hess. Philadelphia: Fortress Press, 1976, pp. 147–61.

Stokes, G. Allison. "Bibliographies of Psychology/Religion Studies." *Religious Studies Review* 4:4 (October 1978): 273–79.

———. "Helen Flanders Dunbar." In *Notable American Women, The Modern Period, A Biographical Dictionary.* Cambridge, MA: Harvard University Press, Belknap Press, 1980, pp. 210–12.

"Stokes, Isaac Newton Phelps." *Who Was Who in America.* Vol. 2, 1943–50. Chicago: A. Marquis Co., 1950.

Tavris, Carol. "The Hundred Year Cover-up: How Freud Betrayed Women." *Ms.* magazine, March 1984, pp. 78–80.

Tillich, Paul. "The Impact of Pastoral Psychology on Theological Thought." In *The Ministry and Mental Health.* Edited by Hans Hofmann. New York: Association Press, 1960, pp. 12–20.

———. "Psychoanalysis, Existentialism, and Theology." *Pastoral Psychology,* October 1968, pp. 9–17.

———. "The Relationship of Religion and Health: Historical Consideration and Theoretical Questions." *The Review of Religion* 10:4 (May 1946): 348–84.

———. "The Theological Significance of Existentialism and Psychoanalysis." In *Theology of Culture.* Edited by Robert C. Kimball. New York: Oxford University Press, 1959, pp. 112–26.

———. "Theology and Counseling." *Journal of Pastoral Care* 10:4 (Winter 1956): 193–200.

———. "The Theology of Pastoral Care." *Pastoral Psychology* 10:97 (October 1959): 21–26.

*Time.* "Mostly in the Mind." Book review of Dunbar, *Mind and Body.* October 6, 1947.

Washburn, Henry B. "Elwood Worcester." *Dictionary of American Biography,* vol. 22, suppl. 2, pp. 735–36.

**UNPUBLISHED WORKS**

Cunningham, Raymond. "Ministry of Healing: The Origins of the Psychotherapeutic Role of the American Churches." Ph.D. diss., The Johns Hopkins University, 1965.

Hiltner, Seward. "Some Observations on the Early History of the Clinical Pastoral Training Movement, Focusing on Particular Persons." Prepared for the Menninger Foundation Archives, June 1966, revised July 1967. Not for publication. For reading only by authorized investigators.

"New York Psychology Group of the National Council on Religion in Higher Education." Record of Papers and Discussions, 1941–1945. Courtesy of Seward Hiltner.

Nouwen, Henri J.M. "Pastoral Supervision in Historical Perspective." Unpublished manuscript. October 1965.

Oates, Wayne. "The Significance of the Work of Sigmund Freud for the Christian Faith." Ph.D. diss., Southern Baptist Theological Seminary, February 1947.

Powell, Robert C. *Healing and Wholeness: Helen Flanders Dunbar (1902–1959) and An Extra-Medical Origin of the American Psychosomatic Movement, 1906–36.* Doctoral dissertation, Duke University, 1974.

# Index

Abbott, Lyman 180
Academy of Religion and Mental Health 104,
 184, 186
accident-prone personality 88–89
Adams, James Luther 187, 189, 207
Adler, Alfred xiii, 132, 176
Ahlstrom, Sydney xxi, 47–48, 154, 192, 196–
 97, 213
Alexander, Franz 88, 124
Allen, A.A. 31
Allen, Charles 6
American Association of Pastoral Counselors
 31, 185
American Association of Theological Schools
 183–84
American Association of University Women
 xxiii
American College, Salonika, Greece 132
American Episcopal Church, Nice, France
 81–82
American Foundation of Religion and
 Psychiatry 104, 106, 184, 186, 204
*American Magazine* 103, 205
American Medical Association of Vienna 73
American Neurological Association 181
American Psychoanalytic Association 181
American Psychological Association 180
American Psychosomatic Society 203
*American Review* 63
Ames, Edward Scribner 155, 213
Amherst College 181
analytical psychology 181, 210
Analytical Psychology Club of New York 133,
 210
Anderson, George Christian 184
Andover Theological Seminary 48, 182

Andover-Harvard Theological Library 110
Angel, Ernest 214, 216
Association for Clinical Pastoral Education
 xv, 66, 185–86, 201
 Historical Archives 202, 206
 Historical Committee xxii, 198, 206
Association of Mental Hospital Chaplains 184
Augustine 30, 64, 157
Averill, Lloyd J. 8, 189

Babies Hospital of the City of New York, The
 78
Baillie, John 131, 214
Baker, Ray Stannard 25–26, 191–92
Bannister, Robert C. 192
Barrett, Elizabeth 88
Barth, Karl 7, 152, 154
Batchelder, Alice 40, 43–44, 46, 48, 57, 65, 74–
 76, 195, 199
Batten, Loring W. 29
Baylor, Courtney 27
Baynes, H.G. 122
Beard, George 180
Beatty, Donald 67, 116
Becan, L.W. 29
Becker, Ernest 57, 199
Beecher, Henry Ward 14
Beecher, Lyman 196
Beers, Clifford 181
Bell, Daniel 136
Benedict, Ruth xvi, 111, 115, 125, 208
Bennington College 120
Berger, Peter xviii, 8, 168, 171, 188–89, 214,
 216–17
Bernadette, of Lourdes 101, 205
Bernheim, Hippolyte 35

233

235

ogy 122, 130
Fromm, Erich xvi, 111, 113–15, 117, 119–20, 128, 133, 163, 167–68, 170, 183, 186, 207, 215–16
fundamentalism xi, 5–6, 31, 51, 64, 182

Galdston, Iago xxii, 94, 98, 147
Galileo 186
Gallahue, Edward F. 184
Gamaliel 141
Gandhi, Mohandas 12, 190
Gaustad, Edwin S. 188
Gay, Peter 157
Geer, Curtis Manning 29
General Theological Seminary of New York 19, 29, 120, 127–28, 135–36
Gerkin, Charles V. 152, 213
Gerstenberg, Greta (*see* Greta F. Frankley)
Gifford, George E. Jr. 192
Gilded Age, the xv, 9, 12–13
Gladden, Washington 7, 13–15, 25, 177, 190–91
Gladstone, William 88
Glasser, 177
Glickman, Hyman 130
Glickman, Martha Jaeger 111, 113, 115, 123, 127, 130, 134, 137
God 5–6, 9–12, 25–26, 30, 50, 65–66, 74–75, 79–80, 88, 91, 93, 98–99, 106–7, 120, 130, 140–41, 143, 145, 151, 153, 155–56, 166, 176–77, 194, 205, 210, 216
Gordon, Arthur 204
Gospel, the 106, 145, 149–50, 164
Gotthard Booth Society for Holistic Health, the 136, 208
Grace Church on Broadway, New York 83
Grace Community Church, Sun Valley, California 186
Graduate School of Applied Religion 197
Grant, Rosamond (*see* Rosamond Grant Fisher)
Greene, John Gardner 192
Gross, Martin 166–67, 215
Guiles, Austin Philip 52, 74, 76, 86, 182
Gustafson, James M. 184

Hale, Nathan G. Jr. 11, 24, 190, 192–93, 199, 203, 215–16
Hall, Charles F. Jr. xxii, 67, 175, 185, 198
Hall, G. Stanley 180–81
Hammett, Hugh 63, 200–201
Harding, M. Esther 210
Harrell, David Edwin Jr. 31
Hartford Theological Seminary 29–30, 193
Hartmann, Heinz 165, 167
*Harvard Theological Review* 33
Harvard University xxi, 29–30, 48–49, 100, 118, 153, 180
  Divinity School 6, 185

Medical School 29–30
Hattie M. Strong Foundation xxiii
Haugk, Kenneth C. 206
Havens, Joseph 208
Havens, Teresina Rowell 122, 208
Hawthorne, Nathaniel 179
Hebrew scriptures 120, 196
Hess, H. Ober 189
Hewlett, Irma Waterhouse 203
High Commission for Refugees 121
Hiltner, Seward xi, xiv, xvi, xxi, 7, 46, 52–53, 67, 86–87, 109–17, 119, 124, 126–27, 132, 134, 136, 138, 140, 144, 158–59, 164, 183–84, 186–90, 198–99, 206–8, 212, 214
Hiroshima 172
Hitler, Adolf 123, 137, 160
Hodge, Charles 180
Hofmann, Hans 211, 213
Holifield, E. Brooks xiv, 46, 54, 57, 187–88, 190–91, 196, 198–99
Hollinger, David 136–37
Holmes, Oliver Wendell 179
Homans, Peter 46, 195–96
Hong, Barry A. 206
Hook, Sidney 136, 165, 187, 215–16
Hooker, Ransom 77
Horney, Karen 128
Horton, Walter Marshall 153–55, 182, 213
Howe, Reuel 67
Hoyt, Ethel Phelps Stokes 77–84, 86, 202
Hoyt, John Sherman 77–79, 202
Hudson River State Hospital for the Insane (Hudson River Psychiatric Center) 81
Hughes, Daphne 111, 127, 132
Hughes, H. Stuart 158, 214
human experience 41, 62, 64, 133, 137, 139, 152, 155, 160, 164–65, 171–72, 194, 213
Hutchinson, William 8–10, 153–54, 189–90, 213
hypnosis 13, 35–36, 180

Indiana University 42–43
Inner Guide, the 122
Institute for Social Research 49
Institute of Pastoral Care 66, 183
Institutes of Religion and Health xiv, 104, 186
Interchurch World Movement 47, 51, 196–97
International Congress for Mental Hygiene 75, 182
International Student Service 121
*Inward Light* 122, 130

Jaekle, Charles R. 67, 187
James, Edward T. 208
James, William 20, 43–45, 153, 180–81, 190
Janet, Pierre 35, 48
Jefferson, Thomas 12
Jesus 6, 17, 21–22, 24, 27–28, 30, 32, 64, 101, 109, 128, 140, 145, 150, 177, 209

237

239

240